COLORADO CABINS LODGES & COUNTRY B&Bs

by

Hilton and Jenny Fitt-Peaster

Rocky Mountain Vacation Publishing, Inc.

Boulder, Colorado

Photo Credits:
Front cover: a cabin at Rockmount, one of many in Estes Park, Colorado, with the Continental Divide in the background © Hilton Fitt-Peaster, Boulder, Colorado. Front cover inset composite photo: a cabinsuite

at Streamside Cabins, Estes Park, Colorado, and a skier © Jim Osterberg, Photostock, Estes Park, Colorado.
Back cover
Horseback riding in Rocky Mountain National Park, Colorado, and Hiking in autumn above Bear Lake, Rocky Mountain National Park, Colorado, © Osterberg.

Cover design: Gloria Wadzinski, Graphic Designer, Boulder, Colorado.

Library of Congress Catalog Card Number: 99-93057

Publisher's Cataloging-in-Publication

Fitt-Peaster, Hilton.
    Colorado cabins, lodges & country B&Bs: scenic getaways for every season / by Hilton and Jenny Fitt-Peaster. -- 4th ed.
    p. cm.
    Includes index.
    ISBN: 1-883087-05-8
    4th ed. of: Colorado cabins, cottages & lodges.

    1. Vacation homes--Colorado--Guidebooks.   2. Colorado--Guidebooks.
3. Colorado--Description and travel --1981--Guidebooks. I. Fitt-Peaster, Jenny.
II. Title. III. Title: Colorado cabins, lodges and country B&Bs
IV. Title Colorado cabins, cottages and lodges.

TX907.3.C5F588 1997   647'.94788

Printed in the United States of America by Millennia Graphics, Colorado Springs, Colorado
5 4 3 2 1

Contents

The Index is cross-referenced to 20 special interests, to help you find cabins that match your vacation plans. The 20 special interests are:

Swimming Pools
Fishing
Horseback Rides
Golf
Raft Trips
Recreational Lake/Reservoirs
Mountain Bike Trails
Downhill Skiing
XC Skiing
Snowmobiling
Hunting
4-Wheel Drive Tours/Rentals
Group Meeting Areas
Hot Tub/Spas
Snacks Served
Meals Served
Pets OK on Leash
Guest's Horses Permitted
RV Sites
Tent Sites

Colorado

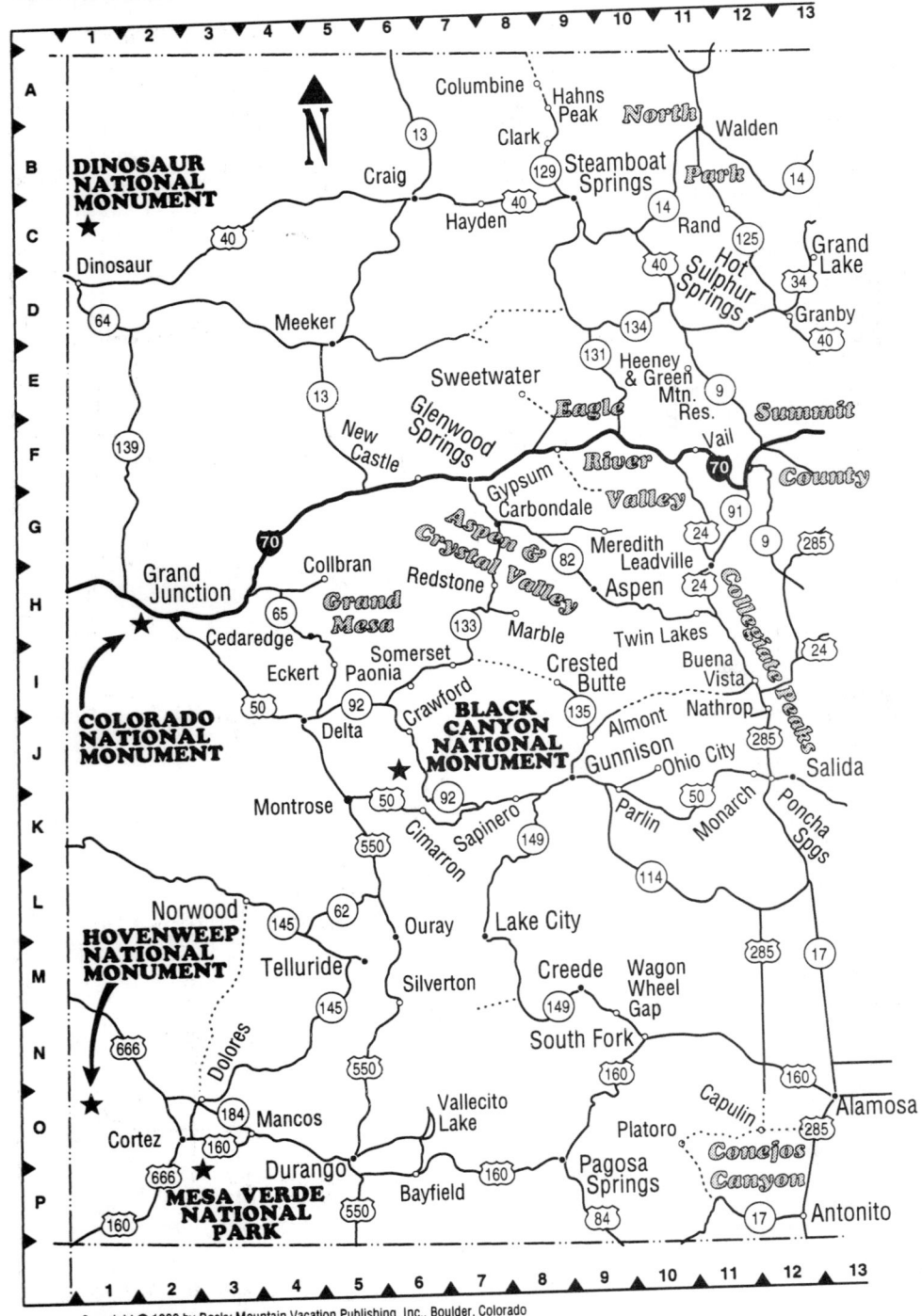

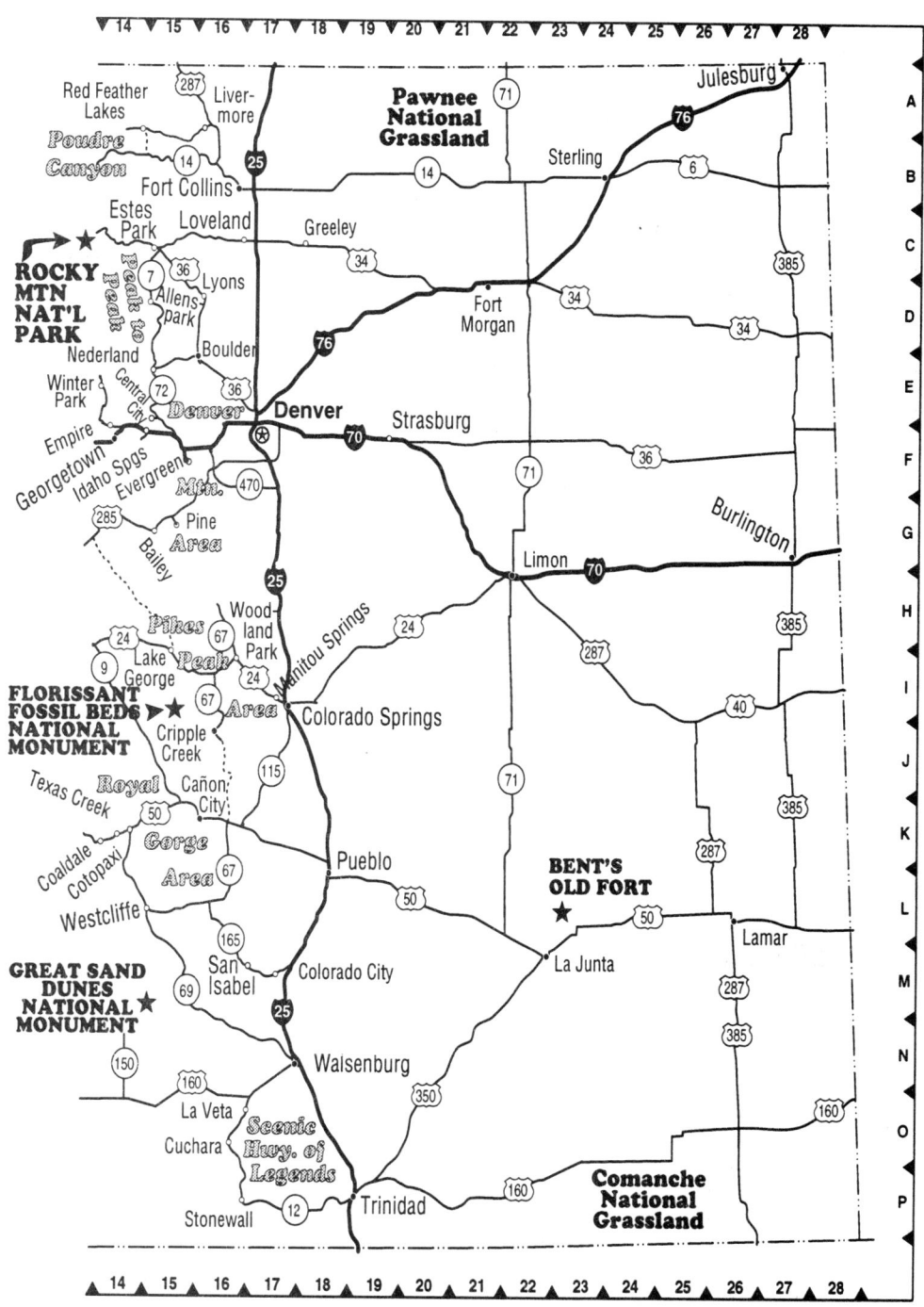

Note: not all highways, roads and towns appear on map

List of Towns & Areas

Preface

There is something special about staying in a cozy log cabin with a crackling fire in the fireplace, surrounded by beautiful Colorado mountain peaks.

WE WROTE THE BOOK ON COLORADO CABINS: THIS IS IT!

It took us years to search out and find these small "cabin resorts." We had to do it in person because there were no mailing lists or books on vacation cabins or mountain lodges. Many are hidden off the beaten track. We found places which third generation Colorado natives didn't know about. To share our discoveries, we wrote the first definitive guide to Colorado's cabins, cottages and lodges in 1993.

NOW WE SHARE OUR SECRETS WITH YOU.

This is our fourth edition — up-dated, expanded, rewritten and improved. A quick look at this one-of-a-kind book will answer your questions about Colorado's cabins, cottages, lodges, suites and country B&Bs.

On these pages, you'll find that romantic cabin getaway, the perfect family reunion cottage, remote trout stream lodge or winter recreation getaway. The variety is wide, ranging from rustic to opulent, timberline to trailhead, historic to modern, in-town to remote wilderness. Your dining options range from cozy kitchenettes to hearty family-style ranch fare to spectacular gourmet meals. No two places are alike. The possibilities are endless!

Colorado is an outdoor recreation paradise. You'll find activities such as hiking, mountain biking, cross-country skiing, snowshoeing, whitewater rafting, fly fishing, kayaking and more in fabulous locations throughout our state — many available right where you stay.

Consider a fall, winter or spring vacation getaway, when rates can be lower, reservations easier, things are quieter when fewer people are around and the scenery is even more spectacular.

When you select a cabin, cottage, lodge, suite or country bed and breakfast tell your friendly hosts you found them in this book.

LET YOUR ADVENTURE BEGIN!

We thank these people who helped with this book: Rebekah Fitt-Peaster (our daughter) and Associate Publisher since 1992, Kathe Conti for creative editing, Gloria Wadzinski for cover design, Tammi Dellaphina, for proofreading, Rodney Sauer of RDD Consultants, Inc. for computer layout design, Arthur Fitt of FittWare (our son) for making our computer database (he programmed) talk with our word processing program, and to all the helpful cabin, lodge and country B&B owner/operator-hosts in this book who double checked the accuracy of their information and supplied artwork.

We hope our book helps you find the right family resorts for your fun and recreation. ENJOY COLORFUL COLORADO!

Hilton and Jenny Fitt-Peaster
Authors, March 1999

How to Use This Book

The book is easy to use. It is organized into chapters. Each chapter covers a town or are. They are arranged A to Z. Within each chapter, fun things to do are listed first followed by the properties A–Z.

Use the List of Towns & Areas beginning on page vi to locate the town or area which interests you. Many towns are grouped together into a common geographic area. The first page of each chapter details information about the area. Map coordinates are also shown. Use these to help locate the town on the map at the front of this book on pages iv and v. These map coordinates are the same ones used on the official State of Colorado highway map.

Definitions—Types of Accommodations

We realize you may not be familiar with the terms we use in this book, so here are definitions for you.

Resort means any "cabin resort" or accommodation listed in this book. We are talking about "Mom-and-Pop" resorts. To some people, "resort" means a world-class, all-inclusive (or exclusive), expensive place. We use the term "resort" more broadly.

Cabin, Cottage, Chalet or **Guest House** — what you call them oft' depends on where you're from. Cabins are usually log or log-sided; cottages are frequently frame construction. Most units are free-standing, while others may be duplex cabins or cabinsuites. Here, we use "cabin" to mean all of these.

Vacation/Mountain Home generally describes an accommodation unit with three or more bedrooms, separate living areas (kitchen, living room, dining room) and more modern amenities than a cabin. This is truly a "home away from home." Often these homes are used for multi family getaways or small retreats.

Housekeeping means equipped with cooking facilities such as a kitchenette or kitchen, cooking and eating utensils so you can keep house. Unless stated otherwise, your hosts will not provide daily maid service. Accommodations with cooking facilities are not supplied with food, so remember to bring your own as it is seldom sold at the resort.

Modern means a bathroom (toilet and hot shower or tub) are inside the cabin.

Rustic either describes atmosphere or style, or means a bathroom is not inside the cabin, but usually in another building.

Primitive means no electricity.

Camper Cabin usually located at a campground, means an inexpensive, non-housekeeping, rustic and sometimes primitive cabin. Bring your own sleeping bags or blankets. Camper cabins are usually not heated — think of them as a "wooden tent." A brand of camper cabin is a Kamping Kabin™, which is a trademark of Kampgrounds of America, Inc. In this edition, we have eliminated places that only have camper cabins.

Lodge Room and **Suites** include linens, a bathroom in the room or a shared bath down the hall. Rooms in a lodge are usually entered from inside the building. Some lodge rooms are more akin to a small apartment or suite of rooms, which may include a kitchen.

Bed & Breakfast Rooms may be in a lodge, inn or owner's home, and always includes breakfast.

Rates

Cabin and room prices constantly change, both seasonally and annually, therefore we provide a price range. The 1999 rates for two people per night in the high- or on-season are indicated. Please note the rates listed are the best available information at time of publication. As we cannot guarantee rates, we strongly urge you to double check what you will pay, deposits, cancellation policies and other items and features that are important to you when making your reservations.

Abbreviations

After Credit Cards:

V means Visa
M means MasterCard
A means American Express
D means Discover

Glyphs Used in Book

At the Resort:

 Hot Tub/Spa in a central area

 Hot Tub/Spa in a private area for your exclusive use

 Some Meals served (inquire if Breakfast, Lunch, or Dinner)

 Well behaved Pets are okay on leash

 Well behaved Pets are okay on leash for a fee or security deposit

 Group Meeting area either indoor or outdoor.
    In the index i indicates indoor and o outdoor

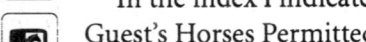 Guest's Horses Permitted

 RV Sites

 Tent Sites

On Resort or within a 15 minute drive:

 Swimming Pool

 Fishing

 Horseback Riding (guided)

 Golf Course (not mini golf)

 Rafting (guided)

 Recreational Lake or Reservoir for Boating or Fishing

 Mountain Bike Trails

 4-Wheel Drive Tours/Rentals

 Downhill (Alpine) Skiing

 Cross Country (XC, Nordic) Skiing

 Snowmobile Trails

 Hunting

Hiking—we did not include a glyph for hiking as it is generally available for all ages and abilities throughout colorful Colorado.

Index

An alphabetical index to all the accommodations in this book is in the back. In the index, under each of the 20 special interest glyphs defined above, you will find a • if that activity is located at the resort, or a number which is the average driving time in minutes if that activity is located near the resort. If the resort allows pets there will be either a • to indicate pets permitted or a $ if there is a fee or security deposit required for a pet. (If an activity is located more than 15 minutes drive from the resort, it is not shown.)

So, for example, if you want to find a resort that has a hot tub (central or private) and is near cross-country skiing, simply look down those two glyph columns until you find a place that has a • under the hot tub glyph and either a • or a number under the cross country skiing glyph. If you want to take your dog with you on your ski trip (but not into the hot tub), also look under the pets permitted glyph until you find a place marked under all three of these items you desire.

Reservations, Facilities, and Fun Things To Do

Be aware that reservations are recommended, sometimes months in advance for holiday weekends and during peak summer and winter seasons of June 15th to August 20th and the week between Christmas and New Years. Depending on location, other busy times include the fall hunting seasons of mid-September to mid-November. In winter for properties near ski area, President's Day weekend and Easter weekend and spring vacation should also be reserved well in advance.

These are generally small resorts operating in a restricted season. When you make a reservation, they are holding space for you and turning down subsequent requests. If you have to cancel, the resort operator may not be able to re-book your space on short notice so you will be obligated to pay for it. To protect yourself from unforeseen emergency cancellations, consider buying cancellation insurance from a travel agent, even if you don't book through that agent.

When selecting accommodations for your vacation, phone the owner/operator to check what they have to offer: price, facilities, reservation deposit/refund policy, non-smoking units available, pet policy, and so on. Season opening dates may change, depending on the weather.

Facilities at cabin resorts and lodges may include a store with some groceries, ice, firewood, and camping and fishing supplies. They may also offer a game room, recreation hall, gifts and souvenirs, pool, hot tub, playground, basketball, volleyball, miniature golf and a snack bar or restaurant. Best of all, the owner/operator lives on site — they should care about you and can serve as your personal hosts providing for your safety and security.

Activities in which you can participate may include fishing, guides and outfitters, nature walks, hiking, climbing, hay rides, water sports, barbecue cookouts, potluck dinners, ice cream socials, campfire programs, movies, slide shows, whitewater raft trips and kayaking, four wheeling, square dancing, sightseeing, tours, gold panning, rockhounding and horseback riding. In the fall, viewing the aspen colors and small and big game hunting are popular pursuits. Winter brings snowmobiling, cross-country and downhill skiing, ice fishing, sleigh and snow-cat rides and snuggling up by a cozy fire. Inquire about rental equipment and instructions for activities when you talk with the owner/operator.

Groups, Reunions and Weddings

In addition to looking for the indoor and outdoor group meeting area glyphs and a mention of these activities on a place's page, remember to also use the Index in the back of our book for this purpose.

For additional information on groups, reunions and weddings, look at our Web site www.coloradodirectory.com and go to the Groups & Reunions section.

Licensed Guides and Outfitters

For fishing or hunting fun, a professional can increase your success and save you time. In addition to outfitting services mentioned in this book, you can find a special Licensed Outfitters section on our www.coloradodirectory.com Web site.

Updates and Corrections

Look on our Web site at www.coloradodirectory.com where we can readily provide you with the latest updates and corrections. We welcome your input.

Altitude Awareness

In Colorado's high country, skies are bluer and stars are brighter because of our altitude. Our air is thinner, with less oxygen, than at sea level, especially above 8,000 feet. Until your body adjusts, go easy on physical activity; drink more water than usual; minimize your intake of alcohol, caffeine and salty foods; and eat high-carbohydrate foods, such as grains, fruits and vegetables. There is less atmosphere to screen out ultraviolet rays, so remember to use sunscreen, sunglasses and a hat with a brim for shade. If you adopt the proper attitude toward Colorado's altitude, you and your family will have the most enjoyable vacation experience possible.

Aspen & Crystal River Valley

Including Carbondale, Marble, Meredith & Redstone
— Map: G-8, H-8 & G-10

Aspen is a renown ski resort, an historic mining town, a relaxing mountain retreat and a cultural hot spot with its art galleries and glittering stars who vacation here. The town began as a remote mining camp in 1879 and became one of the richest silver producing areas in the world until the silver market crashed in 1893. In the Roaring Fork Valley, Aspen offers a winter wonderland for all outdoor enthusiasts and in summer hosts a music festival, theater, ballets and other entertaining events. Fishing spots, hiking and mountain biking trails abound on public forest lands near this mountain town. The Maroon Bells is said to be one of the most photographed peaks in North America and is a must-see. Down the road in the Crystal River Valley is towering Mount Sopris. Its peak reaches 12,953', and dominates the vista of the charming town of **Carbondale**. Formerly the only stagecoach stop on the 40-mile run to Aspen, Carbondale takes pride in its specialty shops, local arts and crafts and fine restaurants. Pick from one of many nearby mountain bike trails, fish the Roaring Fork River for its large trout or enjoy the scenery on the Crystal River. Thirty miles from Aspen and 12 miles from Glenwood Springs, this valley, surrounded by the White River National Forest, offers unique charm and secluded, untouched beauty. For a retreat even further off the beaten path, try the Redstone-Marble area with its mining past, ghost towns and dramatic mountain scenery. **Redstone** was founded by John Cleveland Osgood at the turn of the century as a model community to house employees of his coal mines. Although the workers and their families lived in simple cabins, Osgood built the luxurious Cleveholm Castle for himself, furnished with Tiffany chandeliers and Italian paintings. **Marble** was best known for its quarries, which produced a pure marble that rivaled Italy's Carrerra marble. Some of it was used in the Lincoln Memorial monument and the Tomb of the Unknown Soldier. The difficulties of mountain transportation closed down the quarries, but you can still visit them.

Fun Things to Do

- Aspen Art Museum (970) 925-8050
- Aspen Golf Course & Cross-Country Center (970) 925-2145
- Avalanche Ranch Antique Shop, Redstone (970/963-2846
- Crystal Glass Studio, Carbondale (970) 963-3227
- Historic Wheeler Opera House, Aspen (970) 920-5770
- Main Street Gallery, Carbondale (970) 963-3775
- Redstone Art Center (970) 963-3790
- Snowmass Golf Club & Cross-Country Center (970) 923-3148
- T Lazy 7 Ranch stables and snowmobiling, Aspen (888)875-6343

Avalanche Ranch Cabins

Avalanche Ranch offers 45 acres of lush countryside overlooking the Crystal River, surrounded by the Elk Mountain Range and the White River National Forest. The original 1913 farmhouse, featured in several national publications, offers four of the most romantic rooms in the rockies, appointed with authentic antiques and folk art. The cozy log cabins, offering abundant views, have full kitchens, sleeping lofts, porches, private yards, picnic tables and barbecues. All rooms are non-smoking and televisions are only available upon request.

This is an excellent place for children — they can play in the tree house and the kid's cabin, or with the ranch animals. Take a mini-cruise with the canoe on the ranch's pond. Explore trails that skirt the valley on foot, by mountain bike, on horseback, on snowshoes or on cross-country skis. Horseback riding is within 5 miles. The historic towns of Redstone and Marble are nearby, while five major downhill ski resorts, including Aspen/Snowmass, are within an hour's drive. The famous Glenwood Springs Hot Springs pool is less than an hour away. Local trout fishing is world-renowned in the Crystal, Roaring Fork and Frying Pan rivers.

Avalanche Ranch provides an ideal setting for romantic getaways, family reunions and weddings. There are no TV's in the cabins or rooms, but available upon request. Smoking is not permitted in the ranch buildings and pets are allowed only with cabin guests. The ranchhouse rents for $295-$385 (plus).

Location: On Highway 133, near milepost marker 56.

12 Cabins with Kitchen	Phone in Lobby	Sharon Boucher, Owner & Cheryl Schmidt,
1 Vacation Home	All Units Nonsmoking	Manager
1 Room with Fireplace	Recreation Room	12863 Hwy 133
5 Rooms with Wood Stoves	Elevation: 7000	Redstone CO 81623
Central Woodstove	Credit Cards: VMD	887/963-9339
Central Campfire Area	Rates: $70-$165	970/963-2846
	Open: All Year	Fax: 970/963-3141
		E-mail: aranch@rof.net
		www.coloradodirectory.com/avalancheranch/

At the resort:

At resort or within 15 minutes:

BRB Crystal River Resort

Rocky Mountain splendor at its finest! B-R-B is located at the base of spectacular, 13,000-foot Mount Sopris on the lively Crystal River which has some of the best fishing in Colorado. The resort has recently updated its modern log cabins with new carpet, stoves, ovens and heating systems. Each has a kitchen, linens, a fire pit, a picnic table and a barbecue grill; some have fireplaces. The cabins can accommodate up to 10 people. All cabins face the scenic river and some are a few steps from its banks. Come for the tranquil mountain scenery, stay for all the outdoor recreation. Numerous trees surround the resort and you'll be lulled to sleep at night by the steady, soothing sounds of the Crystal River.

On-site, play horseshoes, basketball, volleyball, badminton, ping pong, tether ball and at the playground. Fish along the half-mile of accessible river frontage or try the gold medal fishing in nearby Frying Pan River. The main lodge has a small grocery store and gift shop. Local hunting is some of the best in the country. Horseback riding trails, four-wheel driving roads, mountain biking trails and river rafting trips are nearby. The open-air hot tub and swimming pool are a welcome retreat after a day of adventuring. Glenwood Springs natural hot springs pool is only 18 miles away. History buffs will want to tour the historic towns of Marble and Redstone just up the road as well as the hand-hewn log school built in the late 1800s and open till 1946 right on the resort.

RV sites and indoor/outdoor group meeting areas are also available.

Location: On Highway 133 (West Elk Scenic Byway), near milepost marker 62, six miles south of Carbondale.

---

13 Cabins with Kitchen
2 Rooms with Fireplaces
Central Campfire Area

Pay Phone Available
Elevation: 6600
Credit Cards: VMD
Rates: $60-$85
Open: All Year

Umar and Ruth Sultan & Parveen Riaz,
Owners
7202 Hwy 133
Carbondale CO 81623
800/963-2341
970/963-2341 & Fax
E-mail: brb@sopris.net
www.coloradodirectory.com/brbcrystalriver/

At the resort:

At resort or within 15 minutes:

Chair Mountain Ranch

At the base of Chair Mountain, secluded among the pine trees along the beautiful Crystal River, this 8-acre ranch is a peaceful mountain retreat, with fully equipped, two bedroom housekeeping cabins with full bathrooms. Kitchens with all the utensils you require and plenty of bedding and linens are supplied. Sit on the cabin's porch and read a book or just watch nature unfold before you on the pond. A newly renovated 1,200-square foot upstairs, two bedroom apartment with a full kitchen and bathroom is also available. Relax in front of the fireplace in the spacious living room with a spectacular view of the mountains. For those who like to rough it, try the rustic camping cabin with no water and a bath house close by.

Romp with the whole family on the large grassy area in the summer, perfect for football, baseball, volleyball, horseshoes and basketball. Picnic in the covered picnic area with its marble barbecue pit. A laundry room is available for your convenience. Fish for gold-medal trout on ranch grounds along the Crystal River. Take a brave dip in medicinal hot springs pouring out of the mountainside into the river a few miles down the road. Visit historic Redstone with its quaint shops. Add a splash of excitement by whitewater rafting on the Roaring Fork or Colorado rivers. Check out the local riding stables that offer everything from breakfast rides to several-day pack trips. Excellent deer and elk hunting in the area. Hike or bike on the abundant, scenic trails.

Pets are allowed for an additional fee.

Location: Take Marble turnoff from Highway 133.

5 Cabins with Kitchen	Phone in Lobby	Dave & Linda Adams, Owners
1 Lodging Room	Recreation Room	0178 CR 3
1 Camper Cabin	Elevation: 7640	Marble CO 81623
1 Room with Fireplace	Credit Cards: VMD	970/963-9522 & Fax
Central Campfire Area	Rates: $25-$110	www.coloradodirectory.com/chairmountainranch/
	Open: 5/25 to 11/15	

At the resort:

At resort or within 15 minutes:

Mountain Chalet Aspen

Located at the base of Aspen Mountain Ski Area and only 300 yards from the gondola, this chalet features 44 custom-designed rooms and four two-bedroom apartments. Each room has a private bath, phone, baseboard heat, color cable television and a small refrigerator. The apartments also have a living room with a fireplace, a full kitchen, one and a half baths and sleep six. Some of the rooms have fireplaces and breakfast is included in all room rates.

Amenities at the Mountain Chalet include an outdoor heated swimming pool, hot tub, steam room, sauna, exercise room and free underground parking. The chalet is also adjacent to downtown Aspen's mall, many fine restaurants, numerous art galleries and unique shops. Ski Aspen Mountain or take one of the free shuttles to the other nearby ski mountains. In the summer, those same shuttles will take you to the beautiful Maroon Bells where you'll want to bring your camera to capture some of the most spectacular views in the state. Partake in the Aprés Ski around a cozy fireplace with a variety of hors d'oeuvres every Monday, or a cup of coffee anytime. Winter breakfasts are all you can eat — perfect for the skier. In other seasons, you'll dine on lighter fare of fresh fruit, yogurt, cereals, toast, sweet rolls, juice and coffee. Whether you come here in during the snow season to enjoy Aspen's winter wonderland, or in the summer to bask in the sunshine, the Mountain Chalet offers you an affordable place to stay, with a touch of luxury to keep you coming back.

The banquet facilities of one to three rooms accommodate up to 200 people, idea for weddings, meetings and receptions. A commercial kitchen is available. All rooms are non-smoking.

Location: In Aspen on East Durant.

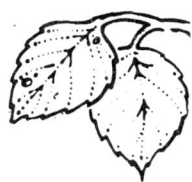

51 Lodging Rooms	Phone in Rooms	Stan Hajenga, General Manager
24 Beds in Bunkhouse	Bed & Breakfast Available	333 East Durant
9 Rooms with Fireplaces	All Units Nonsmoking	Aspen CO 81611
Central Hot Tub	Recreation Room	800/321-7813
Central Fireplace	Elevation: 7900	Fax: 970/925-7811
	Credit Cards: VMAD	E-mail: mtchalet@sopris.net
	Rates: $60-$380	www.coloradodirectory.com/mtnchalet
	Open: All Year	

At the resort:

At resort or within 15 minutes:

Prospect Mountain Ranch

On a 100-acre meadow surrounded by 13,000-foot peaks, Prospect Mountain Ranch is a real working horse ranch and feels like it's close to heaven. The rustic housekeeping cabins overlook the Crystal River. Eight of the ten cabins have wood burning stoves for heating and cooking. Campsites with no hookups and hot showers are also available near the river.

Anglers cast into the two miles of river frontage near their cabins, while children under 8 are welcomed to try their luck in the trout pond on site. Everyone will enjoy the opportunity to ride horses with the cowboys here. See the local sights while hiking or mountain biking. Take a four wheel drive road to Marble Quarry and Old Crystal Mill. The ranch is also close to Redstone Castle, Glenwood Hot Springs and Aspen. Within a short drive are restaurants, family evening entertainment and lakes for boating. Less than a hour's drive are a museum, a golf course and white water raft trips.

Rates are the same for two to four people. Pets are allowed at the campsite for no additional charge.

Location: Turn off Highway 133 near milepost marker 46 onto County Road 3.

Prospect Mountain Ranch

---

10 Cabins with Kitchen	Elevation: 7600	John & Teresa Armstrong, Managers
8 Rooms with Wood Stoves	Credit Cards: None	PO Box 1163
Central Campfire Area	Rates: $30-$40	Carbondale CO 81623-1163
	Open: 5/15 to 10/4	970/963-2323 summer
		970/925-1994 winter
		www.coloradodirectory.com/prospectmtnranch/

At the resort:

At resort or within 15 minutes:

Redstone Cliff's Lodge

Overlooking the rushing waters of the Crystal River, Redstone Cliffs Lodge offers cozy comfort and modern convenience in its cabins and motel rooms. Rooms feature custom lodge pole beds, quilts and a western mountain atmosphere. The 13 cabins have fully equipped kitchenettes, private baths and color cable television. Choose between mountain and river views.

Surrounded by White River National Forest, Redstone Cliff's Lodge is close to mountain biking, horseback riding, hiking, snowmobiling and white water rafting. The historic town of Redstone offers high country charm, spectacular views, soaring cliffs, mountain vistas, Colorado wildflowers and year-round activities. Be sure to visit the quaint shops, art galleries and fine restaurants in town. Soak in the outdoor hot tub and enjoy the stone terrace overlooking the river while you vacation here.

All rooms are non-smoking.

Location: In Redstone on Redstone Boulevard.

13 Cabins with Kitchen	Pay Phone Available	Susan & Eric Yoder, Owners
13 Motel Rooms	All Units Nonsmoking	0433 Redstone Blvd
Central Hot Tub	Elevation: 7250	Redstone CO 81623
Central Campfire Area	Credit Cards: VM	970/963-2691
	Rates: $65-$95	Fax: 970/963-7369
	Open: All Year	E-mail: susan@redstone-cliffs.com
		www.coloradodirectory.com/redstonecliffs

At the resort:

At resort or within 15 minutes:

T Lazy 7 Ranch

Family owned and operated since 1938, T Lazy 7 Ranch is only five minutes from Aspen and is spread over 500 private acres. It's seclusion is enhanced by a quarter of a million acres of surrounding national forest and wilderness. Not to be confused with neighboring Colorado dude ranches, T Lazy 7 operates on a unique, informal level. The lack of structure allows you to enjoy your vacation at your own pace in recently renovated rustic cabins. Six lodges contain three or four cabin like apartments, each with modern kitchens, baths, and fireplaces. The unique decor emphasizes quality, rustic furnishings and original handmade hardware throughout.

The ranch is located near the base of beautiful Maroon Bells, the most photographed peaks in North America! Three miles of private fishing streams, stocked beaver ponds, rolling pastures, thick stands of aspen and pine, waterfalls, horses, and animals grace this exquisite valley. Ranch activities include horseback riding, fishing, and partaking in western chuckwagon parties. Pick among any number of guided horseback rides from breakfast rides, to Maroon Bells lunch rides, to Tennessee Walker day rides. In the winter snowmobile to historic mining sites or frolic on the world-class downhill slopes in Aspen. At the resort, enjoy a year-round heated swimming pool and jacuzzi.

Guest are welcomed to stay from two nights to a relaxing month. Pets are permitted in selected cabins.

Location: On Maroon Creek Road, 5 minutes from downtown Aspen.

16 Cabins with Kitchen	Pay Phone Available	Landon & Rick Deane & Bill McEnteer
1 Vacation Home	Elevation: 8400	3129 Maroon Creek Rd
1 Lodging Room	Credit Cards: VMD	Aspen CO 81611
9 Rooms with Fireplaces	Rates: $70-$120	88/T7LODGE(888/875-6343
9 Rooms with Wood Stoves	Open: 5/25 to 10/5	970/925-7254
Central Hot Tub		Fax: 970/925-5616
		E-mail: tlazy7@rof.net
		www.coloradodirectory.com/tlazy7guestranch/

At the resort:

At resort or within 15 minutes:

Yolande Placer Cabins

Located on Fryingpan River, just 2 miles past Ruedi Reservoir, Yolande Placer cabins are rustic yet modernized. The six housekeeping units have bathrooms and double beds. One new, large cabin has beautiful views and sleeps up to six. Another cabin, which has a fireplace, can accommodate up to eight.

Anglers will appreciate the convenience of fishing the river right outside their door or the nearby reservoir. Other fishing spots include the Chapman Dam and DeemerLake. Famous Glenwood Springs Hot Pool, once a favored place among the Ute Indians to relax, is just a scenic hour drive away. Open May to October, Yolande Placer is in the midst of great hunting, hiking, horseback riding and mountain biking country.

Two full service RV sites are also available.

Location: From Highway 82, in Basalt take Fryingpan River past Ruedi Reservoir, about two miles.

6 Cabins with Kitchen	Phone in Lobby	Dennis, Monika & Carl, Betty South, Owners
1 Room with Fireplace	Some Units Nonsmoking	24635 Frying Pan Rd
Central Campfire Area	Elevation: 8000	Meredith CO 81642
	Credit Cards: None	970/927-3296
	Rates: $60-$125	www.coloradodirectory.com/yolandecabins/
	Open: 5/1 to 11/1	

At the resort:

At resort or within 15 minutes:

Black Canyon Area

Including Cimarron, Crawford & Montrose —
Map: K-6, J-6, K-5

Bordered by Gunnison National Forest, **Cimarron** is known for its old narrow-gauge railroad, with a part of the original trestle crossing the creek. The 469-foot Morrow Point Dam and Cimarron Canal supply water for the arid Uncompahgre Valley. Cimarron River yields a variety of trout. Just east is the Curecanti National Recreation Area where breathtaking scenery emphasizes the series of dams created to alter the Gunnison River's course. Nearby Marrow Point Reservoir is a mixture of jagged rock jutting out over calm water. Named for the former Ute Chief Curecata, the area also boasts 20-mile long Blue Mesa Reservoir. The lake is ideal for sailing and windsurfing. Its 96 miles of shoreline offer up rainbow, brook and brown trout, mackinaw, and kokanee salmon. **Crawford** is a town where cowboys still wear Stetson hats and spurs, and cattle drives take place down Main Street. An adventurer's paradise, Crawford offers outstanding big game hunting, excellent fishing, four-wheel drive tours and hiking in Gunnison National Forest. Crawford Reservoir, good for rainbow trout and perch, also has swimming and boating. **Montrose** is the gateway to the San Juan Skyway and the Ridgway State Recreation Area. Take a scenic day trip to Telluride, Grand Mesa, Blue Mesa, Owl Creek Pass and Silver Jack Reservoir. The Black Canyon to the west is the most stunning day trip of all: as deep as 2,700' and as narrow as 1,300', the canyon was shaped by the churning waters of the Gunnison River. A 50-mile long chasm, the Black Canyon's sheer, shadowy rock walls drop more than a half mile to the river creating a somber and memorable site. Ute Indians did not enter the canyon, preferring to stay on the rim and hunt and when you visit, you'll see why — there are difficult trails down. Take raft trips through the steep canyon to see otherwise inaccessible sites. The Montrose area offers some of the best fishing in Colorado on the Gunnison, San Miguel and Dolores rivers. Keep an eye out for the many golden eagles, red-tailed hawks, prairie falcons and great horned owls that live here. The Ridgway State Recreation Area provides boating, fishing, and swimming opportunities. Visit the Ute Indian Museum, dedicated entirely to one tribe, to understand a bit of the region's rich history.

Fun Things To Do

- Black Canyon of the Gunnison National Monument (970)641-2337
- Branding Iron Steakhouse & Stables, Crawford (888) 921-HORSE
- Crawford Reservoir & State Park (970) 921-5721
- Curecanti National Recreation Area, Gunnison (970) 641-2337
- District Forest Service Office, Gunnison (970) 641-0471
- Ute Indian Museum, Montrose (970) 249-3098
- West Elk Trading Post, Crawford (970) 921-6311

Prock Elk Ranch

Prock Elk Ranch offers you the opportunity to stay in its newly built log cabin in the midst of an elk herd! The cabin sleeps four and has modern facilities and an efficiency kitchen. The cabin offers privacy and a king bed, a queen hide-a-bed and decor that is definitely "elkie." If you are looking for elbow room and have the desire to get away from people this is the ideal location as there is only one cabin on the property.

At night, gather around the campfire and listen to the sounds of nature under a star-filled sky. Start your day by viewing the magnificent San Juan Mountains and watching the 150 head of domestic elk from your front porch. Gear up to go hiking or four wheeling in the Black Canyon of the Gunnison. Stop for a picnic and drink in the awe-inspiring wilderness. Visit nearby Ouray, otherwise known as the "Little Switzerland of America." After an energetic tour of the unique shops there, try swimming in the natural hot springs. Or enjoy sweet solitude by dropping a line in the nearby Ridgeway Damn for a little fishing. In the fall, turn your attention to the elk once again to hear their haunting bulging melodies. Be sure to bring your camera to tour the largest working elk ranch in the area. You can even pet the bottle baby "Lulu" or see a massive full antlered bull elk at this unique vacation destination.

The cabin is non-smoking.

Location: About 8 miles south of Montrose. Turn east on Uncompahgre Road, pavement ends or from 5, milepost marker 117 just past Colona, Buckhorn Road.

1 Cabin with Kitchen	Phone in Lobby	Roger & Linda Prock, Owners
	Bed & Breakfast Available	22710 Uncompaghre Rd
	All Units Nonsmoking	Montrose CO 81401
	Elevation: 7200	800/249-7828
	Credit Cards: VM	970/249-7828
	Rates: $75	E-mail: prock@rmi.net
	Open: All Year	www.coloradodirectory.com/prockelkranch/

At the resort:

At resort or within 15 minutes:

Rocky Mountain Homestay Guest House

Uniquely situated between the desert landscapes of eastern Utah and the heart of the Rocky Mountains, Rocky Mountain Homestay Guest House offers a year-round rural experience. The new guest house features carpeted bedrooms with ample closet space, a vaulted ceiling, new appliances, tiled living room, bath and kitchen. This 760 square foot, separate house sleeps up to six comfortably in two bedrooms and is wheelchair accessible. A separate porch offers fabulous, unobstructed views of Grand Mesa and the peaks of the West Elk Mountains. For bed and breakfast guests, the room rate includes morning complimentary baked goods, coffee and tea.

The guest house is located on a 15 acre "ranchette" originally homesteaded in 1890 as a 160 acre parcel. Several original buildings add historic charm. The grounds include pasture, wetlands, ponds, flower gardens, a vegetable garden, an old apple orchard, a grape arbor and a yard with trees for your relaxation in the shade. The guest house is located just outside of Crawford on the western flank of the West Elk Mountains and is ideally near numerous recreational activities. The following range from a five minute to a two hour drive: big game and bird hunting on public lands, lake fishing and boating on Crawford Reservoir, trout fishing on the Gunnison River, hiking, cross country skiing and horseback riding in the Gunnison National Forest, and touring the Black Canyon of the Gunnison National

Monument. Take a fall foliage tour on the West Elk Scenic Byway, golf in Cedaredge and Delta or take in any of the numerous cultural events in the area.

The guest house is smoke-free. Guest horses are welcomed.

Location: Off State Highway 92, 2 miles west of Crawford; or 8 miles east of Hotchkiss.

---

1 Cabin with Kitchen	Phone in Rooms	Peter McCarville & Elizabeth Skelton,
	Bed & Breakfast Available	Owners
	All Units Nonsmoking	3867 Hwy 92
	Elevation: 6400	Crawford CO 81415
	Credit Cards: None	970/921-3867
	Rates: $85	E-mail: rmhomestay@aol.com
	Open: All Year	www.coloradodirectory.com/rockymountainhome stay

---

At the resort:

At resort or within 15 minutes:

Stewart Homestead Cabin

In the picturesque Onion Valley, 9 miles southeast of Crawford, Stewart Homestead Cabin offers a quiet, peaceful rest with no phone or television to distract you from relaxing. The cabin features a full kitchen and bath, glass door wood stove for cozy winter days and can sleep up to nine. This homestead cabin offers you a chance to see what life was like 100 years ago will all the conveniences of today.

Nearby are the Blue Mesa, Black Mesa, Gould and Crawford Reservoirs for fishing and water sports. A visit to the stunning Black Canyon of the Gunnison will prove to be unforgettable. Activities in this area include horseback riding (you can bring your own horse), mountain biking, hiking, fishing, cross-country skiing and snowmobiling. Your hosts encourage you to bring your family and share the adventure!

Location: Nine miles southeast of Crawford on Highway 92, between milepost marker 40-41 on the Westhoop Scenic Byway.

Carol Bowker

1 Cabin with Kitchen	Elevation: 7800	Jim & Susan Ayer
1 Room with Woodstove	Credit Cards: None	4156 B Rd
Central Campfire Area	Rates: $85	Crawford CO 81415
	Open: All Year	970/921-6751
		Fax: 970/921-6751 call 1st
		www.coloradodirectory.com/stewarthomesteadcabins

At the resort:

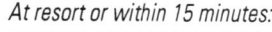

At resort or within 15 minutes:

Western Recreation Ranch & Branding Iron Steakhouse and Stables

The new housekeeping cabins at Western Recreation Ranch overlook Smith Fork Stream. The four cabins sleep two to nine. The working cattle ranch is on 300 acres. Be sure to ask about the occasional cattle drives when making your reservations.

Horses are welcomed to accompany you and there is a roping arena available to guests. Dine at the steak house located on the ranch that features a dance pavilion for special events. The ranch is also close to a hunting outfitters, perfect for your backcountry treks in the fall hunting seasons. The Crawford area is great for hiking, mountain biking or horseback riding — yours or theirs. Take the whole family on a hay ride and experience the real West.

Rustic tent and RV sites are also available only 100 yards from the stream. Pets are also welcomed here.

Location: Off Highway 92 on the north side of Crawford on Dogwood Avenue. One mile down Smith Fork Creek.

3 Cabins with Kitchen
3 Rooms with Wood Stoves
Central Campfire Area

Phone in Lobby
Elevation: 6500
Credit Cards: VM
Rates: $80-$100
Open: 5/25 to 11/15

Clair & Nola Hicks, Owners
PO Box 162
Crawford CO 81415-0162
888/921-Horse (4677)
970/921-4-FUN (386)
Fax: 970/921-4387
E-mail: lfmilliron@aol.com
www.coloradodirectory.com/westernrecranch

At the resort:

At resort or within 15 minutes:

Central City to Georgetown
Including Black Hawk, Empire, Golden & Idaho Springs —
Map: F-14 & F-16

Once known as the richest square mile on earth, **Central City** is again enjoying a boom. A historic mining town where fortunes were made and lost, this mountain city now has legal gambling mixed in with Victorian houses, the fanciest opera house in the west and abandoned mines. The entire city, just a mile up the road from **Black Hawk**, is part of a National Historic District. Because Central City attracted more than 20,000 people in the 1860s, it became a cultural center for Colorado. The Central City Opera House, which opened in 1878, still runs a nationally renown summer season. Gambling has brought people back in droves and the city is once again filled with dance hall music and the clink of coins. Hiking around Central City and Black Hawk is not recommended because the hillsides are dotted with abandoned mine shafts. Take a tour instead at the Lost Gold Mine and see how early settlers lived at the Thomas House. The first major gold strike in Colorado on Jan. 7, 1859, was in **Idaho Springs** by George Jackson. Today would-be miners should check out the still operating Phoenix Gold Mine. south of town, on Flirtation Peak is the Bridal Veil Falls where the largest water wheel in the state was built in 1893. Idaho Springs was named for the geothermal pool and baths fed by waters considered scared to the Utes who once relaxed here. Drive the Mt. Evans Scenic and Historic Byway 14 miles to the summit of the 14,264' peak. Just before the toll gate stop at historic Echo Lake Lodge for some of their home-made pie and a cup of coffee. Along this, the highest paved highway in America look for bighorn sheep, elk and goats among alpine tundra and 1000-year-old bristlecone pines. The "Oh My God Road" links Central City to Idaho Springs and passes by hundreds of abandoned mines and mills. St. Mary's Glacier, only 15 minutes away, is a popular, year-round ski and snowboard area for those who don't mind hiking in with their equipment so they can ski a snow bowl in August. Encompassing the town, Arapaho National Forest offers endless alpine hikes which turn into great cross-country skiing trails in the winter.

Fun Things To Do

- Arapaho National Forest (970) 887-4100
- Central City Opera House (303) 292-6700
- Clear Creek Ranger District Office (303) 567-2901
- Echo Lake Lodge, Idaho Springs (303) 567-2138
- Edgar Mines, Idaho Springs (303) 567-2911
- Georgetown Loop Railroad (800) 691-4FUN
- Gilpin County Historical Museum, Central City (303) 582-5283
- Phoenix Gold Mine, Idaho Springs (303) 567-0422 - See Page 22
- Teller House & Tours, Central City (303) 582-3200

Phoenix Gold Mine Tour

Catch gold fever at Phoenix Gold Mine Tour, a working gold mine. This tour offer a glimpse at the human side of mining. The excitement Al, the owner, has for mining is passed on to each tour participant. As the tour winds through the many tunnels he touches on the history, changing technology and shares his families personal anecdotes. Walking through the mine you will see Resurrection Vein a relatively new section of the mine, producing 2 ounces of gold per ton and frequent pockets of pure gold. Young and old will enjoy the slow passed walking tour. In the heart of the historic Idaho Spring Mining District, The Phoenix Mine is operated by the oldest continuous gold mining family in Colorado. Authentic miners teach gold panning by a beautiful mountain stream, anything you find you can take home with you. After the mine tour and the gold hunting enjoy a picnic lunch (you'll need to bring your own) in the splendor of the mountains. Be sure to stop in the gift shop as it offers books written by Al, gold panning supplies and gold jewelry.

Open all year, seven days a week from 10 a.m. till 6 p.m. Group tours and rates are available with advanced reservations. There is Plently of parking for buses and motorhomes.

Location: Thirty minutes from Denver on I-70 to exit 239, then one mile west of Idaho Springs on I-70 frontage road, the 3/4 miles south on Trail Creek Road.

Alvin & Pat Mosch, Owners
PO Box 3236
Idaho Springs CO 80452-0537
303/567-0422
www.coloradodirectory.com/phoenixgoldmine/

Call of the Canyon

Enjoy elegance in the rough at Call of the Canyon's luxury cabins at the base of 14,258-foot Mount Evans. The knotty pine cabins, built in the 1950s, have full kitchens, fireplaces and other amenities. Surrounded by Arapaho National Forest, the cabins are only 25 feet from a mountain creek. Settle under a down comforter on the queen-sized bed at night and listen to the rushing sound of West Chicago Creek right outside your window. In the early morning, if you're quiet and lucky, you might meet Hal, the giant rainbow trout who lounges about in the pool under the bridge.

Activities include mountain biking, hiking and fishing — but don't catch Hal! Take an excursion to the ice fields of St. Mary's Glacier in the summer where some hikers go for back country, downhill skiing in July. Go whitewater rafting nearby and then relax in Idaho Springs' hot springs afterwards. Winter is great for cross-country skiing here and the resort is a short drive from the ski resorts at Winter Park, Loveland and Keystone. Be sure to drive up Mount Evans — the highest road in America — where you might spot herds of bighorn sheep and mountain goats grazing above timberline. Other wildlife you might spot are deer, hawks, ravens, marmots, bear, elk and if you're really lucky, cougars. One critter you'll be sure to met is Pinhead, the resident cat at Call of the Canyon.

Location: Just over six miles from Idaho Springs, turn right off Highway 103, between mile-post marker 6-7 onto County Road 114, on West Chicago Creek.

---

2 Cabins with Kitchen	Phone in Lobby	Richard Eakins, Owner
1 Vacation Home	All Units Nonsmoking	155 CR 114
3 Rooms with Fireplaces	Elevation: 9000	Idaho Springs CO 80452
	Credit Cards: VM	800/257-4783
	Rates: $85-$100	303/567-0170
	Open: All Year	E-mail: webmaster@canyoncabins.com
		www.coloradodirectory.com/callcanyoncabins/

At the resort:

At resort or within 15 minutes:

Club Hotel, The

This turn-of-the-century hotel has 14 restored, charming and comfortable rooms. The hotel serves a healthy, wholesome complimentary breakfast in the special guest dining room.

The Club Hotel is a National Historical Landmark in the heart of Idaho Springs, The hotel's larger dining room boasts a beautiful, one of a kind, granite rock fireplace. A recreation room with board and card games, television and VCR is also available to guests. Doc Holiday spent an entire summer here and President Roosevelt visited often. Hot Mineral Springs is a mere half mile away. Area activities include white water rafting, horseback riding, taking mine tours, visiting museums, biking on paved paths and taking train tours. The hotel is within 30 minutes of five major downhill ski resorts and the casinos of Central City and Black Hawk are only 15 minutes away.

All units are non-smoking.

Location: Only 20 minutes from Denver on I-70, take exit 239, 240 or 241.

14 Lodging Rooms	Rates: $95-$135	Mike & Rita Dickey, Owners
Central Hot Tub	Open: All Year	PO Vox 3009
Central Fireplace		Idaho Springs CO 80459-3009
Bed & Breakfast Available		303/567-9391
All Units Nonsmoking		Fax: 303/567-9434
Recreation Room		www.coloradodirectory.com/clubhotel
Elevation: 7500		
Credit Cards: VMAD		

At the resort:

At resort or within 15 minutes:

Conestoga Wagon Cabins & RV Campground

Just five miles west of historic Empire, Conestoga Wagon Stop sits in the tall pines of the Arapaho National Forest. Originally built in the early 1930's as mining cabins, the newly remodeled, five cabins are available all year. Each fully furnished cabin has a kitchenette with cookware and utensils. You'll enjoy the beautiful view of Clear Creek River near your cabin, and the peaceful sound of rushing water will lull you to sleep every night. RV camping and tent sights are also available.

Both your horse and pet are welcome at Conestoga Wagon Stop. Area activities include fishing right at the resort, river rafting, horseback riding, golfing, boating on lakes and mountain biking — all within a short drive. In the winter, you can enjoy downhill and cross-country skiing, snowmobiling, ice fishing and hunting. The mountainside property was once mined and an existing miner's cabin sits on top of the property along wiht an old mining road which is accessible during the summer months.

RV sites are also available.

Location: Off I-70, five miles from Empire on Highway 40 near milepost marker 250.

4 Cabins with Kitchen	Pay Phone Available	Pam Holzer, Owner & Troy Claudio
1 Vacation Home	Elevation: 9650	PO Box 334
Central Campfire Area	Credit Cards: VM	Empire CO 80438-0438
	Rates: $45-$75	888/428-9604
	Open: All Year	303/569-3066
		Fax: 303/569-3066
		www.coloradodirectory.com/conestogacampcabins/

At the resort:

At resort or within 15 minutes:

Indian Springs Resort

Indian Springs Resort is a world famous natural hot mineral springs facility which also offers 68 rooms. The hotel rooms have one double or two twin beds, the inn rooms have one king bed or two double beds, and the lodge rooms have one double bed, one king bed, two double beds, or suites. All room guests have free use of the swimming pool and a V.I.P. discount card for the resort's other amenities.

The resort's facilities include men and women's geo-thermal cave baths, mineral water swimming pool, private outdoor Jacuzzi baths and indoor private baths. Club mud, spa services with massage, facials and more are also available. There is a full service restaurant on-site. Seven different ski resorts are within an hour's drive. Other area activities include casino gambling in Central City and Black Hawk, exploring the downtown Idaho Springs national historic district and the Argo Gold Mill, the Georgetown Loop Railroad and driving the Mt. Evens Scenic & Historic Byway.

Twenty-six RV sites with electricity and water are also available. Some rooms are non-smoking and some are handicap accessible. The resort caters birthday parties, meetings, parties and weddings from 20 to 100 people.

Location: Twenty minutes from Denver on I-70, take exit 239, 240 or 241 on Soda Creek Road.

INDIAN SPRINGS RESORT

68 Lodging Rooms	Elevation: 7600	Jim E Maxwell, Owner
Central Hot Tub	Credit Cards: VM	PO Box 1990
Some Units Nonsmoking	Rates: $45-$83	Idaho Springs CO 80452-1990
	Open: All Year	303/989-6666 Denver
		Fax: 303/567-9304
		E-mail: info@indianspringsresort.com
		www.coloradodirectory.com/indianspringsresort

At the resort:

At resort or within 15 minutes:

Van Eden Ranch Retreat, B&B and Mountain Cabin

The motto at Van Eden is: "Big enough to serve you, small enough to care." The ten bedroom moss rock lodge features private baths, hardwood floors and fireplaces. One room has a jetted tub and Primestar TV. This romantic, bed and breakfast lodge also has some non-smoking rooms. Plus there is a log vacation home that sleeps up to 16 people and has a kitchen.

Imagine waking up to a delicious breakfast before relaxing by a mountain stream, hiking the forest and meadow or horseback riding along a picturesque trail. Tobaggon run and sleigh rides in winter. The first floor of the lodge has a large outdoor deck and cozy lounge with a moss rock. Western horseback rides with either steak or vegetarian cuisine (homemade by prior arrangement) or box lunches are also available. A true riding experience that's not nose to tail, so you can spread out, trot and even gallop, if you wish. Your guides will give you lessons to help you have a good time. Surrounded by the Arapahoe-Roosevelt National Forest, the ranch is secluded and quiet, up two and a half miles of private road. For a relaxing vacation, soak in the seasonal hot tub before getting a refreshing, professional massage.

Van Eden is ideal for small groups. Your horse is welcome to vacation with you.

Location: Thirty-five miles west of Denver & 4.5 miles South of Idaho Springs off I-70, exit 241A.

1 Vacation Home	Phone in Lobby	Pat & James Fleming, Owners
8 Lodging Rooms	Bed & Breakfast Available	PO Box 1169
16 Beds in Bunkhouse	Some Units Nonsmoking	Idaho Springs CO 80452-1169
1 Room with Hot Tub	Recreation Room	303/567-2566
1 Room with Fireplace	Elevation: 9000	E-mail: vaneden@juno.com
1 Room with Woodstove	Credit Cards: VM	www.coloradodirectory.com/vanedenranch
Central Hot Tub	Rates: $50-$100	
Central Campfire Area	Open: All Year	

At the resort:

At resort or within 15 minutes:

Collegiate Peaks Area

Including Buena Vista, Granite, Leadville, Monarch, Nathrop, Poncha Springs, Salida & Twin Lakes — Map: I-12, J-12, H-12, K-12, J-13 & H-11

The small town of **Buena Vista**, nestled at the base of the Collegiate and Sawatch Mountain Ranges, is named for its "good view." In the Upper Arkansas River Valley, Buena Vista and its surroundings were once home to the Ute Indians. Lt. Zebulon Pike, who passed through in 1806, found evidence of some 3,000 Utes. Like other Colorado towns, miners came when they learned of gold strikes in the area and ranchers eventually followed. The city has a rowdy past, once hosting 36 bars and a hanging judge. Now Buena Vista is the jumping off point for some of the best river rafting in Colorado. Brown's Canyon, 8 miles south, is often called the whitewater capital. The impressive Collegiate Range, lies to the west has the most concentrated number of peaks above 14,000' in Colorado, abounds with hiking trails, mountain bike trails and riddled with ghost towns. **Salida** grew quickly in the 1880s when the railroad made it a rail hub. A rip-roaring town, Salida had a famous madam, Laura Evans, who ran a bordello in town from 1896 to 1950! Today, it's still a roaring town, roaring with rapids, that is. Salida boasts the headquarters for the Arkansas River Valley State Park. The town has one of the largest, indoor, hot springs. The Arkansas River is a launching point for some of the best whitewater rafting and is the most boated in the country with rapids ranging from easy to challenging. Accessible from Salida are the Rainbow and Colorado trails for mountain bikers and hikers can enjoy. In the winter try skiing at the much-praised, less-visited Monarch Ski Resort whose basin traps 300 inches annually fluffy powder. In 1880 **Leadville** was the 2nd largest city in Colorado, now it's a quit community with many Victorian-style buildings and mining sites still stand as mementos of the silver boom. The town is a designated National Historic District with eight museums to preserve it's rich history. **Twin Lakes**, at the base of Independence Pass, are natural, glacier-made lakes, measuring 90' deep, almost 2 miles wide and 6 miles long. You can fish from the shoreline or a boat. The majestic mountain backdrop makes this a photographer's dream.

Fun Things to Do

- American Adventure Expeditions (800)288-0675
- Arkansas Valley Adventure Rafting (800) 370-0581
- Black Diamond Expeditions (800) 880-0299
- Buffalo Joe River Trips, Buena Vista (800) 356-7984
- Crazy Horse Jeep Rentals (800) 888-7320
- Good Times Rafting (800) 808-0357
- High Country Camper & Canoe Rentals (719) 395-6041
- Monarch Crest Tram Ride (719) 539-4091
- River Runners Ltd., Salida (800) 525-2081
- Twin Lakes Nordic Inn Restaurant (800) 626-7812

Arkansas Valley Adventures Rafting & Cabins

This family oriented rafting, lodging and camping resort offers it all in one location! The cabins here boast a view of the spectacular Collegiate Peaks. Use Arkansas Valley Cabins are your mountain retreat for a quick, weekend getaway, or for a long summer vacation. Three of authentic log cabins are available with kitchens and two without kitchens. Each cabin has an outdoor grill and picnic table. Rustic tent camping — bring your own gear or rent it here — is also available. Hot showers are available for campers.

The resort is dedicated to making your whitewater rafting adventures unforgettable. These trips are fun for the whole family and nine different options are available, from a relaxing float trip to a continuous, heart-pounding adventure. Half-day trips are offered with and without a steak lunch. Full day and multi-day trips are also available. The Arkansas River offers some of the best whitewater rafting in the country. Other activities here including fishing, hiking, mountain biking, volleyball and horseshoes — all on site.

The company's guides are certified in First Aid and CPR — safety and fun are their first priorities. Ask about the weeknight rates for cabin rentals. Pets are allowed for no fee with advanced arrangements.

Location: Fourteen miles north of Buena Vista and seventeen miles south of Leadville on Highway 24 near milepost marker 197

3 Cabins with Kitchen	Pay Phone Available	Duke Bradford, Owner
2 Cabins without Kitchens	Recreation Room	40671 Hwy 24
Central Woodstove	Elevation: 9000	Buena Vista CO 81211
Central Campfire Area	Credit Cards: VM	800/370-0581
	Rates: $60-$65	719/395-2338
	Open: 5/1 to 10/15	Fax: 719/395-3845
		E-mail: dcbradford@yahoo.com
		www.coloradodirectory.com/arkansasvvalleyadventures

At the resort:

At resort or within 15 minutes:

Bunny Lane Cabins

Bunny Lane offers three cabins with kitchenettes and wood burning stoves for heat. The one and two bedroom cabins are modern and semi-modern in pioneer log cabins, each ideal for nightly or weekly rentals. A historic lodge room is also available for groups.

Outstanding scenery and tall shade trees surround Bunny Lane Cabins, making for a quiet and secluded vacation spot. The cabins are near Chalk Creek and only 200 yards from Wright's Lake, both of which have great trout fishing. Enjoy the roaming bunnies, peacocks, goats and chickens. Sorry, but no guest pets are allowed. Walk to the nearby Colorado Continental Divide Trail. Within a short drive are horseback rides, whitewater rafting, museums, golfing, lakes for boating, downhill skiing, cross-country skiing, snowmobiling and hunting. Both restaurants and family, evening entertainment are within a 5 minute drive. End your day with a soothing soak in the nearby hot springs.

All units are non-smoking.

Location: Up Chalk Creek on County Road 291.

3 Cabins with Kitchen	Phone in Lobby	Jeff Determan, Owner
1 Room with Fireplace	All Units Nonsmoking	17290 CR 291
3 Rooms with Wood Stoves	Elevation: 8400	Nathrop CO 81236
	Credit Cards: None	719/395-2800
	Rates: $50-$85	E-mail: Jeffery@bemail.com
	Open: All Year	www.coloradodirectory.com/bunnylanecabins/

At the resort:

At resort or within 15 minutes:

Cabin at Quiet Waters

A lovingly restored 1929 log cabin, the Cabin at Quiet Waters rests on four secluded acres along Cottonwood Creek. The cabin has two bedrooms plus a futon and sofa, two living areas, a well equipped kitchen, one bath and a phone. It sleeps six or more. This retreat is furnished with comfortable and cozy down comforters, a wood stove, videos, games and books for a snowy winter retreat. In the summer, enjoy the hammocks, campfire and picnic area and inviting front porch.

At the base of Mt. Princeton, Cabin at Quiet Waters has a stocked pond for fishing. Enjoy a cup of coffee in the sunny morning room before heading outdoors to picnic in the meadow, fishing in the creak or pond, watch deer graze in the backyard or simply relax in the fresh mountain air. Mountain bike and ice fish on site. Nearby activities include four wheel drive tours, white water raft trips, museums, golf courses, boat rentals, cross country and snowmobile trails and hunting.

Pay for six nights and get the seventh night free. This is a non-smoking cabin. Guest horses are welcomed but other pets are not allowed.

Location: Just off Cottonwood Pass Road (County Road 306), 4 miles west of Buena Vista.

1 Cabin with Kitchen	Phone in Rooms	Susie & Charlie Blackwell, Owners
1 Room with Woodstove	All Units Nonsmoking	30595 Overlook Run
	Elevation: 8300	Buena Vista CO 81211
	Credit Cards: None	888/842-5338
	Rates: $150	719/395-4928
	Open: All Year	Fax: 719/395-4928
		E-mail: qwaters@amigo.net
		www.coloradodirectory.com/qwaters/

At the resort:

At resort or within 15 minutes:

Collegiate Peaks Vacation Home Rentals

In the heart of Buena Vista, these weekly vacation homes have something for everyone. Victorian Secret Cottage has two bedrooms decorated in an elegant, historical style. Furnished with a washer and dryer, Berber carpet, a deck, views and fenced yard, you'll feel right at home here. Alpine Retreat condo offers two bedrooms in brand new comfort with a double skylight and a hot tub, available from Memorial Day to Labor Day. Apple Tree Chalet condo has three bedrooms, a gas fireplace, deck and hot tub in the summer. All rentals have fully equipped kitchens with dishwasher, oven and range, microwave and a full-sized refrigerator with freezer. Color cable television, VCR with videos, books, games, and phone are in each home as well as on-premise secure storage for bicycles or skis.

All the amenities of Buena Vista are minutes away, from restaurants and shops, to museums, parks and local special events such as the Quilt Show, Gold Rush Days and rodeo. Outdoor activities abound here, including white water rafting, fishing, boating, hiking, mountain biking, gold panning, horseback riding, and touring ghost towns in four wheel drives. Also nearby are tennis courts, a golf course and hot springs. In the winter, you can ski at Monarch resort, snowmobile, cross-country ski, snowshoe, ice fish and hunt.

All accommodations are weekly rentals and no smoking or pets are allowed.

Location: In the heart of Buena Vista.

3 Vacation Homes	Phone in Rooms	Marilyn & Tom Ross, Owners
Central Hot Tub	All Units Nonsmoking	PO Box 922
	Elevation: 7900	Buena Vista CO 81211-0922
	Credit Cards: VMAD	719/395-2459 (days best)
	Rates: $125	Fax: 719/395-8374
	Open: All Year	E-mail: Katrina@about-books.com
		www.coloradodirectory.com/victoriansecret/

At the resort:

At resort or within 15 minutes:

Colorado Vacation Homes

Colorado Vacation Homes rents fully equipped, private vacation homes in magnificent mountain settings where you'll be surrounded by tall pines, aspens and sparkling streams. The new, clean, quality homes sleep from 2 to 10 people. Choose between 8 properties. Near the South Fork of the Arkansas River, Bear's Den has a great room with cathedral ceilings, a gas stove, completely equipped kitchen, 3 bedrooms, a sleeping loft and 2 baths. Brown's Cabin, which sleeps up to 6, is luxurious log home 8 miles west of Poncha Springs. A three-sided verandah surrounds Brown's Cabin and inside are natural wood walls, vaulted ceilings with a master bedroom king bed and full bath. The River Ranch Home, just 8 miles from Salida on five pastoral acres, has panoramic views of the mountains from its spacious deck, accommodate up to 9 people and is wheelchair accessible. Chimney Rock Chalet, a ranch style vacation home at the base of Mt. Princeton, sleeps 8, fully equipped kitchen, washer and dryer provide all the comforts of home. Creekside Cabin, with 3 bedrooms and 2 baths is 10 miles west of Salida, sleeps 8 and the half acre of lawn is a great place for the kids to play.

All homes are located in the heart of the Rockies, from Garfield/Monarch — just four miles from the ski area — to the base of Mt. Princeton near the historic ghost town of St. Elmo. Whether planning a reunion or group gathering, one of these homes will be just right for you. In the summer, opportunities for hiking, mountain biking, fishing, horseback riding and white water rafting abound. In the winter, cross-country ski, snowshoe, snowmobile, and downhill ski within a short drive from any of the homes.

A two night minimum is required.

Location: The Office is on Highway 50 West.

2 Cabins with Kitchen	Phone in Rooms	Stephen Hall, Owner
6 Vacation Homes	Some Units Nonsmoking	7405 Hwy 50 W Ste 123
2 Rooms with Fireplaces	Elevation: 8000	Salida CO 81201
2 Rooms with Wood Stoves	Credit Cards: VM	800/845-5502
	Rates: $130-$200	719/539-7211
	Open: All Year	Fax: 719/539-7297
		E-mail: sphall@chaffee.net
		www.coloradodirectory.com/covacationhomes

At the resort:

At resort or within 15 minutes:

Crazy Horse Camping Resort & Jeep Rentals

This is a great resort for family reunions with its family oriented activities. Crazy Horse Camping Resort offers two new, modern, log sided cabins with kitchens and the mountains at your doorstep. Five camper tent-cabins are also available.

The resort is located at a scenic old stagecoach stop. Activities on-site include whitewater raft trips, Saturday barbecues, Sunday pancake breakfasts, ice cream socials and horseback rides. Rent a Jeep or ATV on-site and tour ghost towns, abandoned mines and the picturesque back country. Amenities include a large, heated swimming pool, lounge, pavilion, arcade and a store with gifts, fishing licenses and tackle. A restaurant is located here to make your stay worry-free.

Crazy Horse Camping Resort loves having groups! Numerous tent and modern RV sites are also available. Some units are non-smoking. Pets are permitted on the campground.

Location: Five miles north of Buena Vista on Highway 24 near milepost marker 205.

2 Cabins with Kitchen	Pay Phone Available	Peter & Karen Griffith, Owners
5 Camper Cabins	Some Units Nonsmoking	33975 US 24 N
Central Campfire Area	Recreation Room	Buena Vista CO 81211
	Elevation: 8300	800/888-7320
	Credit Cards: VMAD	719/395-2323
	Rates: $30-$75	Fax: 719/395-2401
	Open: 4/15 to 11/1	E-mail: crazyhorse@sni.net
		www.coloradodirectory.com/crazyhorsecamp/

At the resort:

At resort or within 15 minutes:

Forest Creek Cabins

The cabins at Forest Creek are located in a quiet, secluded area away from traffic about a half mile west of Buena Vista. The fully self-contained, all non-smoking cabins have full-size kitchens for your cooking convenience. The rough cut pine exteriors, knotty pine interiors and vaulted ceilings are tastefully decorated for the '90s. Some of the furniture is custom made of aspen logs for a full Colorado mountain experience. The whole family will appreciate the board games left in each cabin for your enjoyment. Forest Creek Cabins offers a vacation off the beaten path on Cottonwood Pass.

Surrounded by the Collegiate Peaks, Forest Creek has a small creek running through the property. Try your luck catching some of the tasty trout at Cottonwood Lake nearby. The cabin resort is close to all area attractions, including hiking, biking, downhill and cross country skiing, and snowmobiling in the Collegiate Peaks mountain ranges and rafting the Arkansas River.

Multiple night and weekly rentals are available. A deposit is required with your reservation. Reservations are advised.

Location: Once in town, drive exactly 2 miles west of the only traffic light toward Cottonwood Pass. On Country Road 306.

4 Cabins with Kitchen	Recreation Room	Brian Hopple, Owner
All Units Nonsmoking	Elevation: 8000	16115 CR 306
	Credit Cards: VM	Buena Vista CO 81211
	Rates: $95-$175	800/603-7690
	Open: All Year	719/395-4819
		www.coloradodirectory.com/forestcreekcabins

At the resort: *At resort or within 15 minutes:*

Gold Camp Recreational Resort

Gold Camp offers a diverse selection of lodging for groups and individuals. Choose between cabins, and motel rooms Two cabins have cooking facilities and one has a fireplace. The six lodge rooms are bed and breakfast accommodations. The lodge rooms range from one to three bedrooms, and have full kitchens, decks and incredible views. A bunkhouse that sleeps 12 is also available.

The resort also has a restaurant for hot meals, a store and rental equipment available. Corporate and family groups will find the new Challenge Course Program, featuring the Alpine Tower (a 50-foot self standing high rope course pictured), giant swing and a low element challenge course, a way to have fun, create team work and promote physical fitness. Twenty-five rock climbing routes are on-site. This is a great place for mountaineers of all skills, from beginners to experts. Learn how to orienteer in the wilderness. Gold Camp offers clinics, lessons and tours for all the adventure sports offered on-site, including fishing, horseback

riding, whitewater rafting, rock climbing, mountain biking, cross-country skiing, snowmobiling and snowshoeing. Learn to walk on water in a hydro broncs. Nearby is a museum, golf course, downhill ski area, ice fishing and hunting as well as lakes for boating. A soak in the hot tub is a must after a challenging day!

platform tents and tent sites are also available. Pets are allowed in the campground at no additional cost. Guest horses are also welcome.

Location: Between Buena Vista and Leadvile on Highway 24 near milepost marker 197.

2 Cabins with Kitchen	Phone in Lobby	Mikki & Bob Keele, Resort Dir
6 Vacation Homes	Bed & Breakfast Available	40579 N Hwy 24
2 Lodging Rooms	Some Units Nonsmoking	Buena Vista CO 81211
9 Camper Cabins	Elevation: 8500	800/709-0418
12 Beds in Bunkhouse	Credit Cards: VMAD	719/395-3234
1 Room with Fireplace	Rates: $30-$75	E-mail: info@goldcamp.com
Central Campfire Area	Open: All Year	www.coloradodirectory.com/goldcamp

At the resort:

At resort or within 15 minutes:

Ice Palace Inn Bed & Breakfast

Step into the past at the Ice Palace Inn where the six romantic guest rooms are elegantly decorated with Victorian antiques, Ice Palace mementos, quilts, feather beds, ceiling fans and exquisite private baths. The inn was built at the turn-of-the-century using lumber from the famous Leadville Ice Palace. Some of the rooms, named for the original ice palace, such as The Grand Ballroom Suite. The Skating Rink and the Crystal Carnival, have views of Mount Massive and Turquoise Lake.

This Leadville bed and breakfast also has a hot tub for your relaxing pleasure. Start your day with a gourmet breakfast and end it with afternoon teas, coffee, hot chocolate and goodies which are offered daily. Enjoy these amenities in the parlor, in front of the fireplace or in the game room. Discover the variety of shops, galleries and restaurants within walking distance in Leadville. Summer and fall activities include sailing, taking a ride on the highest standard gauge railroad in the country, mountain biking, hiking, golfing, fishing, taking a carriage ride or historical tour, white water rafting, boating, hot air ballooning, gold panning and much more. Visit the town's museums, antique shops, tennis courts, swimming pool, running and bicycle races, art and music festivals. In the winter, ski, ice skate, snowmobile, sled, snow shoe, ice fish and take a sleigh ride.

The inn is non-smoking and no pets are allowed.

Location: From Denver take I-70 to Colorado Highway 91, 24 miles to Leadville. From Colorado Springs take Highway 24 north to Leadville. Highways 24 and 91 turn into Harrison Avenue, drive west on West 8th street to Spruce, Ice Palace is the the the left.

6 Lodging Rooms	Phone in Lobby	Kami & Giles Kolakowski, Innkeepers
Central Hot Tub	Bed & Breakfast Available	813 Spruce Street
Central Fireplace	All Units Nonsmoking	Leadville CO 80461
	Recreation Room	800/754-2840
	Elevation: 10430	719/486-8272
	Credit Cards: VMAD	Fax: 719/486-0345
	Rates: $79-$119	E-mail: ipalace@sni.net
	Open: All Year	www.coloradodirectory.com/icepalace/

At the resort:

At resort or within 15 minutes:

Liars' Lodge Bed & Breakfast

Liars Lodge is a family friendly bed and breakfast resort. Located on 23 piñon covered acres on the banks of the Arkansas River, this modern lodge has five rooms. All rooms have a queen bed with a private bath, and many have sleeping lofts for kids. Two rooms have decks and two have jacuzzi tubs. Choose between rooms with river views and those with mountain views. Check in treats and an evening beverage are included with your room.

Activities in the area surrounding Liars Lodge include rafting, kayaking, hiking, fishing, four wheel driving and mountain biking. Visit one of the nearby ghost towns for a glimpse of the past. A boat launch is on-site. Liars Lodge sits on the Arkansas River and boasts over a third of a mile of virtually exclusive river frontage. In addition to a full breakfast, the lodge provides a "snack sack" for those spending a day outdoors having fun. Buena Vista is only a mile away, but you'll feel like it's worlds away.

Children five and older with well behaved parents are welcomed! Smoking is permitted on the outdoor decks only. Pets are not allowed unless the lodge's two Labradors approve in advance.

Location: One mile north of Buena Vista on County Raod 371 (Colorado Avenue).

this big...

.between the eyes

5 Lodging Rooms	Phone in Rooms	Carl & Connie Bauer, Owners
2 Rooms with Hot Tubs	Bed & Breakfast Available	30000 CR 371 (Colo Ave)
Central Fireplace	All Units Nonsmoking	Buena Vista CO 81211
Central Campfire Area	Recreation Room	888/LIARS LODGE
	Elevation: 8000	719/395-3440
	Credit Cards: VM	E-mail: mail@liarslodge.com
	Rates: $85-$115	www.coloradodirectory.com/liarslodge
	Open: All Year	

At the resort:

At resort or within 15 minutes:

Love Ranch

Mark & Josephine "Jo" Love purchased and named it Love Ranch in the 1920s. Mark Love guided Teddy Roosevelt into the mountains before his untimely death in 1930. Jo went on to establish a unique guest ranch that became a treasured retreat for thousands of visitors, including many historical figures and writers, like Dwight D. Eisenhower and author Alex Haley. Jo passed away in the '70s, but her spirit and traditions live on at the ranch today. Love Ranch is in the beautiful Chalk Creek Canyon between Mt. Princeton and Mt. Antero, part of the San Isabel National Forest. Currently 8 rustic and modern cabins and 1 private apartment make up the Ranch. Modestly furnished cabins accommodate from 2 to 7 people; rent weekly during the summer. Honeymoon, Knotty Pine, Hermit, Woodsy, and Cozy are some of the cabins, which all lie next to Chalk Creek. Partial amenities include a refrigerator, microwave, toaster, coffee maker, and hotplates plus firepits and picnic tables.

Anglers will enjoy the plentiful fishing for rainbow and brook trout in the ranch stream and in the two lakes just a mile from the cabins. Nearby activities are endless: rafting, horseback riding, swimming at the hot springs, hiking, biking, climbing 14,000' mountains, 4-wheeling, visiting the St. Elmo ghost town, rock-hounding for crystals, wildlife viewing, hunting, skiing, snowshoeing, snowmobiling, and relaxing by campfires. Visit the towns of Buena Vista and Salida for golfing and dining.

A great place to hold a family reunion, outside wedding or wilderness retreat. Also, running specialized retreats and planned adventure vacations throughout the year plus guided fishing trips.

Location: Six miles south of Buena Vista on Highway 285, then 8 miles west on County Road 162. About 18 miles north of Salida on Highway 285.

8 Cabins with Kitchen	Phone in Lobby	Chris Phillips & Doug Baumgardner,
1 Vacation Home	Some Units Nonsmoking	Managers
1 Lodging Room	Elevation: 8500	18670 CR 162
1 Room with Fireplace	Credit Cards: VM	Nathrop CO 81236
10 Rooms with Wood Stoves	Rates: $35-$125	719/395-2366
	Open: All Year	E-mail: LRanchCO@sni.net
		www.coloradodirectory.com/loveranch/

At the resort:

At resort or within 15 minutes:

Mount Elbert Lodge & Cabins

Step out of today's often hectic world into an earlier time at Mount Elbert Lodge for year-round fun in the Colorado Rockies. On Lake Creek at the base of Mt. Elbert, this former, turn-of-the-century stage stop lodge is easily accessible, yet remotely private. The comfortable, log housekeeping cabins feature separate kitchen and living spaces, private bathrooms, and porches that encourage relaxing in the sun. The bed and breakfast lodge has five rooms, including the "Mount Elbert" room, with a southern exposure and a private balcony; and the "Twin Peaks" room, with a view of the valley from its east and south windows. The lodge's common area offers a woodstove for cozy winter retreats. There are no televisions, radios or phones so you can truly get away from hectic city life.

The lodge serves healthy and wholesome complimentary breakfasts. Step out your cabin door and choose a hike to the peaks (trailhead to Mount Elbert begins at the lodge), wander the mountain meadows, mountain bike rides though San Isabel National Forest or sit on the porch and soak up the glorious Colorado sun and sky. Aspen and Leadville offer shopping, dining and exploring in old mining towns. Climb several other "fourteeners" nearby in the summer. Enjoy excellent lake, reservoirs and stream fishing and some of the country's best whitewater rafting. In winter the landscape changes from green to white so you can cross-county

ski or snowshoe from your back door. Alpine skiing is only a 45 minutes drive. Other winter activities include ice skating and ice fishing.

Location: Off Highway 82. About 4.5 miles west of Twin Lakes village.

6 Cabins with Kitchen	Phone in Lobby	Scott Boyd & Laura Downing, Owners
5 Lodging Rooms	Bed & Breakfast Available	PO Box 40
2 Rooms with Hot Tubs	All Units Nonsmoking	Twin Lakes CO 81251-0040
4 Rooms with Fireplaces	Recreation Room	800/381-4433
Central Woodstove	Elevation: 9700	719/486-0594
	Credit Cards: VMAD	Fax: 719/486-2236
	Rates: $59-$88	E-mail: mtelbert@amigo.net
	Open: All Year	www.coloradodirectory.com/mountelbertlodge/

At the resort:

At resort or within 15 minutes:

Piñon Valley Ranch

Encircled by lovely mountain views and located on a 73-acre spread, off the highway and peaceful, Piñon Valley Ranch has quiet country cabins equipped with either a kitchenette or full kitchen. A television and VCR are provided in the cabins for in-room movie viewing. Broadcast channels are not available. The kitchenette cabin sleeps four while the full kitchen cabin can accommodate up to six comfortably (more if you want to be cozy). With only 2 cabins on 73-acres there are few people and an abundance of nature and tranquility.

The Ranch is a mere 20 minutes from Monarch Ski Resort and 15 minutes from Salida's soothing hot springs pool. Restaurants, jeep tours, a bowling alley and golf course are all nearby. Area activities include whitewater rafting, mountain biking, horseback riding, fishing and hunting.

No pets are allowed at the ranch. Cots are available for an extra fee.

Location: Off Highway 50, about 2 miles west of junction 50 & 285, then north on County Road 250 (first county road after junction) a quarter mile beyond County Road 140. Not as far west as Maysville.

2 Cabins with Kitchen	Phone in Lobby	Paul & Cheri Jensen, Owners
1 Room with Fireplace	All Units Nonsmoking	8309 CR 250
	Elevation: 7500	Salida CO 81201
	Credit Cards: None	719/539-6729
	Rates: $55-$65	Fax: 719/539-9370 Fax & Recorder
	Open: All Year	www.coloradodirectory.com/pinonvalleyranch

At the resort:

At resort or within 15 minutes:

River Suites at Monarch Shadows

Just minutes from the Monarch Ski Area, River Suites offers new, first class chalets nestled in aspen groves. The one and two-bedroom suites have full kitchens with microwaves and ice makers. You'll also appreciate the private hot tubs outside the bedroom door, satellite television, VCRs, wood burning stoves, phones, king beds and queen sleepers in each of the units. Just outside your front door is a redwood lined river walk to enjoy and quiet beaver ponds to wander among.

In addition to the amenities of Monarch Ski & Snowboard Area nearby, the River Suites are near whitewater rafting, fishing, four wheel driving, horseback riding, golfing, mountain biking, mountain climbing and hiking. Within a short drive are restaurants and family evening entertainment in historic downtown Salida.

All the suites are non-smoking.

Location: Between Salida and Monarch on Highway 50 West.

8 Cabins with Kitchen	Phone in Rooms	Bill & Patricia Zapel, Managers
8 Rooms with Hot Tubs	All Units Nonsmoking	16724 Hwy 50 W
8 Rooms with Wood Stoves	Elevation: 8500	Salida CO 81201
Central Campfire Area	Credit Cards: VMA	800/464-6953
	Rates: $125-$200	719/539-6953
	Open: All Year	Fax: 719/539-6773
		E-mail: riversuites@monarch-shadows.com
		www.coloradodirectory.com/riversuites

At the resort:

At resort or within 15 minutes:

Sagewood Cabins

High in the heart of the Collegiate Peaks Range, at the foot of Mt. Harvard (14,000+ feet) Sagewood offers quaint, quiet, country log cabins located on a small family ranch. A true Colorado getaway, the cabins, adjacent to the San Isabel National Forest, have no televisions or telephones (the office phone is available if you need it). These country style cabins are full of antiques. Some cabins have fireplaces; all have private baths and lofts. Each is set up for basic housekeeping with dishes, cooking utensils and linens.

Area activities include hiking, biking, fishing, horseback riding, four-wheel driving trails and exploring ghost towns. In the winter, come for snowmobiling and skiing. Year-round, enjoy shopping or resting and relaxing away from it all. Stay for a night, a week or a month.

Reservations are recommended. Sagewood is normally open from May through November; however, the season may begin earlier or later due to weather conditions. Call ahead for open dates.

Location: Eleven and a half miles north of Buena Vista on Highway 24, near milepost markers 199/200, a quarter mile west of the highway.

3 Cabins with Kitchen	Phone in Lobby	Kristen Ahlstedt, Owner
2 Rooms with Fireplaces	Elevation: 9000	38951-B N Hwy 24
	Credit Cards: None	Buena Vista CO 81211
	Rates: $65	719/395-2582
	Open: 5/1 to 11/15	www.coloradodirectory.com/sagewoodcabins/

At the resort:

At resort or within 15 minutes:

Twin Lakes Nordic Inn

An authentic century-old stagecoach stop and former brothel, the Twin Lakes Nordic Inn has been romantically restored with imported Austrian featherbeds and antiques. All of the rooms offer different styles, views and architecture. Some have their own baths; others have shared baths.

The inn's restaurant, open all day, specializes in authentic German cuisine, beers and wines and fireside dining. A video room with a film library is available for those evenings when you want to relax indoors. Ask your host to arrange river rafting trips on the Arkansas in the summer. Explore the ghost town of Interlaken on the south side of the larger twin lake and accessible only by horseback, mountain bike, skis or on foot. In the heart of the Pike-San Isabel National Forest on the shore of Twin Lakes, the Nordic Inn is an ideal base camp for cross-country and alpine skiing, fishing, hiking, hunting and windsurfing. Twice a year, be sure to attend the "Hookers Ball" — but only with an appropriate costume!

Location: In Twin Lakes, off of Highway 82, near milepost marker 79.

1 Cabin with Kitchen	Phone in Lobby	John & Carol Slater, Owners
13 Lodging Rooms	Bed & Breakfast Available	PO Box 410
Central Fireplace	All Units Nonsmoking	Twin Lakes CO 81251-0410
	Recreation Room	800/626-7812 x
	Elevation: 9227	719/486-1830 & fax
	Credit Cards: VMD	www.coloradodirectory.com/twinlakesnordicinn
	Rates: $48-$70	
	Open: All Year	

At the resort:

At resort or within 15 minutes:

Twin Peaks Cabins

Twin Peaks Cabins are at the edge of the forest and offer a lovely view of the south side of upper Twin Lakes. These modern, fully equipped, log-sided housekeeping cabins have the mountain peaks of the Sawatch Range looming at their door step. The large unit has 4 bedrooms with queen-size beds, 2 baths, a deck and can sleep up to 10 persons. The small cabin is ideal for a couple, with a double bed, small refrigerator toaster oven and double hot plate for cooking. The medium size cabin has two rooms: a kitchen/living room and bedroom with two double beds. None of the cabins has televisions or telephones; however, there are books, magazines, and games to pass the time.

The gift shop on-site features leather and fur items including sheepskins, steer hides and alpaca; and southwestern gifts. For the sports enthusiasts there is a basketball court, volleyball/badminton net, and horseshoe pit. The kids will love the sandbox complete with shovels and play toys. Bring your boat to take advantage of the good fishing in lakes, boat ramps within minutes. Fish for brook, lake, and

brown trout in the many streams, some within walking distance. Hiking trails begin near the cabins and offer enough scenery to keep photographers busy for years! The cabins are a quarter mile west of Twin Lakes on the road to Independence Pass, the "high road" to Aspen.

Location: Off of Highway 82, near milepost marker 78. A quarter mile west of Twin Lakes

3 Cabins with Kitchen	Phone in Lobby	Fred & Judy Woodcock, Owners
	Elevation: 9200	PO Box 86
	Credit Cards: VM	Twin Lakes CO 81251-0086
	Rates: $45-$80	719/486-2667 & fax
	Open: 5/15 to 11/30	www.coloradodirectory.com/twinpeakscabins

At the resort:

At resort or within 15 minutes:

Woodland Brook Cabins

These modern, housekeeping cabins offer mountain seclusion with in-town convenience. Set off of the highway in a cottonwood and Ponderosa pine grove, Woodland Brook is quiet and relaxing. Pick between two-bedroom and one-bedroom cabins with fully equipped kitchens, color cable televisions, sleeper sofas and fireplaces or efficiency cabins with kitchenettes and color cable television. All cabins are provided with pots, pans, dishes and linens.

Fish the lakes and streams of this pleasant valley, or visit historic ghost towns and mines. Woodland Brook is a good base camp for winter skiing at Monarch and Cooper ski areas, both only 45 minutes away. The area also features snowmobiling and cross-country skiing. During the summer, be sure to experience some of the best kayaking and whitewater in the U.S.A.! Other activities include hiking, and golfing. Good game hunting in the fall. The resort's bubbly hot tub is wonderful after a day of mountain adventures.

Your pets are welcome to vacation with you here! A one night advance deposit is required when placing your reservation. A discount of 10 percent is offered on stays of 5 days or more. Discount ski tickets are available for guests. Firewood is furnished.

Location: Within the city limits of Buena Vista, a few blocks off of Highway 24, near milepost marker 210.

14 Cabins with Kitchen	Phone in Lobby	Riaan & Marjorie van Niekerk, Owners
8 Rooms with Fireplaces	Elevation: 8000	PO Box 418
Central Hot Tub	Credit Cards: VMAD	Buena Vista CO 81211-0418
	Rates: $60-$85	719/395-2922
	Open: All Year	Fax: 719/395-8672
		E-mail: wbcabins@chaffee.net
		www.coloradodirectory.com/woodlandbrookcabins

At the resort:

At resort or within 15 minutes:

Conejos River Canyon

Including Antonito, Capulin & Platoro — Map: P-13 & O-11

The southern San Luis Valley city of **Antonito** is rich in culture and history from the Ute Indians and the Spanish who called the valley home. Antonito lies between the Conejos and the San Antonio rivers at an elevation of 7,888' and is the gateway to the beautiful, 40-mile Conejos River Canyon where outdoor enthusiasts can fish, hunt and hike. The upper Conejos River offers excellent trout fishing and the lower part is good for rainbows, browns and the occasional northern pike. Near the Conejos Headwaters is the community of **Platoro**. The Platoro Reservoir has wonderful fishing for browns, rainbows and some kokanee soon after the spring thaw and is stocked with rainbow trout in the summer. No matter the river or lake, fishermen will always have something biting their line in Conejos River Canyon area. Antonito was once the "mainline" of the infant Denver and Rio Grande railroads. Today, Antonito is the main station for the Cumbres & Toltec Scenic Railroad — the highest and longest narrow-gauge railroad in the North American continent — an authentic railroad trip to Chama, New Mexico, that brings Colorado history to the present day. Nearby the town of **Conejos** boasts the oldest church in Colorado, Our Lady of Guadeloupe Church. The Rio Grand National Forest offers rolling hills, river canyons, and thick pine and aspen forests to explore.

Fun Things to Do

- Cumbres & Toltec Scenic Railroad (719) 376-5983
- Mountain Home Lodge Restaurant, Store & Snowmobile Rentals (800) 758-8379
- Our Lady of Guadeloupe Church (719) 376-5985
- Rio Grande National Forest Headquarters (719) 852-5941

Conejos Cabins

Near the Continental Divide on an easily-traveled 23-mile gravel road, Conejos Cabins has ten riverside cabins. The large, family cabin can sleep up to 18 people. The two bedroom cabin can accommodate up to 8, while the small cabin with one bedroom sleeps 4. Cabins have dishes, cooking utensils and bedding while larger cabins have fireplaces furnished with wood. Cook your daily meals inside or out-side on the handy grills. The resort is surrounded by mountains, on the Conejos River and an old gold mining town.

Plan to rent fishing boats to cruise the nearby Platoro Reservoir. Rent a horse nearby or bring your own for a ride to the high mountain lakes in the surrounding area where the fishing is pristine.

First night's deposit is required within 10 days of making a reservation.

Location: Take Highway 17 west from Antonito 23 miles, near milepost marker 17, to Horca. Go north 23 miles on gravel road #250, follow the river up to the cabins.

9 Cabins with Kitchen	Pay Phone Available	Bob, Dixie & Troy Peterson, Owners
1 Vacation Home	Elevation: 9750	PO Box 519
5 Rooms with Fireplaces	Credit Cards: VM	Antonito CO 81120-0519
	Rates: $50-$55	719/376-2547
	Open: 5/28 to 10/15	E-mail: infodesk@conejoscabins.com
		www.coloradodirectory.com/conejoscabins/

At the resort:

At resort or within 15 minutes:

Conejos River Guest Ranch

With a mile of river frontage, Conejos River Guest Ranch is situated in the Rio Grande National Forest on twelve acres. Enjoy a bed & breakfast adventure in the 104 year-old lodge with a classy western decor and exterior wrap-around deck. The lodge rooms have private baths, and a choice of king, queen or double bed, and a hide-a-bed. A full, scrumptious breakfast is included as well. Or choose a comfortable housekeeping cabin featuring a fully-equipped kitchen sleeping from five to eleven people. Some of the cabins include a cozy woodburning stove. All guests can enjoy the common den area in the lodge with a fireplace, satellite television, game table, bar, and mini-library.

During your stay, be sure to take advantage of horseback riding, basketball, volleyball, horseshoes, hiking, relaxing by the river, and, of course, fishing—all on the premises. Children will enjoy the stocked children's fishing pond and wandering farm animals. Boxed lunches are available daily for your outdoor excursions. Browse through the gift shop for your perfect southwest sovenier. Take a tour of the Rio Grande Forest or the Great Sand Dunes National Monument. Ride on the Cumbres & Toltec Narrow Gauge Railroad; your hosts can make reservations for you. Big game hunting in season is especially popular. Rent a snowmobile or cross-country skis for winter sports. After a full day of activity, enjoy the "Best food in the Canyon" at the restaurant. Campfires and chuckwagon meals are spontaneously planned by your hosts. They would be delighted to help organize and customize your next party, meeting or family reunion.

Advance reservations are recommended. A 50% deposit is required.

Location: At 25390 Highway 17, near milepost marker 26, in Antonito.

6 Cabins with Kitchen	Pay Phone Available	Shorty Fry, Manager
8 Lodging Rooms	Bed & Breakfast Available	PO Box 175
3 Rooms with Wood Stoves	Recreation Room	Conejos CO 81129-0175
Central Fireplace	Elevation: 8700	719/376-2464
Central Woodstove	Credit Cards: VMAD	E-mail: info@conejosranch.com
Central Campfire Area	Rates: $79-$110	www.coloradodirectory.com/conejosriverguest/
	Open: 3/1 to 11/15	

At the resort:

At resort or within 15 minutes:

Cottonwood Meadows Cabins & Fishing Guides

The modern housekeeping cabins at Cottonwood Meadows are in the midst of San Luis Valley's prime fly-fishing country. The cabins are comfortably equipped with a kitchenette, cooking and eating utensils and baths with a tub or shower. The large cabin on the banks of the Conejos River sleeps up to 7 persons. Anglers will want to make this their base camp for catching tasty, trout suppers!

Take guided fishing trips into the Rio Grande National Forest, including the Conejos River and its many tributaries (License #1161). If you crave solitude while casting, fish all day in backwoods streams. Most Cottonwood Meadow trips are limited to no more than two guests per guide. Our season generally runs from may through October with July, August, and September being the prime months for the dry-fly enthusiast. In addition to guided fishing trips, take a horseback ride or go on an overnight trip into the wilderness. Bring the family along and visit other nearby attractions; including the Cumbres & Toltec Scenic Railroad, the Great Sand Dunes National Monument and the Rio Grande Gorge.

Location: 5 miles west of Antonito on Highway 17, near milepost 35.

5 Cabins with Kitchen	Pay Phone Available	Randy & Naomi Keys, Owners
	Recreation Room	34591 Hwy 17
	Elevation: 7600	Antonito CO 81120
	Credit Cards: VMAD	719/376-5660
	Rates: $49-$100	www.coloradodirectory.com/cottonwoodmeadows
	Open: All Year	cabins/

At the resort:

At resort or within 15 minutes:

High Plains Drift Inn Bed & Breakfast

Experience the 1800s at this working horse and cattle ranch where the plains meet the Colorado Rockies. High Plains Drift Inn offers one cabin with a cooking facilities, seven bed and breakfast ranch rooms and a bunk house that sleeps 16 — ideal for family reunions and hunters. The panoramic view from the ranch is so breathtaking, you'll hardly believe your eyes. Mountains completely encircle the valley, with some snow-capped peaks adding to the luster.

You won't need to leave this resort to enjoy a great vacation! The inn is also home to an historical western working town where you can spend the day watching and participating in 36 lifestyle demonstrations of the 1800s. In the Blacksmith shop you can watch as hot forged metal is formed and shaped on an anvil or the 1800s drill press. Wander over to the General Store and learn how gold nuggets were used on a scale weight for trade. Try out quill and ink writing and take an evening buggy ride. This is a fun learning experience for children and adults alike. In addition, the inn offers chuckwagon suppers with guitar and harmonica music, driving cattle, horseback rides, lye soap making. Relaxing activities include pitching horseshoes and counting baby goats! Across the valley from the ranch is Great Sand Dunes National Monument. Wildlife, including bighorn sheep, mule deer, elk and antelope, abound here. Other outdoor activities include hiking, fishing, four wheel driving, mountain biking, snowshoeing, snowmobiling and more.

Package vacation prices include all meals, horseback riding and activities. Pets and horses are allowed with advanced arrangements. The ranch is also open daily to the public. Ask about the special rates for groups and extended stays over three days.

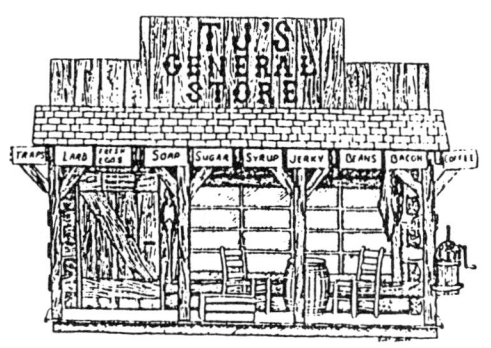

Location: Fifteen miles south of Monte Vista on County Road 6, pavement ends, continue 2.4 miles on gravel, then west on driveway.

1 Cabin with Kitchen	Bed & Breakfast Available	R.V. & Margaret Robertson
7 Lodging Rooms	Recreation Room	PO Box 203
16 Beds in Bunkhouse	Elevation: 8040	Capulin CO 81124-0203
Central Fireplace	Credit Cards: None	800/365-4681
Central Woodstove	Rates: $178	www.coloradodirectory.com/highplainsdriftinn
Central Campfire Area	Open: All Year	

At the resort:

At resort or within 15 minutes:

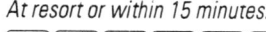

Lodge at Platoro, The

Snug in the high mountains of southern Colorado Texan Court Cabins features housekeeping cabins and lodge rooms. Their cabins sleep from two to four people and are completely furnished with kitchens and private bathrooms. Each lodge room sleep two and has private bathrooms. The cabins are surrounded by the San Juan Mountains with breathtaking views and nestled near the Conejos River for your audio visual delight.

The lodge features a game room with a pool table, gift shop and coin laundry. There are ample mountain biking trails in the area and with the resorts bike rental facility its easy to plan a last minute excursion. The area offers some of the best hunting and fishing in the state. Bring your boat and enjoy Platoro Reservoir, the highest man made lake in North America, a short drive away. In addition to the reservoir there are over 100 lakes in the area, an anglers delight. Bird enthusiast will be delighted and photographers should bring extra film. There are guided fishing and horseback riding tours leaving right from your cabin. The resort is open through the first rifle season in October.

A deposit of one night is required with reservations. Stay seven nights and only pay for six. Children under 5 years old stay free. Pets are welcome to join you.

Location: Take Highway 17 west from Antonito 20 miles, near milepost 17, to Horca. Go north 23 miles on gravel road #250, follow the river up to the cabins.

10 Cabins with Kitchen	Pay Phone Available	Marice & Glenn Lindsey, Owners
3 Lodging Rooms	Bed & Breakfast Available	FDR 250 at Platoro
Central Hot Tub	Some Units Nonsmoking	Antonito CO 81120
Central Fireplace	Recreation Room	719/376-2321
Central Campfire Area	Elevation: 10000	www.coloradodirectory.com/lodgeatplatoro
	Credit Cards: VM	
	Rates: $35-$300	
	Open: 5/15 to 11/1	

At the resort:

At resort or within 15 minutes:

Mountain Home Lodge

Located in southern Colorado in the scenic Conejos Canyon 22 miles west of Antonito, Mountain Home Lodge has breath-taking scenery year-round. Choose between one and two bedroom, modern, light housekeeping units. Both have full kitchens and separate living areas. The one bedroom units have a king bed and a queen hide-a-bed. The two bedroom units have a king bed, two single beds and a queen hide-a-bed.

Mountain Home Lodge has a restaurant, gift shop, and laundry facilities on the premises for your convenience. In the winter, take a snowmobile tour and ride to the top of the Continental Divide for an unforgettable adventure. In the summer, take in the breathtaking scenery of the San Juan Mountains via horseback. This area offers excellent big game hunting and gold medal waters for trophy trout fishing. The Conejos River has been designated a Wild Trout River by the state of Colorado. The lodge is less than 30 minutes from the famous Cumbres Toltec Narrow Gauge Steam Railroad — a ride on this is a trip through the past as well as panoramic vistas. Be sure to take time out for a dip in the hot tub after your day's adventure.

Location: On Highway 17, milepost marker 17.

12 Lodging Rooms	Pay Phone Available	Betty & Sherman Matthys, Owners
3 Rooms with Fireplaces	Some Units Nonsmoking	0047 FDR 250
Central Hot Tub	Recreation Room	Antonito CO 81120
Central Woodstove	Elevation: 8650	800/758-8379
	Credit Cards: VMAD	719/376-5393
	Rates: $70-$70	Fax: 719/376-2245
	Open: All Year	www.coloradodirectory.com/mountainhomelodge/

At the resort:

At resort or within 15 minutes:

Ponderosa Campground & Cabins

The combination of pine trees, cottonwood trees and the Conejos River make this a beautiful vacation spot. Stay in newly remodeled, housekeeping cabins surrounded by large cottonwoods, pines, firs and willows. Gather firewood in the area. A place for leisure with its clean, crisp mountain air, Ponderosa Cabins includes one mile of access along the rushing Conejos River and rests at the foot of the scenic Cumbres Pass. In the summertime, the climate is dry in the day and cool at night.

Hot showers, clean restrooms and a coin laundry are on-site for your convenience. A game room with board games, pool table and video games are on the property. With the river just steps away, fishing opportunities abound. Mountain biking and hiking trails are a short distance away. Kayaking and rafting is excellent here in June.

RV and tent sites and an indoor, group meeting area are also available.

Location: On Highway 17 at milepost marker 19.

5 Cabins with Kitchen	Pay Phone Available	Karl Casebeer, Owner
Central Fireplace	All Units Nonsmoking	19600 W Hwy 17
	Recreation Room	Antonito CO 81120
	Elevation: 8500	719/376-5857
	Credit Cards: VM	www.coloradodirectory.com/ponderosacampcabins/
	Rates: $47	
	Open: 5/26 to 9/30	

At the resort:

At resort or within 15 minutes:

Twin Rivers Cabins & RV Park

Away from the hustle and bustle, at the mouth of the beautiful Conejos Canyon where the fishing and hunting are excellent, are Twin Rivers' country-decorated cabins. Choose from 8 rustic housekeeping cabins sprawled about Twin Rivers' 12 acres ranging in size from a studio to 2 bedrooms. Each is furnished with linens, dishes, cooking utensils and color television, plus an outdoor bar-b-que grill and picnic table.

Fly fish right at your doorstep in the park's two stocked streams. Or cast your line in nearby reservoirs, mountain lakes, rivers and streams. Play volleyball, badminton, or horsehoes while letting the kids romp in the playground. A tackle and gift shop are on the property for supplies, ice and souvenirs. Arrange for a catered chuckwagon dinner or a good old fashioned hay ride. The Rio Grande National Forest and San Juan Mountains are within 10 miles for outstanding hiking and mountain biking. Take a trip to Taos, New Mexico or the Great Sand Dunes National Monument, both just an hour away. Guest horses are allowed.

RV and tent sites in the shade, an indoor, group meeting area, group activities and catering are available. Ask about the family rates.

Location: 5 miles west of Antonito and the Cumbres & Toltec Scenic Railroad depot, on Highway 17, near milepost marker 34.

8 Cabins with Kitchen Central Campfire Area	Pay Phone Available Recreation Room Elevation: 7600 Credit Cards: VMD Rates: $45-$65 Open: 5/1 to 11/15	Jim & Linda McGee, Owners 34044 Hwy 17 Antonito CO 81120 888/689-6787 719/376-5710 Fax: 719/376-5954 E-mail: twnrvrs@fone.net www.coloradodirectory.com/twinriverscabinsrv park/

At the resort:

At resort or within 15 minutes:

Creede

Map: M-9

Isolated and picturesque, **Creede**, at 8,854', is in Mineral County where 95 percent of the land is national forest or wilderness. Prospector Nicholas Creede discovered silver here in 1889 and one of his mines, the Amethyst, produced $2 million one year. What attracted hundreds of miners also brought crooks: "Soapy" Smith opened the Orleans Club to separate miners from their riches. He was eventually banned from Creede which was also home to other famous westerners, including Calamity Jane and Bob Ford, the man who shot Jesse James in the back. Today, the old mining town atmosphere still exists in restaurants, shops and the Creede Repertory Theater. The Wheeler Geologic Area, 24 miles northeast, is a photographer's dream: unusual volcanic rock formations have earned it the name City of Gnomes. From the Rio Grande Reservoir, 30 miles away, to Creede, people raft and fish for the plentiful German brown trout along the Rio Grande headwaters. The Bachelor Historic Loop, a 17-mile ride through the unique silver mining district and two ghost towns, and the Silver Thread Scenic Byway, which runs from South Fork through Creede northwest to Lake City, are two ways to enjoy the backcountry without crowds. Along the Silver Thread Scenic Byway, State Highway 149, are some of the most majestic valleys in all of Colorado — the distances between mountain peaks appears vast and mesmerizing.

Fun Things to Do

- Creede Ranger District (719) 658-2556
- Creede Repertory Theater (719) 658-2540
- Creede Underground Firehouse (719) 658-0811
- Rio Grande National Forest & Weminuche Wilderness (719) 658-2556
- Underground Mining Museum (719) 658-0811

Antlers Rio Grande Lodge

Antlers Rio Grande Lodge, a year-round resort, is a picturesque mountain retreat nestled between the banks of the sparkling Rio Grande River and the Silver Thread Scenic Byway. Most of the secluded modern cabins and motel rooms have gas heat, two double or queen-sized beds, a bathroom with a shower and fully equipped kitchenettes. Enjoy a cup of coffee or a night cap on the porch swing outside your cabin door. If you want a more unique experience ask about their rustic cabins across the Rio Grande River. You'll have to carry your gear over the foot-bridge; but it's worth the effort. At night you'll feel a million miles from civilization with only the sound of the river to lull you to sleep.

For those days when you don't want to explore the outdoors, ranch facilities include a rec room with snack bar (planned for 1999), children's playroom and television room with VCR and movies. Fish right from your front door or cross the foot-bridge to the quiet side of the ranch for your fishing. A fish fry/potluck dinner is a weekly event. You can purchase supplies at the lodge store. The Lodge's 70 acres borders the Rio Grande National Forest, providing unlimited opportunities for year round enjoyment. Other activities include hiking, rafting, biking and horseback riding and in winter cross-country skiing, snow cat tours, snowmobiling and alpine skiing at Wolf Creek Ski Area.

Antlers Ranch offers group rates. Ideal for small groups and reunions. Horses are welcomed for a fee and must be declared at registration. Three corrals available for your horse.

Location: five miles southwest of Creede, just off Highway 149, near milepost marker 26.

13 Cabins with Kitchen	Pay Phone Available	Patti & Charles Powers, Owners
9 Motel Rooms	All Units Nonsmoking	26222 Hwy 149
3 Rooms with Wood Stoves	Recreation Room	Creede CO 81130
Central Fireplace	Elevation: 8720	719/658-2423
Central Campfire Area	Credit Cards: VM	Fax: 719/658-0804
	Rates: $67-$96	E-mail: antlersrio@aol.com
	Open: 5/15 to 10/25	www.coloradodirectory.com/antlersriograndelodge/

At the resort:

At resort or within 15 minutes:

R Running Bar C Guest Ranch & Circle Divide Outfitters

This guest ranch offers true western hospitality in a magnificent setting. Ten comfortably furnished one to three bedroom cabins are available. All cabins have kitchens and private bathrooms.

The cabins are clustered near the main lodge which houses the ranch office and Ralph & Charlie's Restaurant which is open to the public. You'll enjoy the old-fashioned home-style cooking offered here. The ranch has wilderness trips, day trips, overnight camping and pack trips, as well as horseback riding and guided mountain biking tours. At the ranch, you'll be close to fishing and plenty of wild-life viewing. Three generations have been taking hunters into the heart of the Weminuche Wilderness, one the nation's most remote forest and high meadow elk ranges. Nearby Creede is home to the nationally known Creede Repertory Theatre and its Victorian Main Street is lined with art galleries, quaint shops and fine restaurants. The Underground Mining Museum is a must!

Ask about the off-season rates. Pets are allowed at no extra fee with advanced arrangements. Guest horses are welcomed.

Location: Seventeen miles west of Creede in the historic silver mining region of Mineral County.

10 Cabins with Kitchen	Pay Phone Available	Ted & Debby Dooley, Owners
Central Fireplace	Recreation Room	PO Box 186
Central Campfire Area	Elevation: 9000	Creede CO 81130-0370
	Credit Cards: VM	719/658-2253
	Rates: $50-$90	www.coloradodirectory.com/rrunningbarc/
	Open: 5/1 to 10/31	

At the resort:

At resort or within 15 minutes:

Soward Ranch

Off the beaten path in a scenic valley on the Rio Grande River, Soward Ranch has been in the same family for over 100 years — a true Colorado centennial farm. The ranch was homesteaded in 1886 before the time of Creede in what was originally known as Antelope Park. Surrounded by mountains, the large resort and cattle ranch has six lakes with outstanding views. Each cabin, located apart from the others to ensure privacy, are modernized with a full bath, gas heating for cooking and electricity. If you want to rough it, try the ranch's pioneer cabin. Dishes, silverware, utensils, bedding and linen are furnished in all cabins. A central shower and coin washer and dryer are available to all guests.

Fishing for trout on the property along several miles of creeks, on the Rio Grande and at three small private lakes is excellent. Soward Ranch is also close to many other state-stocked lakes, reservoirs and streams. Take a quiet hike along secluded trails and enjoy mountain serenity at its best.

Advance reservations are required. The Soward Ranch has been a quest ranch since 1932.

Location: Fourteen miles southwest of Creede, off of Highway 149, near milepost marker 28.

10 Cabins with Kitchen	Phone in Lobby	Margaret M. Lamb & Scott Lamb
1 Vacation Home	Recreation Room	PO Box 130
3 Rooms with Fireplaces	Elevation: 9000	Creede CO 81130-0130
1 Room with Woodstove	Credit Cards: None	719/658-2295
Central Campfire Area	Rates: $50-$110	www.coloradodirectory.com/sowardranch
	Open: 5/26 to 10/7	

At the resort:

At resort or within 15 minutes:

Thirty Mile Resort

To reach this resort, you have to drive through a national forest campground. Situated next to the Rio Grande National Forest and the headwaters of the Rio Grande in the beautiful San Juan Mountains. Thirty Mile Resort has nine housekeeping cabins set in the woods and two lodge rooms. All the cabins have woodstoves for heat and cooking. This authentic 1930s style fishing and hunting camp has a central shower and generates its own electricity. The individual hand-built cabins are comfortably furnished for simple living in the peaceful aspen-spruce forest. The accommodations have neither telephones or televisions — the perfect place to get away from it all and experience a little peace and quiet. Run by a third-generation Colorado family they run the business which reflect a philosophy which protects the areas natural resources.

Thirty Mile Resort sits at the edge of the wilderness where you can hike, mountain bike, boat and horseback ride to your heart's content. Travel along the trails through the stunning Weminuche Wilderness. A short drive away are river rafting trips and a museum explaining the area's fascinating history. The owners pride themselves on being committed to preserving the natural environment. Thus, small pets are not allowed as they attack the bears. Fish right on the property and then cook your fresh trout in a cast iron skillet on a woodburning cookstove.

Gather around the evening campfires and spin your tales with other guests.

All units are non-smoking. Reservation recommended, there is a minimum stay of one week except during the off-season.

Location: Thirty miles west of Creede on Rio Grande Reservoir Road. Entrance through U.S. Forest Service, then 30 miles past campground.

---

9 Cabins with Kitchen
2 Lodging Rooms
9 Rooms with Wood Stoves
Central Campfire Area

Phone in Lobby
All Units Nonsmoking
Elevation: 9400
Credit Cards: None
Rates: $75-$92
Open: 5/28 to 9/30

Charlotte Trego, Owner
SW of Creede
Creede CO 81130
719/658-2294
www.coloradodirectory.com/thirtymileresort

At the resort:

At resort or within 15 minutes:

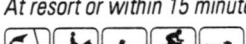

Crested Butte

Map: I-9

Surrounded by sheer beauty, **Crested Butte** is the place to white water raft and enjoy nature's splendor. This town's history is embedded in the coal mining of the 1800s and its future rests on fragile wildflowers and soaring mountain peaks. Home of the Fat Tire Bike Week, the oldest bike festival in the world, the town is near mountain bike trails over scenic passes and four wheel drive roads to old ghost towns. Try fly-fishing in nearby streams or golfing a championship course. Savor campfire cuisine or gourmet restaurants after catching a play or climbing a peak. As the wildflower capital of Colorado, Crested Butte basks in gentle mountain warmth, an inspiration for recreationalists and nature lovers alike. During the winter, Crested Butte, Mt. Crested Butte and Crested Butte Ski Area are connected by a free shuttle. With an average of 229 inches of snow each year, this is a great place for winter sports, including snowmobiling, downhill and cross country skiing, snowboarding and ice skating. Explore the mountains around Crested Butte in the summer on foot, horseback, mountain bike or with a four wheel drive vehicle. Crested Butte is on the West Elk Loop Scenic Byway. Outdoor activities abound in the national forests and wilderness areas that encircle this unique mountain town.

Fun Things to Do

- Country Club & Golf Course (970) 349-6127
- Crested Butte Country Club (800) 628-5496
- Crested Butte Mountain Resort (800) 647-3119
- Crested Butte Nordic Center (970) 349-1707
- Mountain Bike Hall of Fame Museum (970) 349-7382
- Three Rivers Outfittings, Rafting & Fly Shop (888) 761-3474

Crested Butte International Hostel

Looking for budget accommodations in the ski town of Crested Butte? The International Hostel is ideal for you! The new facility opened during the 1997-98 ski season and it is safe, clean, attractive and an affordable place for people of all ages to stay. The hostel accommodates 52 people in four, six and eight person rooms. In summer there is a "couples" room with a queen size bed. Each room is equipped with bunk beds, individual locking storage drawers, a desk and chair, and all have great views. Sheets and towels can be rented for a minimal fee, or you can supply your own. Pillows and blankets are included. Large bathroom facilities are down the hall. Facilities for those with disabilities are also available.

Hostel guests will enjoy the great room with its fireplace, small library, games, television, VCR and collection of local information. The common kitchen is open for guest use and will cut down on your dining out costs. Guests may also choose from a meal plan which offers continental breakfast, lunch to go and nightly meals. A full service, coin laundry is on-site. Ski and bike storage are also provided. Summer days here are filled with mountain biking, hiking, fishing and white water rafting. Numerous festivals are held throughout the year in Crested Butte. Winter is the time for skiers, snowboarders and snowmobilers to play. A stop for the free shuttle to ski area is only 150-feet from the Hostel. The town is filled with good restaurants and interesting stores. Surrounded by national forests and wilderness areas, Crested Butte is the perfect staging ground for any alpine adventure you choose — including relaxing!

The Hostel is a member of the Hostelling International/American Youth Hostels and offers discounts to members. Package rates are available for skiing. Reservations are recommended.

Location: Three blocks north of Elk Avenue, right on Teocalli, on left.

13 Lodging Rooms	Pay Phone Available	Loree & Ward Weisman, Owners
52 Beds in Bunkhouse	All Units Nonsmoking	PO Box 1332
1 Room with Fireplace	Recreation Room	Crested Butte CO 81224-1332
Central Fireplace	Elevation: 8885	888/389-0588
	Credit Cards: VMD	970/349-0588
	Rates: $46-$52	Fax: 970/349-0586
	Open: All Year	E-mail: hostel@crestedbutte.net
		www.coloradodirectory.com/crestedbuttehostel/

At the resort:

At resort or within 15 minutes:

Cristiana Guesthaus Bed & Breakfast

This European style lodge offers 21 rooms with private baths. The rooms are furnished with comforters and quilts, pine furniture and rocking chairs. Choose between smaller rooms with one queen bed, or larger rooms with one queen bed and a double bed or sofa sleeper. Breakfast of homemade cereals, fruit and pastries are served fireside daily.

Cristiana Guesthaus is close to the free shuttle to the Crested Butte ski area and town, as well as shopping and fine restaurants. The cozy lobby has a large stone fireplace to relax in front of after a busy day in the snow. Or soothe your tired muscles in the outdoor hot tub with spectacular views of Crested Butte Mountain and the Elk Mountain Range. In summer, hiking and mountain biking trails are nearby. Vacation here in the warmer months and you'll see why this area has earned the name of the Wildflower Capital of Colorado. In the winter, you'll find ample opportunities for downhill and Nordic skiing at Crested Butte. The town sits on the doorstep of five wilderness areas in the heart of the Rocky Mountains. A former mining town, Crested Butte has retained its Victorian character and architecture and the inn is located within the National Historic District. Bike and ski storage are offered on-site.

Smoking and pets are not permitted in the Guesthaus.

Location: In town from Highway 135 turn onto Maroon Avenue.

21 Lodging Rooms	Pay Phone Available	Rosie & Martin Catmur, Hosts
Central Hot Tub	Bed & Breakfast Available	PO Box 427
Central Fireplace	All Units Nonsmoking	Crested Butte CO 81224
	Recreation Room	800/824-7899
	Elevation: 8885	970/349-5326
	Credit Cards: VMAD	Fax: 970/349-1962
	Rates: $67-$91	E-mail: cristian@rmi.net
	Open: All Year	www.coloradodirectory.com/cristianaguesthaus

At the resort:

At resort or within 15 minutes:

Irwin Lodge

Irwin Lodge is a unique, cedar log structure offering year-round luxury in the wilderness just 12 miles west of Crested Butte off Kebler Pass Road. The 24 guest rooms and one master suite all have private baths.

The lodge features an 8,000 square foot common area with a fieldstone fireplace, dining room, bar, game area and hot tubs. The lodge offers horseback riding, fly fishing and mountain bike riding. Near Lake Irwin, it is accessible only by snowmobile or snowcat in the winter. The self-contained resort is home to the largest snowcat powder skiing and snowboarding operation in North America. Here you can indulge in powder skiing to your heart's content. In the summer, come to hike, four wheel drive to historic sites, fish, horseback ride, mountain bike or hunt.

Ask about the winter packages which include guided activities, lodging and meals. This is a great location for intimate banquets and weddings, corporate getaways and other activities for all seasons. All rooms are non-smoking.

Location: Twelve miles from Crested Butte on Kebler Pass Road. Twenty-eight miles west of Paonia Reservoir. Turn west off route 135 onto White Rock Avenue it turns into a dirt road about one mile out. Head right at big "Y" in the road, following signs to Irwin Lodge about six miles up Kebler.

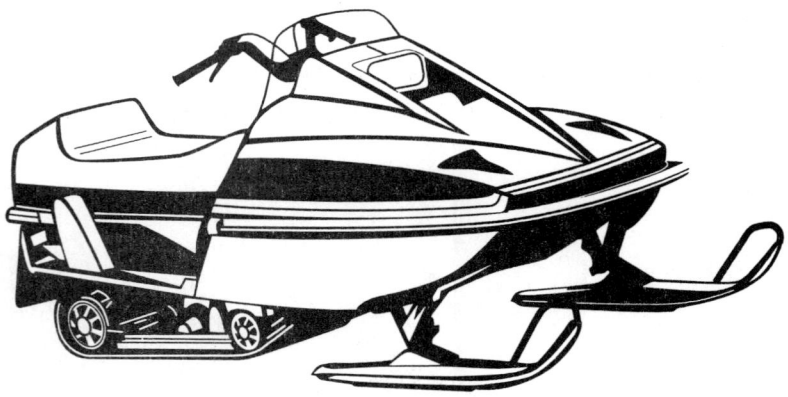

22 Lodging Rooms	Credit Cards: VM	Molly & Larry, Alan Eldridge, Mgrs
Central Hot Tub	Rates: $90	PO Box 457
Central Fireplace	Open: All Year	Crested Butte CO 81224-0457
Central Campfire Area		888/GO-IRWIN(464-7946)
Bed & Breakfast Available		970/349-9800
All Units Nonsmoking		Fax: 970/349-9801
Recreation Room		www.coloradodirectory.com/goirwin
Elevation: 10700		

At the resort:

At resort or within 15 minutes:

Denver Mountain Area

Including Bailey, Evergreen, Golden & Pine Map: G-15, F-15, & F-16

In **Golden,** at the foot of the Rocky Mountain's Front Range, you can tour Coors Brewery and explore Buffalo Bill's Grave perched on top of Lookout Mountain. Further adventures await you in the mountains. In a picturesque setting, **Evergreen** offers all the outdoor adventures possible in the Rocky Mountains. The town boasts a lake that has been a popular ice skating spot for decades and usually opens by Christmas. You'll get to experience what ice skating was meant to be — outdoors in view of snowcapped peaks. Other area activities include hiking, mountain biking, fishing and cross-country skiing. Evergreen also has an 18-hole Denver municipal golf course and the Hiwan Homestead Museum. **Bailey,** just 45 miles southwest of Denver, is surrounded by Pike National Forest. It is an undiscovered mountain hide-away, yet near the big city amenities of Denver. At an altitude of 7,750 feet, it is an excellent area for hunting and fishing. If you love the great outdoors, you'll love vacationing in Bailey year-round! Central City and Blackhawk both have limited stakes gambling casinos just like the days gone by. Central City is a National Historic district and retains its Victorian flavor and several museums, shops and restaurants.

Fun Things To Do

- Buffalo Bill's Grave and Memorial Museum (303) 526-0747
- Coors Brewery Tour (303) 277-BEER
- Evergreen Lake (303) 674-2677
- McGraw Historical Park, Bailey (303) 838-9511
- South Park Historical City Museum, Fairplay (719) 836-2387

Ashley House Bed & Breakfast

Only 20 minutes from Denver, Ashley House Bed & Breakfast is tucked away among the pine trees in the foothills of the Rocky Mountains. This comfortable home offers five rooms to choose among. Each room has a private bath, television, VCR, ceiling fans and magnificent mountain views. The themes of the rooms vary, from the Evergreen Room, an elegant corner room decorated in green with a queen bed, cherry four-poster bed, to the Wedgewood, where the blue decor is restful and peaceful and includes a queen bed, antique dressers and a treadle sewing machine just like grandma used to use. The Amethyst Room done in shades of lavender features a brass queen size bed in a cozy setting. The Rosewood Room, on the ground floor with easy access, has heavy mountain pine furnishings, and a brass chandelier. The largest room is the Gazebo with white wicker furniture surrounded by flowery tones.

Ashley House sits on nine acres with wonderful views of the distant peaks. After your fresh morning breakfast, enjoyed in the downstairs cheery breakfast room or on the deck, prepare to spend a day outdoors. Area activities include fishing, hiking, mountain biking, horseback riding, cross country skiing, golfing and shopping. With ski resorts only 40 minutes away, you can enjoy all the winter ski sports you like. Central City, a historical gambling town, and all the big city attractions of Denver are both just a short drive away. No matter how you spend your day, return to Ashley House and gather around the fireplace in the sitting room, chatting with

other guests and enjoying the refreshments and snacks provided. A television room is open to all where you can put your favorite movie in the VCR — just like home.

All rooms are non-smoking.

Location: From I-70, exit 252 (near El Rancho) to Highway 40 west, 1.3 miles (cross over I-70). Sign on road.

5 Lodging Rooms	Phone in Lobby	Tim Coursey & Ken Martin, Owners
Central Hot Tub	Bed & Breakfast Available	30500 Hwy 40
Central Fireplace	All Units Nonsmoking	Golden CO 80401
	Recreation Room	800/308-2411
	Elevation: 7000	303/526-2411
	Credit Cards: VMAD	Fax: 303/526-2411
	Rates: $89-$110	E-mail: timfc@aol.com
	Open: All Year	www.coloradodirectory.com/ashleyhouse/

At the resort:

At resort or within 15 minutes:

Bauer's Spruce Island Chalets

On 19 roomy acres, Bauer's Spruce Island Chalets provide comfort and convenience throughout the year. All chalets have kitchens or kitchenettes, living rooms, bathrooms, shower-tubs and have from one to four bedrooms. The larger chalets feature fireplaces and cable television.

Most of the chalets surround a large verdant lawn where the whole family can barbecue, picnic and play lawn games, including croquet and badminton. Walk along Cub Creek or fish in the property's small pond and stream. Public park lands to the east are easily accessible for hiking and fishing. In addition, a variety of stores, craft shops, churches, restaurants, art galleries, golf, horseback riding stables and tennis courts are nearby in town. If you desire solitude, take a short drive to scenic areas where you can watch wildlife and birds frolic on the mountainside.

Location: From Highway 74, go through Bergan Park to Evergreen. Turn west on Highway 73, then turn south on Brook Forest Road.

5 Cabins with Kitchen	Phone in Lobby	Ron & Sue & Dave Retterer, Owners
3 Vacation Homes	Elevation: 7200	5937 S Brook Forest Rd
4 Rooms with Fireplaces	Credit Cards: VMA	Evergreen CO 80439-1678
Central Campfire Area	Rates: $65-$180	303/674-4757
	Open: All Year	Fax: 303/670-0783
		E-mail: Info@BSIChalets.com
		www.coloradodirectory.com/bauerschalets/

At the resort:

At resort or within 15 minutes:

Crystal Lake Resort Bed & Breakfast & Trout River Grill

The seven bed and breakfast rooms at Crystal Lake Resort all have private baths and fireplaces. Most rooms have televisions with 99 channels and VCRs. The Rainbow Room, the closest to the lake, features a rustic log theme with a bright contemporary accent and log queen bed. The Buckaroo Room is designed for younger guests with a Cowboys & Indians theme and log bunk beds and connects to the adjoining Garden Room which has a log queen bed and offers easy access to the garden bordered breakfast nook. The Pine Room has a log king bed and its antiques will take you back in time. The Ice Box is much warmer than its name suggests! It was named for the original "Eggert Ice Co." wooden crate pieces found when the room was fully restored. Now the room has original ice handling tools as decorative momentos, along with a log queen bed. The Train Whistle was originally part of the bunkhouse quarters for ice workers and has railroad memorabilia with a log queen bed. The Caboose is a light, airy room just steps away from the soothing flow of the South Platte River with a log queen bed.

Situated next to a 10-acre lake with 2.5 miles of private South Platte River frontage, Crystal Lake is an angler's dream come true. Guided fly fishing and instruction are available for anglers of all skill levels. Explore the resort's 200 acres or venture onto the adjacent 1.1 million acre Pike National Forest and the 800 acre Jefferson County Pine Valley Open Space. A variety of trails for hiking, horseback riding and mountain biking await you. The Trout River Grill offers casual, fine dining with an emphasis on fresh Colorado trout, seafood, game and beef. End the day with a visit to the outdoor Jacuzzi which is open from noon to 10 p.m. daily.

This is an ideal site for group events of up to 1,000. All rooms are non-smoking. The minimum stay in summer is two nights on the weekends, three nights on holidays. Single nights will be considered Sunday through Thursday. Fifty RV sites are also available.

Location: Six miles south of Highway 285, west of Schaffers Crossing at Pine Junction, on County Raod 126 (Pine Valley Road). Just after blinking yellow light, sharp right on Crystal Lake Road for 200 yards.

7 Lodging Rooms	Pay Phone Available	David & Becky Jones, Owners
7 Rooms with Fireplaces	Bed & Breakfast Available	PO Box 529
Central Hot Tub	All Units Nonsmoking	Pine CO 80470
Central Fireplace	Recreation Room	303/838-LAKE (5253)
Central Campfire Area	Elevation: 6990	Fax: 303/838-6689 or1314
	Credit Cards: VMD	E-mail: clinfo@qadas.com
	Rates: $75-$150	www.coloradodirectory.com/crystallakeresort
	Open: All Year	

At the resort:

At resort or within 15 minutes:

Glen Isle Resort Lodge & Cabins

This national historic site on the Platte River has been under the same family ownership since 1923. You will be "roughing it" in well-insulated, well-furnished cabins that sleep from two to 10 people. All cabins contain fully equipped kitchens, private baths, easy chairs, bedding and linens, fireplaces (wood provided) and gas heat. All rooms in the lodge are decorated with antiques. The lodge, built in 1900, is listed on the National Register of Historic Sites and has been owned by the same family for more than 75 years. Lodge rooms are also available. Glen Isle Resort offers a restful, informal and reasonably priced family retreat.

Decorated in antiques, the lodge has a gift and antique shop. Resort amenities include a children's playground, games, a library to browse in, billiard and ping-pong. Spend the days fishing, hiking, horseback riding, bird watching and hunting. Centrally located in Colorado, the resort is near countless points of interest by car.

Pets may accompany you for a fee. A deposit is required with advance reservations. The lodge is open June through mid-September. Some cabins are open all year.

Location: 50 minutes southwest of Denver on Highway 285, near milepost marker 221.

13 Cabins with Kitchen	Pay Phone Available	Barbara Tripp, Owner
6 Cabins without Kitchens	Some Units Nonsmoking	PO Box 128
14 Lodging Rooms	Recreation Room	Bailey CO 80421-0128
14 Rooms with Fireplaces	Elevation: 7830	303/838-5461
Central Fireplace	Credit Cards: None	www.coloradodirectory.com/glenisleresort/
Central Campfire Area	Rates: $48-$95	
	Open: 5/25 to 9/15	

At the resort:

At resort or within 15 minutes:

Durango & Vallecito Lake Areas

Including Bayfield — Map: P-5, O-6

A city created by the railroad, **Durango** retains a "Frontier West" feeling. Surrounded by the San Juan Mountains, this town bustles with activity. Take a walk through living history down Main Street, Durango's National Register Historic District. The famous Durango-Silverton Narrow Gauge Railroad is the country's only coal-and-steam-powered train operating daily. Chug along sheer cliffs, criss-crossing the Animas River on the 45 mile trip to Silverton. The Animas River, or river of lost souls, has wild whitewater rafting during spring run-off and settles down in the summer for family jaunts. Rent a bike for a day and discover why this area is so popular with mountain bikers. Set amidst reddish, sandstone bluffs, Durango is 25 miles north of Purgatory Ski Resort which offers the unpretentious skiing of the southwest. **Vallecito Lake**, located 23 miles northwest of Durango, lies under the snow-capped peaks of the San Juan National Forest. This lake is an angler's delight — fish for rainbow trout, kokanee salmon and northern pike. Several boat ramps and docks surround the 22-mile lake shoreline. The Vallecito Trail and the Pine River Trail access the Weminuche Wilderness where mountain bikes are strictly forbidden, but hikers and horseback riders are welcomed.

Fun Things to Do

- Animas School Museum (970) 259-2402
- Bar D Chuckwagon Suppers (970) 247-5753
- Bartels' Mancos Valley Stage Line (800) 365-3530
- Durango-Silverton Narrow Gauge Railroad (970) 247-2733
- Five Branches Horse Rides, Vallecito Lake (800) 582-9580
- Hillcrest Golf Course (970) 247-1499
- Old Hundred Gold Mine Tour (800) 872-3009
- San Juan Rio Grande National Forest (970) 247-4874
- Tamarron Golf Course (970) 259-2000
- Virginia's Steak House (970) 884-2473

Bear Paw Lodge

When touring southwest Colorado, Bear Paw Lodge offers a serene vacation retreat. The seven clean cabins are snug beneath towering ponderosa pines, blue spruces and aspen. Each unit has a wood burning stove, a full kitchen with a microwave, carpeting, a barbecue facility and most have an outdoor picnic table. Bear Paw Lodge also offers several distinctive private homes near the lodge, some of the two, three and four bedroom vacation homes are on Vallecito Creek.

Children will like playing in the recreation area on-site with its volleyball, horseshoes, swings and sand box. Enjoy excellent springtime fishing and the re-awakening of the valley. See spectacular colors in the fall while hunting deer and elk. Winter in Vallecito Valley looks like a perpetual Christmas card. Enjoy cross country skiing, tobogganing, ice skating, snowmobiling and going on sleigh rides. Bear Paw Lodge is within 1 mile or less of the marina on Lake Vallecito, horseback riding stables, national forest hiking trials, three restaurants and two country stores. Vallecito Lake has 22 miles of scenic shoreline and is bounded by national forest and wilderness areas. You'll also be centrally located for all the sights in and around the Durango area.

All units are non-smoking.

Location: Twenty-eight miles northwest of Durango. Take Highway 160 east to Bayfield, then north on County Road 501. Just northwest of Vallecito Lake.

7 Cabins with Kitchen	Phone in Lobby	Burt & Pat Armstrong, Owners
5 Vacation Homes	All Units Nonsmoking	18011 CR 501
11 Rooms with Wood Stoves	Elevation: 8000	Bayfield CO 81122
Central Campfire Area	Credit Cards: VMA	970/884-2508
	Rates: $70-$150	E-mail: bearpawlodge@rmi.net
	Open: All Year	www.coloradodirectory.com/bearpawlodge

At the resort:

At resort or within 15 minutes:

Circle S Lodge

Journey to a high-country retreat in the picturesque San Juan Mountains. Circle S Lodge is adjacent to the Weminuche Wilderness area on the north end of Vallecito Lake and features nicely decorated private mountain cabins that can accommodate up to nine people. Each completely carpeted cabin includes all linens, a fully equipped kitchen, a microwave, a fireplace, an outdoor grill and a picnic table. For your convenience, they have a laundromat on the premises.

The kids will have fun on the playground and fishing in the small trout pond. Adults can pitch horseshoes or play volleyball, badminton and basketball. Surrounded by so much wilderness, you'll want to rent horses and boats, fish in the lakes and rivers, hike and take pictures. A grocery store and restaurant are within walking distance.

A 50% deposit of rental fee is required for reservations.

Location: Just northwest of Vallecito Lake.

7 Cabins with Kitchen
1 Vacation Home
7 Lodging Rooms
7 Rooms with Fireplaces
Central Campfire Area

Pay Phone Available
Recreation Room
Elevation: 8000
Credit Cards: VMAD
Rates: $60-$90
Open: All Year

Steve Dudley, Owner
18044 CR 501
Bayfield CO 81122
970/884-2473
Fax: 970/884-9845
E-mail: virginiaslodge@animas.net
www.coloradodirectory.com/circleslodge/

At the resort:

At resort or within 15 minutes:

Cool Water Ranch Cabins

Nestled beneath ancient pines beside the beautiful Pine River, also known as Los Piños Rio, are five cottage-style cabins. Two of the cabins have two bedrooms with 2 twin-beds and a double bed. Choose from two studios one with 2 double beds the other with a single double bed. The largest cabin has three bedrooms with 2 twin-beds and 2 double beds. All the cabins, equipped with kitchenettes, pots, pans, dishes and linens, offer modern comforts without modern hassles — no telephones or television, just a peaceful country environment.

Cool Water Ranch is quiet and off the highway, yet close to Vallecito Lake for restaurants and shopping. Enjoy trout fishing from your back door and in nearby mountain streams, lakes and rivers.

Seven day minimum stay required in July and August. Advanced reservations recommended. RV sites are also available.

Location: Two miles south of Vallecito Lake.

4 Cabins with Kitchen	Phone in Lobby	Thomas W. & Judy Beuten, Operators
1 Vacation Home	Elevation: 7500	10643 CR 501
	Credit Cards: None	Bayfield CO 81122-9701
	Rates: $50-$70	970/884-2269
	Open: 5/1 to 9/30	www.coloradodirectory.com/coolwaterranch/

At the resort: *At resort or within 15 minutes:*

D'Mara Resort

For a touch of luxury in the wilderness come to the tastefully decorated cottages of D'Mara Resort. Located on Grimes Creek, just north of Vallecito Lake, each cabin has spectacular views of the San Juan Mountains and can accommodate from 2 to 8 persons. Enjoy the comforts of home with modern kitchens, drip-coffee makers, microwave ovens, televisions, fireplaces or wood stoves with free firewood, linens (provided and exchanged upon request) and outdoor barbecue grills. The Valley View, a spacious two-bedroom cabin, features a large picture window with panoramic views of the valley. The Mountain View, a two-story, two-bedroom home, has a balcony that faces picturesque mountain scenery. The Broookside, a spacious two-story, three-bedroom, two bath home, overlooks Grimes Creek and is beautifully decorated with a native stone fireplace. The Hideaway is a charming two-bedroom secluded cabin located by the rushing Grimes Creek; a perfect honeymoon setting. All cottages are non-smoking and no pets are allowed. The Hideaway is accessible to the disabled.

Your hosts can reserve boat rentals on the lake, arrange rides on the Durango-Silverton Narrow Gauge Railroad and make dinner theater suggestions. Partake in the excellent fishing, skiing, horseback riding, hiking, bird watching and fine dining in the area. And, perhaps most importantly, enjoy simple, peaceful relaxation.

D'Mara Resort

A minimum stay of 5 nights is required. Having a special occasion while visiting? Your hosts can make any arrangements in order to make you celebration as memorable as possible. There are excellent catering services nearby in which anything from a birthday cake to brunch on a pontoon is available!

Location: North of Vallecito Lake.

---

4 Vacation Homes
2 Rooms with Fireplaces
2 Rooms with Wood Stoves

Phone in Lobby
All Units Nonsmoking
Elevation: 7850
Credit Cards: None
Rates: $125-$260
Open: All Year

Mara & David Edwards, Owners
1213 CR 500
Bayfield CO 81122
970/884-9806 & Fax
E-mail: dmara@webtv.net
www.coloradodirectory.com/dmararesort/

At the resort: *At resort or within 15 minutes:*

Durango East KOA, Kamping Kabins™ & Kamping Kottage™

The closest KOA to Durango, these kamping kabins are in a rolling, semi-wooded area high on the Mesa with panoramic views. Kamping kabins are cozy log structures equipped with electric light, lockable doors and log beds complete with mattresses and heating for added comfort. Kamping kabins sleep up to four or six people in one-room or two-room styles, respectively. Bring your own cooking gear and bedding. The Kamping Kottage has a log structure and offers a kitchenette, dining area, bathroom with shower and sleeps up to 4 people. In the evenings site in front of the fireplace or on the porch swing. The abundant piñon pines provide shade and the distinct aroma of southwestern Colorado.

From Memorial Day to Labor Day, enjoy the daily feast of delicious pancake breakfasts. Soak in the heated swimming pool before watching a free nightly movie and enjoying an ice cream social. Take advantage of the miniature golf course, TV lounge and the video game room. The camp store has souvenirs, snacks and groceries. Exercise your pet on the dog walk that follows the creek running through the campground. Some popular area attractions are the Durango-Silverton Narrow Gauge Railroad, Mesa Verde National Park, Vallecito Lake, Durango Pro Rodeo, the Million Dollar Highway and Trimble Hot Springs.

Of course you can always explore the terrain on a mountain bike trail, a horseback ride or a whitewater raft trip nearby.

Kamping Kabins/Kottage book early, so make reservations! Ask about the indoor and outdoor pavilions for group meetings. Durango East KOA is a non-smoking facility.

Location: Seven miles east of the Durango-Silverton Train on the south side of Highway 160, near milepost marker 91.

---

1 Cabin with Kitchen	Pay Phone Available	Jay & Carol Coates, Owners
19 Camper Cabins	All Units Nonsmoking	30090 US Hwy 160
1 Room with Fireplace	Recreation Room	Durango CO 81301-8289
	Elevation: 7000	800/KOA-0793
	Credit Cards: VMD	970/247-0783
	Rates: $38-$95	Fax: 970/247-3655
	Open: 4/15 to 10/15	E-mail: 104117.3442@Compuserve.com
		www.coloradodirectory.com/durangoeastkoa/

At the resort:

At resort or within 15 minutes:

Elk Point Lodge

Relax on the tranquil east shore of Vallecito Lake at Pine River. Elk Point features modern cabins with fully equipped kitchens, tucked away among tall pines. choose between a cabin on the lakefront or with a view of beautiful Vallecito Lake. Some cabins have fireplaces and all bedding and towels are provided (there are even extra blankets in each room). All cabins boast knotty pine interiors, carpet and bathrooms with showers. The cabins are decorated with rustic wood furniture. Firewood is provided. All cabins are off the main road and the only noise to boast of are the pitter-pattering feet of the friendly squirrels.

The lodge has a general store. There is also a recreation room with a pool table, foosball table, games, books and a huge rock fireplace. There is always a puzzle to be completed. Outside is a playground for the kids. Rent horses (Lic. #1820) and fishing boats on the property or fish the lake and Pine River. Culminate the perfect day with a sunset dinner ride. Elk Point Lodge is adjacent to the San Juan National Forest, ideal for horseback riding, mountain biking and hiking. Weminuche Wilderness is 3 miles away, your hosts can help plan pack trips and expeditions for autumn elk, deer and small game hunting. Open all year, the resort offers a selec-

tion of winter sports as well. Snowmobile tours are available or bring your own. Cross-country ski right outside your door. Or just come to relax, watch a beautiful sunset from your porch while barbecuing dinner and listen to the water gently lapping the shore.

Elk Point is wonderful for a fall or winter vacation and less crowded.

Location: Follow paved road around west and north side of Vallecito lake. When pavement ends, keep going south 2 miles on gravel road.

10 Cabins with Kitchen	Pay Phone Available	JR (Larry) & Lark Kokesh, Owners
5 Rooms with Wood Stoves	Recreation Room	21730 CR 501
Central Fireplace	Elevation: 7800	Bayfield CO 81122-9703
	Credit Cards: VMD	970/884-2482 & Fax
	Rates: $60-$135	E-mail: elkpoint@frontier.net
	Open: All Year	www.coloradodirectory.com/elkpointlodge/

At the resort:

At resort or within 15 minutes:

Granite Peaks Ranch

At the end of the road in a pristine environment, Granite Peaks Ranch awaits you. The 3 secluded cabins with kitchens are tucked away at this "gateway to the Weminuche Wilderness." The Lincoln Cabin has 2 rooms with a complete kitchen, bath with shower, living room/bedroom combination with electric heaters and sleeps 2-4 people. The River House and the Creek House are larger cabins with 2 bedrooms, one with twin beds and one with a double bed, each with closets. These cabins sleep 4-7 people. Each cabin has a full bath with a shower and kitchens with cooking pots and pans, dishes, utensils, refrigerator/freezer, mircowave, propane gas heat and fresh mountain water. The hardwood floored living room has 2 sofas, one of which is a sofa bed. Televisions upon request. Linens and towels are provided. Laindry room on premises

Granite Peaks Ranch has been a working cattle and horse ranch for over 50 years. You can access a U.S. Forest Service trail from one of the ranch's gates and experience miles of land for hiking, fishing, Horseback riding and nature watching. Vallecito Lake, with its boating and fishing opportunities, is only 3.5 miles away. Photographers will have a field day capturing the wildlife that traverse the ranch, including deer, elk and an occasional moose! Off ranch activities include white water raft trips, sightseeing tours, fine dining, shopping, horse shows, rodeos, antiquing and arts & craft fairs. All guests will appreciate the natural beauty that abounds at Granite Peaks Ranch.

Vacationing with your horse and pet are an option here with advance permission. There is a fee for overnight stableing. Hunters and reunions are welcomed. Ask about weekly and monthly rates.

Location: Three and a half miles northeast from the east shore of Vallecito Lake along Pine River.

THE MAIN GATE AT GRANITE PEAKS RANCH—C.G.SHILLINGBURGS
BY I.G. SHILLINGBURG ©1999

| 3 Cabins with Kitchen | Phone in Lobby
Elevation: 8000
Credit Cards: None
Rates: $100-$150
Open: 6/1 to 10/31 | Leslie G Schillingburg, Owner
25080 CR 501
Bayfield CO 81122
970/884-2626
Fax: 970/884-2626
E-mail: GranitePks@aol.com
www.coloradodirectory.com/granitepeaksranch/ |

At the resort:

At resort or within 15 minutes:

Historic Wit's End Guest Ranch

Established in the 1860s, this ranch adjoins the 575,000-acre Weminuche Wilderness. Amid a dramatic setting of 14,000-foot peaks in a narrow valley, the cabins, some over 100 years old, have, knotty pine interiors, living rooms, native stone fireplaces, kitchens, porch swings and queen-sized brass beds. The furnishings and decorations are exquisite and unique. The 35 cabins (one bedroom to 4 bedroom) are all near streams, rivers and ponds.

Wit's End provides unlimited activities: carriage rides, fly fishing, moonlight cruises on the lake, mountain biking, tennis and swimming. They also arrange horseback rides, hayrides, rafting, wilderness trips, and much more! Kids will enjoy the complete children's program. The main lodge — the original rock and log structure built in the 1870's — now contains a candle-lit restaurant, library, entertainment center and a dance floor. Listen to live music in the old-world bar, featuring mirrors from the 1836 Crystal Palace in London. Later in the evening, soak in one of the four outdoor hot tubs or the large swimming pool.

Ask about the full American plan (summer or winter package) when making reservations, which includes a scrumptious breakfast, lunch and dinner; and all ranch amenities and activities. The summer package activities include dinner hay

rides and pontoon boat rides; while the winter package offers sleigh rides, snowshoeing, snowmobiling and cross-country skiing. If you're planning a large group vacation, inquire about the 7,000-square-foot cabin along Vallecito Lake. Conference facilities are also available.

Location: Only one mile north of Vallecito Lake.

32 Cabins with Kitchen	Phone in Rooms	Jim & Lynn Custer, Owners
5 Vacation Homes	All Units Nonsmoking	254 CR 500
37 Rooms with Fireplaces	Recreation Room	Bayfield CO 81122-9702
Central Hot Tub	Elevation: 7800	800/236-9483
Central Fireplace	Credit Cards: VMAD	970/884-4113
Central Campfire Area	Rates: $500	Fax: 970/884-3261
	Open: All Year	E-mail: weranch@aol.com
		www.coloradodirectory.com/witsendranch/

At the resort:

At resort or within 15 minutes:

Logwood Lodge B&B and Lodge

This luxurious 3-story, red cedar log home bed and breakfast along the banks of the Animas River is surrounded by 5 acres of quiet and seclusion. The guest rooms are attractively furnished with a southwestern flair and the queen and king beds have colorful home-stitched quilts. Rooms features private bath, phone and large picture windows for viewing the beauty of the Animas River valley. A large river rock gas fireplace warms the elegant living and dining areas. The entire lodge is non-smoking.

Wake up to a full breakfast which could be country fare or a gourmet delight. Enjoy a game of pool, watch a movie, or play a board game in the new recreation room. In the evenings, enjoy the cozy fire and savor their award-winning desserts! Lounge on the wrap-around deck and watch the wildlife and in the evening watch the shadows climb the mountainside. Wet a hook and catch a trout lurking in the waters of the Animas while enjoying the beautiful views and sounds. Only 15 minutes from downtown Durango shopping and dining. The ancient Indian ruins of the Anasazi, Mesa Verde National Park, are an hours drive. Enjoy mountain biking and hiking on nearby trails through the San Juan Mountains. The area also offers excellent golf courses. In winter enjoy downhill skiing at Purgatory Ski Area a 15 minute drive (Logwood is the closest B&B). The area also offers cross-country skiing, snowshoeing, sleigh rides through La Plata Canyon and snowmobiling. Your hosts are happy to supply activity information to make your stay enjoyable.

No pets allowed. Rent the entire lodge with use of kitchen for weddings and family reunions, sleeps 24. Advance reservations are recommended. Ask about their special winter rates and discount ski packages.

Location: Twelve miles north of Durango, off Highway 550, near milepost marker 35.

1 Vacation Home	Phone in Rooms	Paul & Maggie & Ron & Amy Windmueller,
8 Lodging Rooms	Bed & Breakfast Available	Owners
2 Rooms with Fireplaces	All Units Nonsmoking	35060 US 550 N
Central Fireplace	Recreation Room	Durango CO 81301
Central Campfire Area	Elevation: 6700	800/369-4082
	Credit Cards: VMA	970/259-4396
	Rates: $85-$135	Fax: 970/259-7812
	Open: All Year	E-mail: paul@durango-logwoodinn.com
		www.coloradodirectory.com/logwoodlodge/

At the resort:

At resort or within 15 minutes:

O-Bar-O Cabins

Disappear for a while in a secluded setting among numerous pine trees and lush grounds. These nicely decorated, river-front housekeeping cabins have stone fireplaces, covered porches or decks, fully equipped kitchens, linens and towels. Barbecue your favorite meal at the outdoor grills and picnic tables. Each cabin has been remodeled and decorated to offer comfort, while retaining a rustic touch of the past. At 1,300' higher than Durango, expect cooler air and refreshing summer evenings.

Vacation under clear Colorado skies, watch deer and elk roam through the alpine meadows bordered by tall pine trees stretching to the horizon. Be sure to cast your fishing rod on the Florida (pronounced *Flor-EED-ah*) River, right outside your door. The resort is only 12 miles from Durango, with its melodrama dinner theater and Durango-Silverton Narrow Gauge Railroad. Just a stone's throw from the national forest, two large lakes and horseback trails, O-Bar-O boasts many nearby activities, including lake and stream fishing, boating, hiking, horseback riding and fine dining.

Reservations are required.

Location: Twelve miles northeast of Durango, about halfway to Vallecito Lake on the Florida River.

9 Cabins with Kitchen	Pay Phone Available	Herb & Gayle Rose, Owners
9 Rooms with Fireplaces	All Units Nonsmoking	11998 CR 240
Central Campfire Area	Elevation: 7800	Durango CO 81301-8489
	Credit Cards: None	970/259-3649
	Rates: $95-$150	Fax: 970/259-5513
	Open: All Year	E-mail: obaro@compuserve.com
		www.coloradodirectory.com/obarocabins/

At the resort:

At resort or within 15 minutes:

Pine River Lodge

Family owned and operated since 1960, Pine River Lodge features cabins over-looking beautiful Vallecito Lake. The cabins have complete kitchens — dishes, cooking utensils, linens and bedding are furnished and boast aspen-, pine- or spruce-paneled walls. Cabins have either double or queen sized beds. Many are carpeted with a porch or deck for outdoor meals and relaxing. Cabins range from small one-room cabins sleeping two people to 4-bedroom 2-story cabins sleeping 11 people. Some cabins have fireplaces. Remember to bring your own dish and bath soap. Portable barbecue grills are furnished.

Pine River Lodge has an indoor swimming pool, a game room and a large play-ground. The playground includes swings, slides, sandbox, jungle gym, basketball hoop, volleyball area and horseshoes. Be sure to try the excellent fishing in Val-lecito Lake — anglers have set state records for northern pike and brown trout here. Hiking and horseback riding trailheads are all nearby. While visiting, step back in time with a trip on the Durango-Silverton Narrow Gauge Railroad. Visit incredible Mesa Verde National Park. Also enjoy river rafting, seeing a melodrama, playing high stakes bingo and chowing down a Bar D Chuckwagon dinner. In the winter, you can snowmobile and ski close by.

No campers, trailers, or motorhomes are allowed on the premises for sleeping. Children under 2 are free. There is an additional crib and pet fee per night. Special needs should be requested when making your reservation. When making reserva-tions there is a two night deposit required.

Location: Sixteen miles north of Bayfield or 23 miles northeast of Durango. Overlooking Vallecito Lake's southwest shore.

22 Cabins with Kitchen	Pay Phone Available	Donna & Debbie & Ermalee Atkinson,
5 Vacation Homes	Some Units Nonsmoking	Owners
13 Rooms with Fireplaces	Recreation Room	14443 CR 501
Central Campfire Area	Elevation: 7800	Bayfield CO 81122-9701
	Credit Cards: None	970/884-2563 & Fax
	Rates: $65-$88	E-mail: pinriver@frontier.net
	Open: All Year	www.coloradodirectory.com/pineriverlodge/

At the resort:

At resort or within 15 minutes:

Steward Ranch Cabins

In the beautiful La Plata Mountains 8 miles west of Durango, Steward Ranch Cabins are on 40 scenic, private acres in Lightner Creek Canyon. The two clean and modern log cabins each have stone fireplaces, firewood, bathrooms and full kitchens with barbecues and picnic tables outside. Each features wood interiors, carpeting, linens and open-beam ceilings. A vacation here offers the seclusion and beauty of camping in the woods with all the comforts and convenience of home.

Steward Ranch has been a working cattle ranch owned by the same family since 1900! Hollywood has used this scenic location for scenes in two movies: "City Slickers" in 1990 and "The Abduction of Kari Swenson" in 1986.

Location: Eight miles west of downtown Durango, from Highway 160, milepost marker 80, on County Road 207.

2 Cabins with Kitchen	Phone in Lobby	Bonnie Brennan, Owner
2 Rooms with Fireplaces	Elevation: 7200	4385 CR 207 (Lightner Creek Rd)
	Credit Cards: None	Durango CO 81301
	Rates: $62-$70	970/247-8396
	Open: 5/1 to 10/15	E-mail: jbrennan5@hotmail.com
		www.coloradodirectory.com/stewardranch/

At the resort: *At resort or within 15 minutes:*

Vallecito Resort

There's something for everyone in the cool pines of Vallecito Resort. The cabins, ranging from one to three bedrooms, are nestled in tall ponderosa pine trees where it's quiet and restful. The 10 housekeeping cabins are equipped with linens, cable tv, dishes and utensils. There's a small, private cabin for honeymooners and a large cabin suitable for family reunions. Vallecito Resort also has 6 park model trailers for you to rent. Every other day you may exchange dirty towels at the office.

You'll find everything you need here, from a grocery store and playground to a recreation hall, card room, library and craft room. Bring your square dance attire for the exciting evening dances: square (Mainstream-C3), round (all phases), line and country swing. Vallecito Resort boasts national square dance and round dance callers. Weekly activities at the resort include Sunday church services, arts and crafts sessions, potlucks, poker, aerobics, bonfires and ice cream socials. Nearby you can play a game of tennis, golf or go bowling. Fish for state-record trout in the Pine River or take a short drive to Vallecito and Lemon lakes.

RV sites and an indoor meeting area for groups up to 30 people are also available. Every site has a cable tv hookup and telephone. Ask about off-season special rates.

Location: Just south of Vallecito Lake.

9 Cabins with Kitchen	Pay Phone Available	Rex & Jeannie Hornbaker, Owners
1 Vacation Home	All Units Nonsmoking	13030 CR 501
Central Campfire Area	Recreation Room	Bayfield CO 81122
	Elevation: 7600	800/258-9458
	Credit Cards: VMD	970/884-9458 & Fax
	Rates: $40-$160	www.coloradodirectory.com/vallecitoresort/
	Open: 5/1 to 10/1	

At the resort:

At resort or within 15 minutes:

Eagle River Valley

Including Gypsum, Minturn, Red Cliff, Sweetwater & Vail —
Map: F-10, F-9, G-11 & F-11, E-8

Drive through tiny **Minturn** and even smaller **Redcliff**, mining towns steeped in history, on your way to the popular wilderness area of the Mount of the Holy Cross at 14,005'. All the ski resorts, including Vail and Copper Mountain, are accessible from here without the cost of staying in expensive, crowded condos during the ski season. Visit the numerous shops in Vail Village that aim to please the most discriminating tastes. Golfers will want to bring their clubs for some high country games in Edwards, Avon and Vail. Down the road, in the direction of Glenwood Springs is **Gypsum**, another gateway to the unspoiled White River National Forest. The forest is home to the largest elk herd in North America. Sylvan Lake State Recreation Area is not only quite scenic, but a great place to fish for brook and rainbow trout. A short drive from Gypsum, 40-acre Sylvan Lake is the perfect place to bring your boat and catch the big ones! Clear streams, flowing from sky-touching, snow-capped mountains, meander through wildflower meadows and into blue mountain lakes in Eagle County. Enjoy many scenic and exciting moments whitewater rafting, fishing and skiing among the wildlife and rare birds. At the edge of the Flat Tops Wilderness in White River National Forest, **Sweetwater Lake**, offers fishing, hunting, boating, spectacular scenery and is certainly off the beaten path (10 miles up Sweetwater Creek Road, 7 miles north of I-70 off exit 133).

Fun Things To Do

- Beaver Creek Golf Club, Avon (970) 949-7123
- Eagle Vail Golf Club, Vail (970) 949-5267
- Nova Guides, Guided outdoor activities (888) 949-NOVA (6682)
- Sonnenalp Golf Club, Edwards (970) 926-3533

Cross Creek Ranch

This working cattle ranch nestled in the majestic Rocky Mountains, deep in the White River National Forest is a gem. The warmth and charm of this restored 1892 log cabin is an intimate mountain hideaway with a full country kitchen, dining area, family room, stone fireplace, bath with Jacuzzi tub and two bedrooms which sleeps up to six people. A large wrap around deck overlooks a cascading creek where you can fish, grill and relish in some of the high country's most spectacular scenery. In keeping with the tranquil setting and crisp clean air, Cross Creek Ranch is entirely non-smoking. There is a television and VCR, however there is no local reception. There are many pre-recorded videos to choose from.

The picturesque ranch has private access to hiking, mountain biking, hunting, cross-country skiing, snowmobiling and snowshoeing (snowshoes are provided) in the National Forest. The wooded area is alive with elk, deer and other wildlife for your viewing enjoyment. There are three ponds and two streams at Cross Creek Ranch. Make a day out of driving the scenic Glenwood Canyon and relax at the Glenwood Hot Springs Pool. In the fall big game hunting and wildlife watching are popular. Or for winter enthusiasts alpine skiing is at its best at Vail or browse through its unique shops.

Wedding facilities are available. There is a 2 night minimum stay. Enjoy a week's stay and receive a seventh night free. Ask about seasonal rates. Bring your horse with advance arrangements. Friendly service is why people return year after year.

Location: Less than an hour west of Vail & Beaver Creek. Off I-70 between Vail & Glenwood, 13 miles south of Gypsum on Valley Road.

1 Cabin with Kitchen	Phone in Rooms	Susan & David Scott, Owners
4 Beds in Bunkhouse	All Units Nonsmoking	13117 Gypsum Creek Road
1 Room with Hot Tub	Elevation: 8700	Gypsum CO 81637
1 Room with Fireplace	Credit Cards: None	970/524-7557
Central Campfire Area	Rates: $125-$200	E-mail: crosscreekranch@yahoo.com
	Open: All Year	www.coloradodirectory.com/crosscreekranch/

At the resort:

At resort or within 15 minutes:

Golden Eagle Ranch

The homestead log cabins at Golden Eagle Ranch border mountain meadows of colorful aspen and blue spruce. This very private, 160-acre high-country ranch is located in the White River National Forest. The cabins, which sleep two to four people, are next to one of three clear mountain streams.

Bill Walden, a professional sculptor, offers roomy, sunlit studio space and instruction for all ages. Bring your own art supplies or purchase them at the studio. Take some time to fish for the abundant brook, rainbow and cutthroat trout in the ranch's lake and beaver ponds. Fishing and boating enthusiasts will like Lede Reservoir just 2 miles away. Hikers will want to strike out for many of the high lakes in the surrounding mountains. Bring your camera: this is the place to spot golden eagles, red-tailed hawks, elk and deer. Venture to Glenwood Springs Hot Springs pool or go whitewater rafting on the Colorado River 45 minutes away.

Advance reservations and a two day minimum stay is required. Stay a week and get the seventh day free!

Location: From I-70 take exit 140 between Vail and Glenwood Springs, 16 miles south of Gypsum on Valley Road which turns into Gypsum Creek Road, a county-maintained road.

1 Cabin with Kitchen	Phone in Lobby	Linda & Bill Walden, Owners
2 Cabins without Kitchens	Elevation: 8500	PO Box 833
5 Beds in Bunkhouse	Credit Cards: None	Gypsum CO 81637-0833
4 Rooms with Wood Stoves	Rates: $75	970/524-9311
	Open: 6/1 to 11/1	www.coloradodirectory.com/goldeneagleranch

At the resort:

At resort or within 15 minutes:

Minturn Inn, The

Discover an authentic Rocky Mountain lodge nestled between Vail and Beaver Creek Resort. The inn is a completely refurbished 1915 hewn log home offering ten rooms with hand-crafted log beds, cozy quilts and comforters, antler chandeliers, hardwood floors and an elegant, rustic atmosphere. The two premier rooms feature river rock fireplaces, vaulted ceilings, beautiful views, queen size log canopy beds and two-person hot tubs - ideal for special occasions. The two deluxe rooms on the top floor also have vaulted ceilings and mountain views. Rooms on the ground level have easy access. One room, with a cast iron tub and shower, was once the master bedroom of the original house. The other ground floor room in the rear of the inn offers ample space and privacy with twin beds. On the second floor are the cozy lodge rooms with exposed hewn log walls and hardwood floors for a log cabin feeling. Two of the original bedrooms on the second floor, one with twin beds and the other with a queen bed, are ideal for when more than one room is need as these rooms share a bath.

One of the owners is always on the property during the daylight hours to answer questions and meet your needs. A hearty breakfast is prepared for all guests in the inn's kitchen. After a day of fun in the snow, return to the Minturn Inn for après ski and a soothing break in the sauna. For those who would like to try a new sport, snowshoe rentals are available. The town of Minturn is an excellent starting point for exploring both the Holy Cross Wilderness Area and White River National Forest. Hiking, mountain biking, fishing, cross-country skiing and snowshoeing are abundant.

Ask about the off-season rates. The inn is non-smoking and no pets are allowed. Children over 12 are welcomed. No more than two people per room.

Location: Just south of the center of Minturn. Only 5 miles to Vail and Beaver Creek.

---

1 Vacation Home
10 Lodging Rooms
2 Rooms with Hot Tubs
2 Rooms with Fireplaces
Central Fireplace

Phone in Rooms
Bed & Breakfast Available
All Units Nonsmoking
Recreation Room
Elevation: 7800
Credit Cards: VMAD
Rates: $65-$200
Open: All Year

Tom & Cathy Sullivan & Mick Kelly
PO Box 186
Minturn CO 81645-0186
800/MINTURN
970/827-9647
Fax: 970/827-5590
E-mail: mi@vail.net
www.coloradodirectory.com/minturninn/

At the resort:

At resort or within 15 minutes:

Pando Cabins & Nova Guided Year Around Outdoor Recreation

The Pando Cabins are at historic Camp Hale, during World War II the 10th Mountain Army Division's winter maneuver training, now listed on the National Historic Register. The cabins nestled amongst the pines were completed in fall of 1995. These log cabins have 2 bedrooms, a bath, full kitchens and fireplaces. The master bedroom has a queen-size bed, while the second bedroom has a full size bed, the living room has a full size sleeper sofa. Each cabin sleeps up to six people. Watch the sun rise and set on your cabins deck.

Many activities are available just steps away from your front porch. Cast your line into Eagle River or fish in their privately stocked lake. Start your mountain bike ride, cross country ski trip or snowmobile adventure from the trails right on the property. If your planning a ski vacation there are two resorts within 30 minutes drive Vail and Beaver Creek plus Ski Cooper which is only a 10 minute drive.

Pets including your horse are allowed for an additional fee. Cabin guests receive a 15% discount for tours from Nova Guides who feature rafting, fishing, jeeping, ATV, mountain bike, snowmobile, snowcat, wildlife, and wildcat tours depending on the season.

Location: Sixteen miles south of I-70, exit 171, on US Highway 24. Six miles south of Red Cliff and 14 miles north of Leadville.

3 Cabins with Kitchen	Phone in Rooms	Steve Pittel & Greg Caretto, Owners
3 Rooms with Fireplaces	Some Units Nonsmoking	1088 Hwy 24
	Elevation: 9100	Red Cliff CO 81649
	Credit Cards: VMAD	888-949 NOVA (6682)
	Rates: $95-$125	970/949-4232
	Open: All Year	Fax: 970/949-4191
		E-mail: nova@vail.net
		www.coloradodirectory/com/pandocabins/

At the resort:

At resort or within 15 minutes:

Sweetwater Lake Resort

Vacation on the edge of the Flat Tops Wilderness in the grandeur of the White River National Forest. Sweetwater Lake Resort is surrounded by an unforgettable panorama of nature from mountain tops to streams rushing through meadows. Choose between two and three-bedroom cabins with fully equipped kitchens, showers and linens provided. Some of the 7 cabins are on the lake and have fireplaces and decks. One unit has a woodstove. A four-unit motel is also available.

Sweetwater Lake Resort boasts rainbow and German brown trout fishing in both the lake and nearby streams. Also available on site are row-boat rentals, a barbecue picnic area, volleyball court and horseshoe area. There's even a wilderness cooking and packing school here! A.J. Brink Outfitters is based out of the resort and offers horseback rides, wilderness pack trips and winter rides. This is also a great area for big game hunting. Diamond Jack's Western Restaurant on the lake serves breakfast, lunch and dinner daily. Numerous trails begin at the resort, including mountain bike, cross-country skiing and snowshoe trails. Nearby are a museum, golf course, whitewater rafting tours, and snowmobile trails.

Also available are 20 primitive tent and RV camp sites have no hookups. Six of the RV sites are 45 feet and have room for slide-outs. Pets are permitted both in the cabins and at the campsites with advanced arrangements. Guests may also bring their own horse. Wedding and activity planning services are available. Permitted by the US Forest Service Bureau of Land Management.

Location: From I-70 take exit 133, go 7 miles, then turn west, up Sweetwater Creek drive 10 miles.

7 Cabins with Kitchen	Pay Phone Available	Adrienne Brink & Kent Scheu, Owners
4 Motel Rooms	Recreation Room	3406 Sweetwater Rd
4 Rooms with Fireplaces	Elevation: 7700	Sweetwater CO 81637
1 Room with Woodstove	Credit Cards: VM	970/524-7344
Central Woodstove	Rates: $50-$90	Fax: 970/524-9510
Central Campfire Area	Open: All Year	E-mail: brink@gateway.net
		www.coloradodirectory.com/sweetwaterlakeresort/

At the resort:

At resort or within 15 minutes:

Estes Park Area

Including Drake, Glen Haven, Loveland & Lyons —
Map: C-14, C-15, C-16 & D-15

Longs Peak, at a dizzying 14,255', towers over the quaint mountain town of
Estes Park. The eastern gate to Rocky Mountain National Park, Estes Park, at
7,522', started when Joel Estes and his family moved to the valley in 1859.
The public soon learned about the high mountain valley surrounded by
snowcapped peaks when a journalist wrote about scaling Longs Peak.
Crowds came to visit the park and stay at the famous Stanley Hotel, built in
1909. In town, stroll along the streets, sampling the numerous candy stores
and craft shops, play golf, horseback ride or sail. Rocky Mountain National
Park has 415 glacially-carved square miles covered with lakes, wildlife and
wild flowers. Trail Ridge Road, the highest continuous paved road in the
United States, traverses the park and crosses the Continental Divide. From
Estes Park, you can tour the Peak-to-Peak Scenic Highway or drive through
the scenic Big Thompson Canyon east to Loveland. **Loveland** has become
famous for its numerous, nationally renown sculptors whose work can be
seen at Benson Park. The town was named for William Austin Hamilton
Loveland, the man responsible for bringing the Colorado Central Railroad's
line from Cheyenne, Wyoming, through here on its way to Denver. In the
early 1900s, Colorado was the leading sugar beet producing state in the
country and Loveland became the sight of the first sugar mill in eastern Colorado. Nearby Carter Lake offers 100 acres of fishing and water sports. The
new 38-store factory outlet mall is just west of the junction of U.S. 34 and I-
25. Enjoy the easy pace in Loveland, where life moves a little slower in this
"Sweetheart City."

Fun Things to Do

- Enos Mills Cabin, Estes Park (970) 586-4706
- Estes Park Area Historical Museum (970) 586-6256
- Estes Park Golf Course (970) 586-8146
- Loveland Municipal Golf Course (970) 667-5256
- Loveland Museum & Gallery (970) 962-2410
- Loveland Sculpture Works (970) 667-0991
- MacGregor Ranch, Estes Park (970) 586-3749
- Rocky Mountain Adventures, Rafting, Kayaking & Fly Fishing
  (800) 858-6808
- Rocky Mountain National Park (970) 686-1206

Anderson's Wonder View Cottages

Relax on top of the world at Anderson's Wonder View Cottages. These modern cottages and motel, with an outstanding view of the 14,256-foot Long's Peak, are scattered across five acres of peaceful land next to Rocky Mountain National Park. All units have fireplaces, a private deck and cable television. Each cottage, spaced 50 feet apart for privacy, has a grill and a fully equipped kitchen.

Resort facilities include a hot tub, heated pool, putting green, basketball court, horseshoes, shuffleboard, a picnic area and a playground. Year-round color surrounds the cottages: spring brings lush green meadows and wildflowers, while summers offer beautiful scenery and cool, refreshing mountain air. Fall abounds with golden aspen and wildlife, and mild winters showcase pristine snow and scenic splendor.

Cabins have a seven-day minimum rental during summer.

Location: Two and a half miles west of downtown Estes Park, 0.25 miles north of Highway 36 (also known as Moraine Ave.).

out dated interiors

9 Cabins with Kitchen	Pay Phone Available	Tom Peter, Owner
1 Vacation Home	Some Units Nonsmoking	540 Laurel Ln
3 Lodging Rooms	Recreation Room	Estes Park CO 80517-0427
3 Motel Rooms	Elevation: 8000	800/327-0113
16 Rooms with Fireplaces	Credit Cards: VMD	970/586-4158
Central Hot Tub	Rates: $80-$200	Fax: 970/586-4515
	Open: All Year	E-mail: andersons@estes-park.com
		www.coloradodirectory.com/andersonscottages/

At the resort:

At resort or within 15 minutes:

3 day min

Log Cabins

couples

Antler's Pointe Log Cabin Suites "On the River"

This elite mountain retreat caters exclusively to husband-and-wife couples. The romantic, luxury log cabin suites at Antlers Pointe are across a bridge for privacy and rest on the banks of the beautiful Fall River. Each suite features skylights, vaulted ceilings, a king bedroom, a private Jacuzzi for two, and step-in showers for two. Cuddle up with your honey in the cozy parlor with a fireplace and love sofa. The cabins have a southwestern decor and are complete with surround sound CD stereo, color cable television, VCR, and a telephone. The kitchenette is complete for a perfect candle light dinner. Walk out onto your private deck with a gas grill just 20 feet from the water's edge. A welcome basket is in your suite upon your arrival. Nestled beneath a grove of spruce and ponderosa pine, you can enjoy the view of snowcapped peaks, wildlife and wildflowers in your secluded river front yard.

All the activities of Rocky Mountain National Park are less than a mile away. Come to the mountains to jog, hike, mountain bike, and horseback ride. Golfers will appreciate the two picturesque courses in Estes Park. This quaint town also offers plenty of shops to explore and fine restaurants to dine in. In the winter, try snowshoeing and cross-country skiing on the pristine snow.

Ask about the 3-, 4- or 5-day romance packages, perfect for sparkling-up your special time alone. This is an ideal getaway for honeymooners, anniversaries, outdoor weddings or mountain-top marriage renewals. You will find Antler's Pointe to be the "Most Unabashedly Romantic" for your special occasion. Smoking and pets are not permitted. Advance reservations only.

Location: One block south of Fall River Road (Highway 34 West) on Fish Hatchery Road.

8 Cabins with Kitchen	Phone in Rooms	PO Box 245
8 Lodging Rooms	All Units Nonsmoking	Estes Park CO 80517-0245
8 Rooms with Hot Tubs	Elevation: 8000	800/638-8881
8 Rooms with Fireplaces	Credit Cards: VM	970/586-8881
	Rates: $189	Fax: 970/586-2301 NO LIST
	Open: All Year	E-mail: antlers3@juno.com
		www.coloradodirectory.com/anlterspointe/

look new & modern

At the resort:

At resort or within 15 minutes:

Appenzell Inn — A Suites Resort, The

The Appenzell Inn is a new, Swiss-inspired mountain inn offering unique designs in studio, one and two bedroom luxury suites. This is a totally smoke free property throughout all the grounds and building to offer a haven to non-smokers, even those with allergies. You'll be sure to enjoy the in-room Jacuzzi tub, fireplace, king bed, television with VCR, kitchenette and air conditioning. The Suite Heart Loft is ideal for a romantic getaway.

The inn offers a heated, indoor swimming pool, mountain views wherever you look and a guest laundry. This resort is convenient to shopping, golfing and taking strolls on the river walk. All the outdoor activities of Rocky Mountain National Park are only five miles away, including hiking, sightseeing, snowshoeing and cross country skiing. Other area activities include horseback riding, four wheel driving, sleigh riding, bicycling, boating and snowmobiling. Lake Estes is only a short half a mile walk.

The entire property is non-smoking. No pets are allowed.

Location: A half mile from Lake Estes on Big Thompson Avenue.

29 Lodging Rooms	Phone in Rooms	David & Susan Habecker, Owners
29 Rooms with Hot Tubs	All Units Nonsmoking	PO Box 3228
29 Rooms with Fireplaces	Elevation: 7650	Estes Park CO 80517
	Credit Cards: VMD	800/475-1125
	Rates: $90-$220	970/586-1122
	Open: All Year	Fax: 970/586-2626
		www.coloradodirectory.com/appenzellinn

At the resort:

At resort or within 15 minutes:

On the Fall River

Aspen Winds

Experience the splendor of the Rocky Mountains at Aspen Winds. The newly constructed one and two bedroom suites all have either a private balcony or deck overlooking the Fall River with a panoramic mountain view in the background. Suites are furnished with an in-room Jacuzzi or jetted tub, a fireplace, kitchen or kitchenette (no stove), king and queen beds, color cable television with HBO and Cinemax, a VCR, in-room phones and gas grills.

Fish for trout right outside your door in the roaring waters of Fall River. About halfway between the village of Estes Park and Rocky Mountain National Park, Aspen Wind appeals to every vacationer's needs. Wildlife abound here and you might see elk, deer and big horn sheep wandering about. Chipmunks, Abert squirrels, blue stellar jays, Clark's nutcrackers and tiny hummingbirds as plentiful as beaver, coyote, raccoon and marmot here. Outdoor activities abound in the alpine paradise, from hiking and mountain biking to hunting and sightseeing. The outdoor hot tub located just 10 feet from the river is a spectacular way to end your day.

Ask about the available packages. No pets allowed. Some units are non-smoking. Aspen Winds does not accept groups or family reunions.

Location: Halfway between town & Rocky Mountain National Park, just west of Castle Mountain Rd.

8 Lodging Rooms	Phone in Rooms	Linda, Doug & Mike Cook, Owners
8 Camper Cabins	Some Units Nonsmoking	1051 Fall River Court
16 Rooms with Hot Tubs	Elevation: 7700	Estes Park CO 80517
16 Rooms with Fireplaces	Credit Cards: VMAD	800/399-6010
Central Hot Tub	Rates: $129-$169	970/586-6010
	Open: All Year	Fax: 970/586-3626
		E-mail: Aspenwinds@aol.com
		www.coloradodirectory.com/aspenwinds

 # 85-179

At the resort:

At resort or within 15 minutes:

Baldpate Inn, The

If the Baldpate Inn didn't have such spectacular views, charming guest rooms and scrumptious food, they would still be famous for their key collection — the largest in the world! The inn is listed on the National Register of Historic Places and offers three cabins without cooking facilities and 12 guest rooms. All are charmingly decorated. Suites are available with private baths, as well as rooms which have a private sink and a shared bath. Room rates include a gourmet, three course breakfast. Cabins with a fireplace in the sitting room range from one to three bedrooms.

Nestled in the pine and aspen forest on the side of Twin Sisters Mountain, Baldpate Inn offers a wonderful mountain retreat. The inn's dining room is open to the public and serves a soup and salad buffet, homemade breads and pies daily. Huge native stone fireplaces welcome you to friendly conversations, a board game or a quiet time with a book in the inn's library. The Baldpate Inn is located amid unlimited opportunities for hiking, watching wildlife, talking photos, horseback riding, golfing, swimming, boating, shopping and attending special events such as the Rooftop Rodeo and the Scottish Festival. And, of course, take time to explore the key collection with more keys and shapes and uses than you could possibly imagine!

Reservations for dining and lodging are recommended. Family reunions, weekend getaways and small conferences are all welcomed. This is a non-smoking establishment.

Location: Seven scenic miles on Highway 7, south of Estes Park.

3 Cabins without Kitchens	Pay Phone Available	Lois Smith, Owner
12 Lodging Rooms	Bed & Breakfast Available	PO Box 4445
1 Room with Hot Tub	All Units Nonsmoking	Estes Park CO 80517-4445
3 Rooms with Fireplaces	Recreation Room	970/586-KEYS
Central Fireplace	Elevation: 9000	E-mail: baldplateinn@aol.com
	Credit Cards: VMD	www.coloradodirectory.com/baldpateinn
	Rates: $80-$140	
	Open: 5/28 to 10/1	

At the resort:

At resort or within 15 minutes:

Barb's Bed & Breakfast

Come spend some time in a tranquil glen nestled on Little Prospect Mountain. Barb's Bed & Breakfast offers dazzling scenery, a variety of wildlife and four rooms. Nancy's Suite has a private entrance, living room, full kitchen, moss rock fireplace, king bed, color cable television and a private bath. Arlene's Room has a window seat, king bed, color cable television and an oval, jetted tub. The Blue Room features the host's grandmother's quilts on the queen bed. This room shares a bath with the Rose Room which has a queen brass bed and antique walnut furniture.

Be sure to stop in the quaint antique store on-site and browse among the assortment of old world treasures, crafts and dried flower arrangements. After breakfast, and before beginning your day, relax for a while in the knotty pine living room with lots of windows to the mountains and a fireplace to keep you cozy. Spend some time on the deck watching for the local wildlife cavorting on the grounds. Within a few minutes drive are any number of ways to spend your vacation, including horseback riding, white water rafting, golfing, boating, mountain biking, cross country skiing and snowshoeing. You can even fish on site or drive to downhill skiing in an hour. With Estes Park right here, and Rocky Mountain National Park down the road, you'll find plenty to do when you vacation at Barb's Bed & Breakfast.

All rooms are non-smoking. Children are accepted on an individual basis and no pets are allowed. Ask about wedding packages, including the minister.

Location: Just west of the junction of Riverside Drive and the road to the Aerial Tram.

3 Cabins with Kitchen	Phone in Lobby	Barbara & Stan Fisher, Owners
1 Vacation Home	Bed & Breakfast Available	PO Box 540
3 Lodging Rooms	All Units Nonsmoking	Estes Park CO 80517
2 Rooms with Hot Tubs	Recreation Room	800/597-7903
1 Room with Fireplace	Elevation: 7500	970/586-5871
Central Fireplace	Credit Cards: VMAD	E-mail: barbsbnb@peakpeak.com
	Rates: $85-$125	www.coloradodirectory.com/barbsbnb
	Open: All Year	

At the resort:

At resort or within 15 minutes:

Motels are rooms or fewer on Fuller
3 night min?

Big Thompson Timberlane Lodge

Located on six grassy acres between Estes Park and Rocky Mountain National Park, Big Thompson Timberlane Lodge has an inspiring view of the Rocky Mountains. All of the motel, cottage units and 1,200-square-foot log homes have their own heat, carpeting, cable television with HBO and combination baths or showers. Accommodations are available with or without kitchenettes. Eight of the log homes have private hot tubs or jetted tubs. The all-season log homes have gas fireplaces, a washer and dryer, fully equipped kitchens with a dishwasher and microwave — ideal for a family vacation.

The lodge is off the road along the banks of the Big Thompson River, yet within walking distance of restaurants, miniature golf and shopping areas. Cast your line into the lodges portion of the Big Thompson River — privately stocked for guests only. BBQ grills with picnic tables are spread throughout the lawn for outdoor cooking. Local activities include scenic drives to Bear Lake, Fall River Road and Trail Ridge Road. After a day's adventures, refresh yourself in the swimming pool and relax in the large hot tub.

Kids under 2 stay free, and you can have a crib added to the room for an additional charge. No pets are allowed. There is a 2 day deposit required and a 30 day cancellation policy. They cater to couples and families. They accept personal checks for deposits.

Location: Highway 36 (also known as Moraine Ave), west of Estes Park.

16 Cabins with Kitchen
14 Cabins without Kitchens
15 Vacation Homes
13 Motel Rooms
8 Rooms with Hot Tubs
16 Rooms with Fireplaces
Central Hot Tub
Some Units Nonsmoking

Elevation: 7500
Credit Cards: VMAD
Rates: $89-$315
Open: All Year

Curt & Pat Thompson, President
PO Box 387
Estes Park CO 80517-0387
800/898-4373
970/586-3137
Fax: 970/586-3719
E-mail: bttl@peakpeak.com
www.coloradodirectory.com/bigthompsonlodge/

log cabins aval

At the resort:

At resort or within 15 minutes:

Black Canyon Inn

Built in 1927 as a private home, the Black Canyon Inn is made entirely out of rough cut logs from the nearby forests. The inn has retained its natural beauty and mountain feel with its high beamed ceilings, natural oak floors, balcony, and floor to ceiling wood burning fireplace. This main building now houses the inn's restaurant. Two rustic cabins are available May - October only. One cabin has a master bedroom with a queen bed, fireplace, and 3/4 bath, while its living room has a fireplace, full bath and sitting area with mountain views. The other cabin is secluded with 1 bedroom, a deck, queen bed, living room with fireplace, full bath and a kitchenette. The pine lodge offers 3 rooms with private entrances, mountain views and can be connected together. Many of the units have private fireplaces and all have cable TV. Suites are available year-round and have a living room with a fireplace, private decks with mountain or stream views, a fully equipped kitchen with breakfast bar, separate master bedroom with queen bed, master bath with a Jacuzzi tub and separate shower, and housekeeping services. These are spacious accommodations with each 1 bedroom suite having 730 square feet. The suites can be rented as 1, 2 and 3 bedroom units.

Situated on 14 private acres, Black Canyon Inn has a heated pool, a stream-fed pond, picturesque views, and seclusion in a quiet and luxurious mountain setting. The restaurant specializes in fresh seafood flown in from the West Coast. Their extensive continental menu offers a wide variety of entrees, including wild game, meats and poultry, pasta, salad and vegetarian dishes. Hike nearby trails, visit

Rocky Mountain National Park, enjoy wildlife viewing from your private deck and relax in front of a fire.

This unique setting is ideal for a romantic getaway or a wedding reception. Rooms are non-smoking. Ask about winter packages.

Location: a half mile north of Estes Park on MacGregor Avenue.

---

2 Cabins with Kitchen
3 Cabins without Kitchens
18 Lodging Rooms
12 Rooms with Hot Tubs
16 Rooms with Fireplaces
All Units Nonsmoking
Elevation: 7600
Credit Cards: VMA

Rates: $85-$185
Open: All Year

Jim Sloan, Owner
800 McGregor Ave (Devil's Gulch Rd)
Estes Park CO 80517-0856
800/897-3730
970/586-8113 reservation
Fax: 970/586-5123
E-mail: info@blackcanyoninn.com
www.coloradodirectory.com/blackcanyoninn

At the resort:

At resort or within 15 minutes:

Boulder Brook on Fall River

The Fall River tumbles past your back door over trout and cobblestones. Inside the 16 private suites at Boulder Brook you'll appreciate the double-wall construction for privacy, fluffy towels and personal bath amenities as well as the thoughtfully provided corkscrew and wine glasses. Boulder Brook's Spa Room is a luxury not soon forgotten with its open floor plan and its in-room spa that overlooks Fall River. The one bedroom suites have separate bedrooms and a tiled bath with an oversized, jetted tub. All suites have cooking facilities, private decks, fireplaces and king beds. Choose between suites with full kitchens or partial kitchens for your cooking convenience. All units have daily housekeeping services.

Set along the banks of the picturesque Fall River, between Estes Park and Rocky Mountain National Park, Boulder Brook is ideally located to take advantage of the unique shops of Estes Park and the abundance of nature in the national park. Among the area activities are scenic drives and hikes, mountain climbing, bird watching, golfing, ice skating, horseback riding, fishing, sailing and wind surfing, cross country and downhill skiing, sledding and much more. Or simply stay at "home," relishing the luxury of your private room with all of its amenities.

Ask about the special packages, including the Sweetheart Package, the Celebration Package, R&R Package, and the Traditional or Tranquillity Package. Go all out, and splurge on the Sky's the Limit Option with a romantic champagne hot air balloon flight added to any package! Special wedding packages are available too. All suites are non-smoking and no pets are allowed.

Location: Two miles from Rocky Mountain National Park on Fall River Road.

---

16 Lodging Rooms	Phone in Rooms	John Spahnle, Owner
8 Rooms with Hot Tubs	All Units Nonsmoking	1900 Fall River Rd
16 Rooms with Fireplaces	Elevation: 8000	Estes Park CO 80517
Central Hot Tub	Credit Cards: VMAD	800/238-0910
	Rates: $169-$189	970/586-0910
	Open: All Year	Fax: 970/586-8067
		www.coloradodirectory.com/boulderbrook

At the resort:

At resort or within 15 minutes:

Brynwood on the River

Brynwood on the River is nestled between towering ponderosa pines and scenic rock formations. Choose between a 10-room convenience motel and the 16 budget river and theme cottages. The tastefully decorated theme units offer a choice of interiors, such as nostalgic days of flying with the 11th Aero Squadron complete with overhead model planes and walls full of interesting documents, or the Victorian decor of the motel unit, Columbine. Stained glass and charming colonial antiques await you at the Chic-A-Dee, the "Sea Galley" has a salty decor, while the Love Nest cottages features a two person jet tub and a real rock waterfall! All units have cable television with HBO, direct-dial phones and all are carpeted and completely furnished. All cottages are equipped for housekeeping with modern appliances, including coffee makers and microwaves. In addition, all of the cottages have portable outdoor grills, picnic tables and many of them have fireplaces.

Brynwood sits right on the privately stocked Big Thompson River, so anglers will find fishing easily accessible. The resort boasts an aquatic complex with a large, heated pool and a soothing spa. There's even a wading pool for the kids. Within a short drive are horseback riding stables, museums, golf and lakes for boating. Nearby are trails for mountain biking, cross country skiing and snow shoeing. You can even take a sleigh ride in the winter, or try downhill skiing about an hour away. Within 30 minutes, you can ice fish, hunt and snowmobile. With

Rocky Mountain National Park and Estes Park a few minutes away, you'll find plenty to do on your vacation here.

Because Brynwood caters to couples and families looking to getaway from the crowds, they do not accommodate reunions or groups. A minimum stay of five days is required, except to fill in between reservations.

Location: On Highway 36 (also known as Moraine Avenue).

17 Cabins with Kitchen	Phone in Rooms	Cindy Oliver, Own & Ron,Lucy McFate
3 Vacation Homes	All Units Nonsmoking	PO Box 1929
10 Motel Rooms	Elevation: 7600	Estes Park CO 80517-1929
3 Rooms with Hot Tubs	Credit Cards: VMAD	800/279-4488
10 Rooms with Fireplaces	Rates: $114-$245	970/586-4488
3 Rooms with Wood Stoves	Open: All Year	E-mail: info@brynwood.com
Central Hot Tub		www.coloradodirectory.com/brynwood/

At the resort:

At resort or within 15 minutes:

Colorado Cottages

Stay where you are treated like a guest of the family in true country comfort at Colorado Cottages. This is a small, intimate spot for getaways, holidays and family vacations at the edge of Rocky Mountain National Park. The 10 charming country-style housekeeping cottages are either individual or duplexes. Each unit has a full kitchen, fireplace, color cable television with HBO and an in-room library, making it feel just like home. Most cottages have private bathrooms with showers, and some have tub/shower combinations. The cottages sleep between 2-8 people. Linens and towels are furnished, but there is no daily maid service. Arranged in a courtyard fashion on one acre, the cottages have a breathtaking wide open mountain view. Each unit has a charcoal grill and picnic table or lawn furniture for outdoor barbecues. "At home" hospitality is extended to your family with the owners as your personal hosts.

Expect to see plenty of wildlife, from birds in the summer to elk in the fall. Among the many local activities are fishing on the Big Thompson River, hiking, golfing, miniature golfing and horseback riding. Grocery stores, souvenir shops and restaurants are all located within walking distance and in nearby Estes Park, a five minute drive away.

A deposit for your first and last night's stay will confirm your reservation. The cottages are non-smoking. No pets and no groups, please.

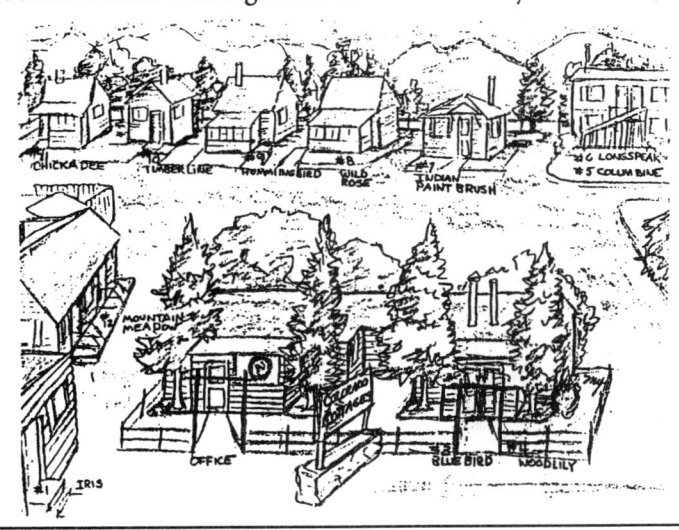

Location: On Highway 36 (also known as Moraine Avenue), just west of Estes Park on the north side of the road.

10 Cabins with Kitchen	Pay Phone Available	Jodi & Mark Adler, Owners
10 Rooms with Fireplaces	All Units Nonsmoking	1241 High Dr
	Elevation: 7850	Estes Park CO 80517
	Credit Cards: VM	800/468-1236
	Rates: $88-$125	970/586-4637
	Open: 5/1 to 9/30	E-mail: coloradocottage@webtv.net
		www.coloradodirectory.com/coloradocottages/

At the resort:

At resort or within 15 minutes:

Min stay - too much #

Dripping Springs Bed & Breakfast Inn and Cabins

Stay at the top of the canyon at this country-style bed and breakfast inn, built in 1936, located on five acres of aspen and pine trees on the Big Thompson River. Dripping Springs offers yesteryear's look with comfy rooms featuring a queen or full bed. Five uniquely decorated rooms have private entrances and baths, while one room shares a baths. Full homemade breakfast are included. None of the rooms have a phone or television. There are also two one bedroom cabins available with a private outdoor hot tub, wood burning stove, kitchen and gas BBQ grill. The views of the canyon and Longs Peak from the deck and grounds are breathtaking.

In a very private location "behind the rock," Dripping Springs is three minutes from Estes Park. Fish on the abundant Big Thompson River frontage at the inn and then soak away your worries in one of the large, outdoor hot tubs as the sun sets behind the mountains. The nearby Rocky Mountain National Park abounds with outdoor possibilities from hiking and horseback riding to sightseeing and alpine picnicking. The lively little town of Estes Park has something to please everyone, including candy and ice cream shops to fine restaurants to theater and boutiques.

All accommodations at Dripping Springs are non-smoking. This Bed and Breakast is an adult resort, the cabins are great for families. There is a two day

minimum stay and a 50% deposit is required when making the reservation.

Location: Three miles east of Estes Park on Highway 34 between milepost markers 66-67 or 16 and a half miles west of the Dam Store on Highway 34 coming from Loveland.

3 Cabins with Kitchen	Phone in Lobby	Oliver & Janie Robertson, Owners
1 Vacation Home	Bed & Breakfast Available	2551 Hwy 34
6 Lodging Rooms	All Units Nonsmoking	Drake CO 80515
4 Rooms with Hot Tubs	Elevation: 7400	800/432-7145
3 Rooms with Fireplaces	Credit Cards: VMAD	970/586-3406
1 Room with Woodstove	Rates: $69-$130	Fax: 979/586-3035
Central Hot Tub	Open: 5/14 to 10/31	E-mail: lnnestes@aol.com
Central Campfire Area		www.coloradodirectory.com/drippingspgsinncabin

At the resort:

At resort or within 15 minutes:

Eagle Cliff House Cabins and Bed & Breakfast

Nestled in ponderosa pines at the base of Eagle Cliff Mountain in Estes Park, this bed and breakfast is a warm, friendly place to stay. The rooms combine soft southwestern decor and colors with the beautiful woods used in American antiques in a warm and hospitable atmosphere. The Heritage Room is decorated with early 1900s antiques and has a queen-size iron bed. The Southwest Room features Indian artifacts and books on the culture of the American southwest as well as a queen-size bed and gas fireplace. Both rooms have a private bath and their own entrance with a shared hot tub on the patio. For a romantic, special getaway, try the Victorian Cottage furnished in period antiques complete with a queen bed, jetted tub, fully stocked kitchenette, gas fireplace and a sunny deck facing the mountains.

A hearty country breakfast is served in the house's sunny breakfast nook. You are welcome to dig into the "never empty" cookie jar at anytime throughout your stay. At Eagle Cliff House, you are within walking distance of Rocky Mountain National Park. Your hosts can help plan everything from a day hike into the

mountains to a overnight backpacking experience into the wilderness. They will also drive you to and from the trailheads, plus they are backpacking consultants and willing to help how they can. The popular resort town of Estes Park is nearby and offers an abundance of western history as well as unique shops and restaurants.

Ask about the individualized service for birthdays, weddings, honeymoons, anniversaries or other special occasions.

Location: On Highway 66 close to the YMCA.

1 Cabin with Kitchen	Phone in Lobby	Mike & Nancy Conrin, Owners
2 Lodging Rooms	Bed & Breakfast Available	Box 4312
1 Room with Hot Tub	All Units Nonsmoking	Estes Park CO 80517-4312
2 Rooms with Wood Stoves	Recreation Room	800/414-0922
Central Hot Tub	Elevation: 7800	970/586-5425
	Credit Cards: None	Fax: 970/577-0132
	Rates: $80-$135	E-mail: m.conrin@worldnet.att.net
	Open: All Year	www.coloradodirectory.com/eaglecliffhouse

At the resort:

At resort or within 15 minutes:

Eagle Manor, The — A Bed & Breakfast Place

Built in 1917, The Eagle Manor is comfortable and tastefully furnished with antiques. The four spacious guest rooms have color cable television. Three rooms have queen beds and the fourth room has twin beds. Two have private baths while two share a bath. The main floor has high ceilings, exquisite oak floors and two fireplaces – mountain luxury at its finest.

The Eagle Manor's great room has a fireplace, big screen television and a billiard table. A hearty breakfast is served in the formal dining room. An indoor swimming pool, an indoor sauna and an outdoor hot tub with a privacy fence round out the amenities here. Be sure to explore all the nearby activities in Rocky Mountain National Park and its surroundings, from fishing and hiking, to shopping, attending the theater and special events and visiting the museum. Special events throughout the year include the Scottish Festival, Rooftop Rodeo, Wool Market to horse shows and the village's Fourth of July celebration.

No smoking or pets allowed.

Location: Intersection of Chapin and Chiquita Lanes north of US highway 34 west, 1st street west of MacGregor.

1 Vacation Home	Phone in Rooms	Mike Smith, Host
4 Lodging Rooms	Bed & Breakfast Available	PO Box 1013
Central Hot Tub	All Units Nonsmoking	Estes Park CO 80517
Central Fireplace	Recreation Room	970/586-8482
	Elevation: 7600	Fax: 970/586-1748
	Credit Cards: VMAD	E-mail: eaglemanor@aol.com
	Rates: $125	www.coloradodirectory.com/eaglemanor
	Open: All Year	

At the resort:

At resort or within 15 minutes:

No photos

Edgewater Heights Cottages

Stay in clean, cozy cottages on the trout stocked Big Thompson River! The eight cabins have fireplaces, color television (no cable), and fully equipped kitchens with microwaves. Outside your door cook your fresh caught fish on the barbecue grill.

Edgewater Heights also has a shady picnic area with a campfire area and horseshoe pits. Soak in the new hot tub overlooking the river. Hike trails begin right on the property. Fish right on the river beyond your cabin door. Just five minutes to the east is downtown Estes Park, Lake Estes, a golf course and fair grounds. Also nearby is Rocky Mountain National Park where you can hike, mountain bike, cross country ski, horseback ride and snowmobile. Other nearby area activities include white water raft trips, visiting the museum, sleigh rides, and places to ice fish and hunt in season.

Pets and children are welcome here.

Location: Two miles east of Estes Park, on Highway 34 near milepost marker 66.

8 Cabins with Kitchen	Pay Phone Available	David Kiser, Owner
8 Rooms with Fireplaces	Some Units Nonsmoking	PO Box 3195
Central Hot Tub	Elevation: 7500	Estes Park CO 80517-3195
Central Campfire Area	Credit Cards: VMD	800/530-3942
	Rates: $79	970/586-8493
	Open: All Year	www.coloradodirectory.com/edgewaterheightscott ages/

At the resort:

At resort or within 15 minutes:

Elkhorn Lodge & Guest Ranch

No photos *Rustic cabins* *Wilderness tent sites*

Just two blocks from downtown Estes Park, the Elkhorn Lodge is an historical treasure — a Registered National Historical Property at the base of Man Mountain, a sacred vision-quest site. You'll experience old-West living in TV-free rooms and outlying cabins. Accommodations are a rustic reminder of yesteryear, with 1890's luxury of indoor baths. The lodge has 39 guest rooms , three housekeeping cabins, 23 non-housekeeping cabins and two vacations homes. Enjoy the views from the Lodge porch, spacious lobbies and meeting rooms. Families will appreciate the reasonably-priced breakfasts and dinners in the 1920s restaurant and the TV room with movies for the kids.

Cabin guests may bring their dogs and all guests can board their horses here. Or take a trail ride with horses from the ranch's stable. One- or two-hour rides, breakfast rides and evening steak rides are available. Other amenities include a swimming pool, stocked fee fishing pond and mountain bike rentals on site.

Originally a stage-coach stop for Estes Park, Elkhorn's Coach House is ideal for 200-person reunions, weddings and other special events. The Coach house also offers chuckwagon dinners, followed by adult socializing and dancing. Wilderness tent sits are also available.

Location: On West Elkhorn Avenue after US Highway 36 turns south at the stop light.

Dude Ranch

3 Cabins with Kitchen	Pay Phone Available	Jerry Zahourek & Kathy Durward
23 Cabins without Kitchens	Recreation Room	PO Box 1560
2 Vacation Homes	Elevation: 7500	Estes Park CO 80517-1560
39 Lodging Rooms	Credit Cards: VMD	970/586-4416 lodge
4 Rooms with Fireplaces	Rates: $85-$92	Fax: 970/586-8304 Apr-Oct
Central Fireplace	Open: 4/15 to 10/31	E-mail: elkhorn@frii.com
Central Campfire Area		www.coloradodirectory.com/elkhornlodge

At the resort:

At resort or within 15 minutes:

Estes Park Bed & Breakfast

The accommodations at Estes Park Bed & Breakfast include either of two king size bedroom suites with a private bath (one suite has an extra sitting/sleeping room) and a choice of king size or twin bedroom. All rooms include in-room color cable television, VCRs upon request, gourmet breakfasts each morning and almost anything else old-fashioned southern hospitality can provide to make your visit memorable.

Be sure to use the hot tub and the barbecue picnic table area while you vacation here. Just minutes away are fishing, horseback riding, white water rafting, golfing, boating, mountain biking, snowshoeing, cross country skiing and sleigh rides. A visit to the shops and galleries of Estes Park is a must when visiting here, as is a trip to the spectacular Rocky Mountain National Park and all its natural beauties.

Ask about the full wedding services and the off-season rates.

Location: West of Morraine Avenue, just south of junction with Elkhorn Avenue.

1 Vacation Home	Phone in Rooms	Vaye & Dick Williams, Owners
2 Lodging Rooms	Bed & Breakfast Available	PO Box 482
Central Hot Tub	All Units Nonsmoking	Estes Park CO 80517
Central Fireplace	Recreation Room	800/492-3425
	Elevation: 7650	970/586-7781
	Credit Cards: VMAD	Fax: 970/586-7782
	Rates: $125-$150	E-mail: stay@estesparkbandb.com
	Open: All Year	www.coloradodirectory.com/estesparkbandb/

At the resort:

At resort or within 15 minutes:

Estes Park Center®/YMCA of the Rockies

Discover why four generations of families return to this magnificent setting every year to rejuvenate spirit, mind and body. Pick between 510 lodge rooms and 205 cabins and vacation homes scatted over 860 acres adjoining Rocky Mountain National Park. Limited cabin availability to non-members of YMCA of the Rockies (mainly available October through May). Each cabin has its own fully equipped kitchen and private phone; many have fireplaces. Linens, bedding, and towels are provided in both the cabins and lodge rooms.

Depending on the season, vacation activities include hayrides, horseback rides, hikes, mountain biking, square dances, miniature golf, tennis and arts and crafts. "SummerFest" offers over two dozen musical events. Kids will love the summer youth day-camp. For relaxation, visit the library or museum, or playing in the indoor swimming pool. During the winter, try ice skating on-site or snowshoeing, and cross-country skiing. Estes Park Center is minutes away from the mountain town of Estes Park. Take scenic drives through Big Thompson Canyon, over Trail Ridge Road in Rocky Mountain National Park or along the scenic Peak-to-Peak Highway.

Reservations are required for groups — the conference and family reunion facilities can accommodate up to 2,500 people. Pets are allowed in cabins only.

Location: West of town on Colorado Highway 36 (also known as Moraine Avenue). Turn south on Highway 66.

185 Cabins with Kitchen	All Units Nonsmoking	Gary Baxter, Managing Dir
21 Vacation Homes	Recreation Room	2515 Tunnel Road
534 Lodging Rooms	Elevation: 8010	Estes Park CO 80511-2550
210 Beds in Bunkhouse	Credit Cards: None	970/586-3341 ext 1010
119 Rooms with Fireplaces	Rates: $48-$231	Fax: 970/586-6078
Central Fireplace	Open: All Year	E-mail: info@ymcarockies.org
Central Campfire Area		www.coloradodirectory.com/ymcaestespark

At the resort:

At resort or within 15 minutes:

Fireside Cabins & RV Park

At the foot of the Rockies, just west of Loveland, are the Fireside Cabins. The cabins, sheltered among many shade trees, over look the "Devil's Backbone" of the mountains. All cabins are air conditioned and have color cable television with HBO and Showtime. Some have queen beds, fireplaces and kitchenettes with cooking utensils. A fully furnished apartment with two bedrooms is also available as a suite for larger families.

Outside, the resort has a playground, horseshoes, volleyball, basketball and badminton for everyone to enjoy. A convenience store and laundry room are also available. RV sites with picnic tables and concrete patios are available year-round as well. Fireside is close to great fishing and many kinds of recreation, including hiking, mountain biking, golfing, boating, and horseback riding. After your day of fun, come back for a soak in the relaxing hot tub. A tanning bed is also available. While vacationing here, be sure to visit the town of Loveland, known for it numerous sculptors whose work grace Benson Park. If you want break from outdoor recreation, try some indoors fun at the close by 38-store factory outlet mall.

RV sites are also available.

Location: Three and a halfmiles west of Loveland and 26 miles east of Estes Park. On Highway 34 near milepost marker 86.

4 Cabins with Kitchen	Pay Phone Available	Alan & Betty Huschka, Owners
4 Cabins without Kitchens	Some Units Nonsmoking	6850 W Hwy 34
8 Rooms with Fireplaces	Elevation: 4800	Loveland CO 80537
Central Hot Tub	Credit Cards: VMD	970/667-2903
	Rates: $50-$100	E-mail: alan@oneimage.com
	Open: All Year	www.coloradodirectory.com/firesidervpark

At the resort:

At resort or within 15 minutes:

Inn of Glen Haven

Step back in time at this historic bed and breakfast inn built in 1919. Faithfully restored to reflect its original charm, this old-world retreat maintains the romantic atmosphere of an intimate English country inn. The rooms are tastefully decorated with antiques, each with its own motif. The Queen Victoria suite has a sitting room with a fainting couch. Five of the rooms have a canopy beds. The Lillie Lantry room is decorated in a peach and green Victorian style with sunny French doors leading to the patio. Some of the rooms are spacious two-room suites with a sitting room and a bedroom. All rooms have private baths.

Continental English breakfast is included with your stay. Overnight guests may also choose to enjoy gourmet candlelight dinners and fine wines in the restaurant or pub. After dinner, relax by the huge moss-rock fireplace in the parlor. Only 7 miles from Rocky Mountain National Park, the Inn of Glen Haven is off the beaten path, yet is on an all-season highway. In the winter, the Twelve Days of Christmas are celebrated each year with "Old English" feasts. The feast is a tradition from the old English Church Kalander starting on December 26th. Explore antique shops in Estes Park and the magnificence of the national park nearby.

Well-behaved children are welcome. Open seven days a week from Memorial day through mid October; and the weeks of December 20th through January 5th

for the twelve days of Christmas Feast. Open weekends the rest of the year; closed March 15th through April 15th. No pets allowed.

Location: Seven miles northeast of Estes Park on Devil's Gulch Road.

6 Lodging Rooms	Phone in Lobby	Tom & Sheila Sellers, Owners
Central Fireplace	Bed & Breakfast Available	PO Box 219
	All Units Nonsmoking	Glen Haven CO 80532-0219
	Elevation: 7500	970/586-3897
	Credit Cards: VM	Fax: 970/586-3707
	Rates: $80-$135	www.coloradodirectory.com/innglenhaven/
	Open: 4/15 to 3/15	

At the resort:

At resort or within 15 minutes:

Jellystone Park of Estes, Yogi Bear's

Welcome to the serenity of the Rocky Mountains. At Jellystone Park of Estes you'll find 35 wooded acres of hillside adjacent to Roosevelt National Forest. The comfortably furnished, housekeeping cabins are shaded by tall ponderosa pine whose scent fills the crisp mountain air. The cabins sleep from two to twelve people. RV sites, with full hookups, picnic tables, barbecue grills and campfire pits, are also available. Wild roses, friendly chipmunks, singing birds and loitering wildlife enhance the friendly atmosphere and add to the beauty of the Meadowdale Valley. Picnic with the whole family at the group picnic areas.

Amenities include modern restrooms, hot showers, a convenience store and a coin laundry. Campground activities include Sunday morning pancake breakfasts, ice cream socials and wagon rides with Yogi Bear. Peaceful and convenient, Jellystone Park is near both Rocky Mountain National Park and Estes Park for wilderness and civilized vacation activities. Explore the adjacent Roosevelt National Forest by hiking, mountain biking or horseback riding the trails that start on site. Play a game of basketball, have fun in the video arcade or challenge your family to horseshoes, volleyball and badminton. To relax, swim in the heated pool and sunbathe on the large deck.

An outdoor, group meeting area is also available. Plan ahead and have Yogi Bear celebrate your birthday or special occasion at your cabin with you and your family. Open May through September.

Location: Five and a half miles southeast of junction Highway 34 and 36, near milepost marker 5.

Yogi Bear ™ © 1995 Hanna-Barbara Productions, Inc. All Rights Reserved

4 Cabins with Kitchen	Pay Phone Available	Tony & Kathy Palmeri, Owners
1 Cabin without Kitchen	All Units Nonsmoking	5495 US Hwy 36
1 Vacation Home	Recreation Room	Estes Park CO 80517
2 Camper Cabins	Elevation: 7800	800/722-2928
1 Room with Fireplace	Credit Cards: VM	970/586-4230
Central Campfire Area	Rates: $37-$65	Fax: 970/577-0474
	Open: 5/7 to 9/27	E-mail: yogibear@frii.com
		www.coloradodirectory.com/jellystone/

At the resort:

At resort or within 15 minutes:

No photos

Lazy R Cottages

From your cottage at Lazy R, you'll be able to gaze upon no less than 16 stunning mountain peaks. The sparkling clean cabins of knotty pine interiors with one, two or three bedrooms, have fully equipped kitchens, color cable television, picnic tables and barbecue grills. Many also have fireplaces stocked with free wood. Two spacious log cabins sleep up to 12 people and boast a private hot tub. The other cabins share a resort hot tub.

After a lovely morning of hiking and exploring, spend a lazy afternoon with your children at the on-site playground. Close to Rocky Mountain National Park, Lazy R is near numerous recreational opportunities, from driving along picturesque Trail Ridge Road to hiking or cross-country skiing in the untouched backcountry.

Location: Highway 36 (also known as Moraine Ave.), one and a half miles from Estes Park.

10 Cabins with Kitchen
4 Vacation Homes
1 Motel Room
3 Rooms with Hot Tubs
11 Rooms with Fireplaces
Central Hot Tub

Pay Phone Available
Elevation: 7800
Credit Cards: VMD
Rates: $69-$245
Open: All Year

Mark Whittlesey & Bob&Gabi Benson
PO Box 1996
Estes Park CO 80517-1996
800/726-3728
970/586-3708
Fax: 970/577-8827
E-mail: lazyr@estes-park.com
www.coloradodirectory.com/lazyrcottages

At the resort:

At resort or within 15 minutes:

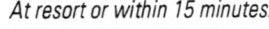

Machin's Cottages in the Pines

In a secluded, beautiful location inside Rocky Mountain National Park, Machin's offers deluxe, immaculately clean cottages which are beautifully decorated. Scattered among tall pines and unusual rock formations, the cottages have fully equipped kitchens, fireplaces stocked with free wood, large picture windows, carpeting and color cable television with HBO. Enjoy the clean, cool mountain air from the porches and patio areas which have outdoor furniture and barbecue grills. All linens are provided and exchanged when necessary.

Kids will like the children's playground on-site. Machin's Cottages is near a small brook and a hiking trail begins on the property. A short 1.25 mile hike from your cottage is Beaver Meadows and the spectacular mountain valley of Moraine Park, where other trails spread out into Rocky Mountain National Park. Fish in the nearby lake and river, or take a 10-minute drive to Estes Park for dining, shopping and golfing.

A minimum of two nights is required. Open May 16-October 1 for late spring and early fall, outdoor family fun. One small pet is allowed, but it must remain on a leash. If bringing a child, ask for highchairs, cribs and bed rails.

Location: Southwest two and a half miles from Estes Park on Highway 36 (also known as Moraine Avenue), then go west a half mile on Eagle Cliff Road.

---

17 Cabins with Kitchen	Pay Phone Available	Lee Machin, Owner
17 Rooms with Fireplaces	Elevation: 8000	PO Box 2687
	Credit Cards: VMA	Estes Park CO 80517-2687
	Rates: $81-$135	970/586-4276
	Open: 5/21 to 10/3	www.coloradodirectory.com/machinscottages/

At the resort: *At resort or within 15 minutes:*

Mountain Haven Inn & Cottages

Mountain Haven offers a haven in the Rocky Mountains where you can enjoy majestic Colorado at its best. On two landscaped acres on the Big Thompson River with a view of snowcapped peaks, the new, fully furnished, two-bedroom cottages have fireplaces, cable television, kitchens and decks. Sit outside at the picnic table and grill dinner in the high country air on the barbecue provided. The Inn offers three bedrooms, two baths (one with a Jacuzzi tub), and a living room with a fireplace and cable television. In addition, those staying in the inn rooms may use the sunroom and the country kitchen/dining area with its dishwasher and microwave.

Fish the Big Thompson River that runs through Mountain Haven. One mile away is Estes Park, the gateway to Rocky Mountain National Park. Estes Park is a resort community that provides many recreational opportunities for visitors, including winter sports, hiking and golfing. Be sure to visit the many shops and restaurants in town during your stay.

The inn and cottages are open year-round for nightly and weekly rentals. Consider holding your family reunion or group retreats here.

Location: Between Estes Park and Rocky Mountain National Park on Highway 36 west (also known as Moraine Ave.).

6 Cabins with Kitchen	Pay Phone Available	Deanna Bleyle & Glenda Brown, Owners
1 Vacation Home	Some Units Nonsmoking	690 Moraine Rt
1 Room with Hot Tub	Elevation: 7500	Estes Park CO 80517
7 Rooms with Fireplaces	Credit Cards: VM	970/586-2864
Central Campfire Area	Rates: $139	E-mail: mtnhvep@aol.com
	Open: All Year	www.coloradodirectory.com/mountainhaveninn

At the resort:

At resort or within 15 minutes:

Mountain Home Bed & Breakfast

A quiet getaway in a new home filled with mountain charm, this bed and breakfast is tucked into a wooded area close to downtown Estes Park. The Country Garden Room is inspired by Monet and decorated with a country charm featuring large windows, a red oak hardwood floor, private bath, king bed, sitting area and television. The Southwestern Suite invites you to relax in a cozy sitting room with a leather love seat recliner and television. The attached bedroom has lodge pole furniture, queen bed and private bath.

Breakfast at Mountain Home may include stuffed French toast, ham and cheese strata or gingerbread pancakes, along with fresh fruit, hot coffee and juice. Outside, 50-foot pine trees keep the house comfortably shaded all summer, or you can enjoy the sun from the front porch in the morning and the deck in the late afternoon. Here you'll be surrounded by views of rock outcroppings, tall pine trees, wildflowers and wildlife. Set in a quiet neighborhood, this bed and breakfast's quiet is only broken by the wind rustling through the trees. You're likely to see deer, elk, black tufted ear squirrels, Stellar's blue jays, hummingbirds and an occasional coyote in the backyard. Take a stimulating walk from here to downtown Estes Park to explore its specialty shops, fine restaurants and art galleries. Be sure to visit Rocky Mountain National Park too for some unforgettable scenery and breathtaking views.

No smoking or pets allowed. Advance reservations may be guaranteed by a deposit of one night's lodging or half the stay.

Location: North on Highway 34 West, north on MacGregor, left on Bighorn, left on Chapin, 1st house on right.

---

2 Lodging Rooms	Phone in Rooms	Johanna Gengler, Owner
Central Fireplace	Bed & Breakfast Available	663 Chapin Lane
	All Units Nonsmoking	Estes Park CO 80517
	Recreation Room	888/686-4600
	Elevation: 7600	970/586-8676
	Credit Cards: VM	E-mail: mtnhomebnb@aol.com
	Rates: $89-$99	www.coloradodirectory.com/mountainhomebnb
	Open: All Year	

At the resort:

At resort or within 15 minutes:

Mountain Shadows Bed & Breakfast

Mountain Shadows Bed & Breakfast offers a romantic escape with everlasting memories. You will appreciate the personal touches of a bed and breakfast in the privacy and luxury of eight cabins. Each of the uniquely decorated units has a king bed, hot tub for two, fireplace, love seat, two person shower, television and private deck. Each of the rooms is individually named and designed for romance. Try Sweethearts Forever with its floral and heart decor, or let your animal magnetism surface in the Safari Escape. Curl up for a nap in Southwest Siesta, or escape to the woods in Mountain Magic.

Each morning, meander up the path to the main house for a gourmet breakfast and breathtaking views. For an additional fee, breakfast can be delivered to your room. Near Estes Park and Rocky Mountain National Park, Mountain Shadows offers plenty of ways to spend your day, from hiking, horseback riding and golfing, to fishing, and shopping. In the winter, come to snowshoe and cross country ski. However you spend your day, this bed and breakfast resort awaits your return with comfort, privacy and an evening full of romance!

Ask about the special romantic packages. No pets are allowed and smoking is permitted on the outside decks only.

Location: Take Highway 36 through Estes Park to Mary's Lake Road, turn left, drive to Riverside Drive, turn left again, Mountain Shadows will be on your left.

4 Cabins without Kitchens	Phone in Rooms	Mark & Kelly Murray, Owners
4 Lodging Rooms	Bed & Breakfast Available	871 Riverside Dr
8 Rooms with Hot Tubs	All Units Nonsmoking	Estes Park CO 80517
8 Rooms with Fireplaces	Elevation: 7200	970/577-0397
Central Hot Tub	Credit Cards: VMD	Fax: 970/577-1334
Central Fireplace	Rates: $185	E-mail: mtnshadows@earthlink.com
	Open: All Year	www.coloradodirectory.com/mountainshadowsbb

At the resort:

At resort or within 15 minutes:

National Park Resort Cabins & Campground

Located next to the Fall River entrance to Rocky Mountain National Park, this resort is on a sheltered, tree-filled mountainside. The housekeeping cabins have fully equipped kitchens, bathrooms with tiled showers, sunken living rooms with fireplaces, picture windows with great views and color cable television. Linens and towels are provided and towels can be exchanged daily at the office. A delightful climate provides warm, sunny days and cool evenings. The pine-scented air, blue skies and grand views all make this a uniquely Colorado vacation.

Across the highway is a grocery store, gift shop, and riding stable. Bordering the national park, the resort has hiking trials, fishing and climbing nearby. Check out the nature walks, films and evening campfires in Rocky Mountain National Park. Estes Park boasts golf courses, sail boats, chuckwagon suppers and other entertainment. After a day spent at play, relax on the deck area in the private and semi-private hot tubs. Sit back, soak your muscles and contemplate the mountain splendor.

RV and tent sites are also available. The Cabins are open all year, while the camping sites are only open from May through September. Pets are welcome for a fee and special pet deposit. Advance reservations are suggested. You must pay first and last night's deposit; there is a 30 day cancellation policy.

Location: Five miles west of Estes Park at the Fall River entrance to Rocky Mountain National Park on Highway 34.

4 Cabins with Kitchen	Pay Phone Available	Dan & Becky Ludlam, Owners
5 Motel Rooms	Elevation: 8300	3501 Fall River Rd
1 Room with Hot Tub	Credit Cards: VMD	Estes Park CO 80517-9801
4 Rooms with Fireplaces	Rates: $70-$140	970/586-4563
Central Hot Tub	Open: All Year	E-mail: rdrunr97@aol.com
		www.coloradodirectory.com/natlparkresort

At the resort:

At resort or within 15 minutes:

River Stone on Fall River

Log Cabin Bldg

new modern

Majestic mountains, towering pine trees and the soothing sounds of a tumbling river surround River Stone on Fall River. The luxury suites are in duplex and triples units. Full and partial kitchens are available. All suites have two person Jacuzzis, fireplaces, king beds, color cable television with VCRs and HBO, washers and dryers and the comforts of home. Every unit overlooks the picturesque Fall River and has a patio with a gas grill for barbecuing.

Return from your day of hiking, horseback riding or sightseeing to sit and relax on your private patio while watching for the elk and deer which frequent the area. At only 2.5 miles from Estes Park and 2 miles from Rocky Mountain National Park, you'll be near all the amenities this area has to offer, from shopping and golfing, to hiking and white water rafting.

Ask about the season rates. No pets or smoking allowed.

Location: Two and a half miles from Estes Park and 2 miles from the north entrance to Rocky Mountain National Park on Highway 34 (Fall River Road).

8 Lodging Rooms	Phone in Rooms	Doug, Linda & Mike Cook, Owners
8 Camper Cabins	All Units Nonsmoking	2120 Fall River Rd
16 Rooms with Hot Tubs	Elevation: 7700	Estes Park CO 80517
16 Rooms with Fireplaces	Credit Cards: VMAD	970/586-4005
Central Hot Tub	Rates: $175-$179	www.coloradodirectory.com/riverstone
	Open: All Year	

At the resort:

At resort or within 15 minutes:

Romantic RiverSong® Bed & Breakfast Inn

Located on 27 wooded acres, RiverSong® is a small country inn at the foot of Giant Track Mountain in Estes Park. Once a luxurious summer home of the wealthy and the scene of "Great Gatsby-like" parties, the Inn now offers quaint bed and breakfast rooms. Each room, named after regional wildflowers, has a private bath, a river-rock fireplace, and large tubs. Each also comes with comfortable bathrobes in case you forget your own. The cozy bedrooms are decorated with a blend of antique and modern furniture. Jacuzzi tubs for two are also available. After a quiet evening in front of a crackling fire, curl up in bed under a warm comforter, lulled to sleep by the magical melody of the mountain stream outside your window. Awaken in the morning to the rich aroma of freshly brewed coffee and freshly made breads and unwind in the evening on candlelight dinners.

Fish the rushing trout stream, relax in the rustic gazebo by a pond, or enjoy the panoramic views from gentle hiking trails with rock benches. Catch site of elk, deer, raccoons, eagles, owls and chipmunks as you wander the grounds. Activities in this area are year-round: snowshoe and cross-country ski in the winter, hike and mountain bike in the summer. Attend a Rocky Mountain Nature Association seminar, or play golf and tennis. Estes Park is well known for all its shops and antiques, as well as its many festivals, including the Scottish Festival, the Rooftop Rodeo, Aspenfest, the Holiday Season Festival and the Spring Snow Festival.

Three rooms are wheelchair accessible. If planning an outdoor wedding ask about the snowshoe winter weddings the owner preforms. The Inn offers picnic basket dinner to enjoy in your room or out on their patio. The Inn is not suitable for small children or pets.

Location: Two blocks south of US Highway 36, at west end of Lower Broadview Road, on the Little Thompson River.

5 Cabins without Kitchens	Phone in Lobby	Gary & Sue Mansfield, Innkeepers
4 Lodging Rooms	Bed & Breakfast Available	PO Box 1910
6 Rooms with Hot Tubs	All Units Nonsmoking	Estes Park CO 80517-1910
9 Rooms with Fireplaces	Recreation Room	970/586-4666
Central Fireplace	Elevation: 7900	Fax: 970/577-0699
Central Campfire Area	Credit Cards: VM	E-mail: riversng@frii.com
	Rates: $135-$250	www.coloradodirectory.com/romanticriversonginn
	Open: All Year	

At the resort:

At resort or within 15 minutes:

Shelly's Cottages

Along the river and away from the road on five acres of quiet mountain splendor, these modern, comfortable cottages have private baths, excellent beds with linens, and full kitchens with dishes. Some cottages have fireplaces, while two "special occasion" units have king-sized beds and private hot tubs in their own gazebos. Another cottage sleeps up to six and also has its own hot tub and fireplace. Cook your freshly caught stream trout on the barbecue grills and eat at shaded picnic tables.

Go for a hike or drive on scenic roads through the high mountain country and dramatic front range canyons. You are only minutes from fine dining, dinner theaters and the sights of Lyons, Estes Park, Rocky Mountain National Park and Boulder.

Special occasion packages come with champagne, breakfast baskets, chocolates and dining certificates.

Location: Four miles northwest of Lyons, 20 minutes from Estes Park, off of Highway 36 near milepost 16.

8 Cabins with Kitchen	Phone in Lobby	303/823-6326
1 Vacation Home	Elevation: 5900	Fax: 303/823-9321
3 Rooms with Hot Tubs	Credit Cards: VMD	E-mail: shellys@csn.net
4 Rooms with Fireplaces	Rates: $60-$160	www.coloradodirectory.com/shellyscottages
Central Hot Tub	Open: All Year	
	PO Box 740	
	Lyons CO 80540-0740	
	800/356-6061	

At the resort:

At resort or within 15 minutes:

Big deck over river

look out dated

Skyline Cottages

Skyline Cottages rests on the Big Thompson River with spectacular views of Long's Peak and the entire front range of the Rockies. The seven cottages and one vacation home are all non-smoking. (Smoking is permitted outside.) Each cottages has color, cable television with Disney, a fully equipped, all-electric kitchen and linens, as well as at least one queen-size Serta Perfect Sleeper bed and all-electric heat. Five of the cottages have woodburning fireplaces set in rustic pine with tile trim. Two are Western-theme featuring patchwork quilts, saddle blanket headboards, chili pepper ceiling fans, and skylights. One of these even has a private spa room attached with a jetted tub right in front of the fireplace. Surrounded by evergreens and blue spruce trees, the cottages can accommodate from one to six people. The vacation home sleeps 12 and has an unusually large kitchen, living room and bedrooms, plus a deck with wicker rocking chairs overlooking the river and mountains. All are carpeted and have an outdoor porches or decks — perfect for admiring the wonderful views while you barbecue dinner.

Fish for trout right outside your cottage. Or relax in the mountain sunshine on your front porch or riverfront deck on the cushioned chairs or love seat. Young guests have their own lounging furniture. Be sure to grill your fresh catch-of-the-day or steaks on the covered, charcoal grills. Tucked between Roosevelt National Forest and Rocky Mountain National Park, Skyline is also a short drive from Estes Park and Hidden Valley Rec Area. Here the activities to choose among seem endless: hiking, horseback riding, golf, the aerial tramway, whitewater rafting, boating, swimming, and, of course, sightseeing. Estes Park entertainment events include theater productions, chuckwagon dinners, rodeos and horse shows. The views as you drive over Trail Ridge Road to the Continental Divide are truly unforgettable.

Location: Two miles southwest of Estes Park on Highway 66.

---

7 Cabins with Kitchen	Phone in Lobby	Sue Lamb, Owner
1 Vacation Home	All Units Nonsmoking	1752 Hwy 66
1 Room with Hot Tub	Elevation: 8000	Estes Park CO 80517
5 Rooms with Fireplaces	Credit Cards: VM	970/586-2886
	Rates: $90-$130	E-mail: skyline-bonanza@worldnet.att.net
	Open: 5/20 to 10/24	www.coloradodirectory.com/skylinecottages/

At the resort:

At resort or within 15 minutes:

log cabins nice scenery

Streamside ... A Village of Cabin Suites

The luxurious suites at Streamside are right on the Fall River and are surrounded by 17 acres of wooded meadow with the mountainside and wildlife enhancing them. AAA rated these elegant cabin suites four diamonds and Mobil gave them three stars. The 19 cabin suites are one and two bedroom with king and queen beds, living rooms with sleeping sofas, full kitchens with microwaves and a dining area. Some feature in-room steam baths, jetted tubs, cathedral ceiling and sky-lights. All cabin suites have fireplaces, color cable television, VCRs, and patios with gas grills.

Streamside is hiking distance from the beauty of Rocky Mountain National Park. Traverse the area on foot, mountain bike, horseback, snowshoes, cross country skis or in your car. Herds of mule deer, elk and big horn sheep are to spectacular to miss! Fish for rainbow trout in the Fall River's rushing waters, a few steps from your cabin suite. Hike Old Man Mountain trail right on the property for 45 minutes to the ancient Arapahoe Indian Nation's former ceremonial site. Near to Estes Park, Streamside is a short drive from the town's many restaurants and numerous, quaint gift shops. No matter how you spend your day, return to Streamside and relax in the new, enclosed, heated swim spa and hot tub.

Minimum stays may apply during holidays and high season. Ask about the 3+ day "Affairs of the Heart" packages for honeymoons, birthdays, anniversaries and other special occasions. All packages include merchant coins ($30-$70) for free shopping, area dining discounts, movie passes, non-alcoholic champagne, roses on the pillows, chocolate mints daily and use of over-sized towels. The 5 and 7 day packages also include two snowshoe/horseback riding passes, and the 7 day pack-

age includes a fruit and cheese tray.

Location: Between Estes Park and Rocky Mountain National Park on Fall River Road.

19 Cabins with Kitchen	Pay Phone Available	Susan & Lynn Coffman, Owners
19 Lodging Rooms	Elevation: 7600	PO Box 2930
6 Rooms with Hot Tubs	Credit Cards: VMAD	Estes Park CO 80517-2930
19 Rooms with Fireplaces	Rates: $125-$215	800/321-3303
Central Hot Tub	Open: All Year	970/586-6464
		Fax: 970/586-6272
		E-mail: resv@streamsidecabins.com
		www.coloradodirectory.com/streamsidecabins

At the resort:

At resort or within 15 minutes:

No photos (handwritten)

Out by Twin Sisters Peak / Mary's Lake (handwritten)

Taharaa Mountain Lodge

Stay in a luxury bed and breakfast just four miles from Rocky Mountain National Park at Taharaa Mountain Lodge. The three suites and nine lodge rooms have a private bath or deluxe shower, fireplaces and a private deck. Two units have private hot tubs. Choose among rooms such as Lark Bunting Room, with a queen bed and decor of a winsome bird motif, to the romantic Taharaa Suite with its stunning views, personal living room, double-sided fireplace and king bed. With many options available, one room is sure to meet your needs. Gourmet breakfasts and evening refreshments are served daily.

The lodge is close to the bustling mountain community of Estes Park, yet quietly secluded with breathtaking natural views of the Mummy Range from its more than five acres atop a beautiful plateau. An exercise and sauna facility, an outdoor spa, great room, comfortable den, solarium, and television room are available for all guests. Explore the walking trails with benches for a casual afternoon stroll. If you desire to explore beyond Taharaa's natural quiet and beauty, this area has much to offer, from all the activities of Estes Park to all the outdoors adventures the national park is famous for: hiking, cross country skiing, fishing and hunting.

The entire lodge is non-smoking and all facilities are handicap accessible. No pets are allowed, though you may offer a pat to the resident chocolate Cocker Spaniel named Rocky. Two guests per room maximum and children under 13 are discouraged. For weddings or catered functions, the facilities accommodate up to 50 day guests.

Location:
Four miles southwest of Rocky Mountain National Park on South St Vrain.

12 Lodging Rooms	Phone in Rooms	Ken & Diane Harlan, Innkeepers
2 Rooms with Hot Tubs	Bed & Breakfast Available	PO Box 2586
12 Rooms with Fireplaces	All Units Nonsmoking	Estes Park CO 80517-2586
Central Fireplace	Recreation Room	800/597-0098
	Elevation: 8500	970/577-0098
	Credit Cards: VMAD	Fax: 970/577-0819
	Rates: $135-$250	E-mail: info@taharaa.com
	Open: All Year	www.coloradodirectory.com/taharaa

At the resort:

At resort or within 15 minutes:

Telemark Resort Cottages

Relax and enjoy the splendor of the outdoors while staying at the cozy cottages at Telemark Resort on the Big Thompson River. Telemark has been here for almost half a century and each year more has been done to insure your comfort and pleasure. Choose from the 10 housekeeping cottages, each having a fireplace, telephone, and cable television. All of the cottages have screened-in porches and/or balconies facing the river.

Within minutes are restaurants, shops and evening entertainment in the charming town of Estes Park. Kids can frolic at the resort's playground while anglers can try trout fishing right on the property. Other nearby activities include horseback riding, river rafting, golfing and boating on the lake. When you need a break from the outdoors, learn a little history of the area at the local museum. In the winter, with the beauty of Rocky Mountain National Park just moments away, you can cross-country ski or go on a romantic sleigh ride. Located all within driving distance to some of the scenic and historic places in Colorado.

Pets are welcomed to accompany you for a fee.

Location: A half mile west of Estes Park on Highway 36.

9 Cabins with Kitchen	Phone in Rooms	Vigdis Lohne, Owner
1 Vacation Home	Elevation: 7522	PO Box 100
10 Rooms with Fireplaces	Credit Cards: VMA	Estes Park CO 80517-0100
Central Campfire Area	Rates: $75-$135	800/669-0650
	Open: All Year	970/586-4343
		www.coloradodirectory.com/telemarkresort

At the resort:

At resort or within 15 minutes:

Tiny Town Cottages

Located on 15 acres, with breathtaking views of the snow-capped peaks of the Continental Divide, these cozy cottages are furnished with everything you need. The one-couple cottages are equipped with fireplaces, kitchens, and king or queen size beds, bath with tub/shower and color cable television with HBO. The Honeymoon Cottage has a two-person whirlpool tub. This property caters to non-smokers only in a totally non-smoking environment.

Enjoy a picnic, BBQ or just relax on the spacious grounds. Try casting your line into the privately stocked quarter mile of the Big Thompson River adjacent to the Cottages, available to guests only. Tiny Town is close to several fine restaurants, a supermarket, laundromat and a miniature golf course. Rocky Mountain National Park, one mile away, offers many scenic roads and trails, wildlife, wildflowers and waterfalls in a spectacular mountain setting.

Tiny Town Cottages caters to adults, singles and couples, who are looking for peace, quiet and privacy. To ensure their privacy, large groups or family reunions are not allowed. A minimum of three to four nights stay is required. Pets are not allowed.

Location: On Highway 36 (also known as Moraine Ave.), one mile west of Estes Park, near milepost marker 5.

20 Cabins with Kitchen	Phone in Lobby	Bob & Helen Mitchell, Owners
1 Room with Hot Tub	All Units Nonsmoking	830 Moraine Ave
18 Rooms with Fireplaces	Elevation: 7644	Estes Park CO 80517-8005
	Credit Cards: VMAD	970/586-4249
	Rates: $49-$110	E-mail: TinyTownEP@aol.com
	Open: 5/15 to 10/15	www.coloradodirectory.com/tinytowncottages/

At the resort:

At resort or within 15 minutes:

Valhalla Resort

Tucked away on 12 tree-studded acres next to Rocky Mountain National Park, Valhalla Resort offers a wide variety of exceptionally clean, comfortable and well-furnished vacation homes, ranging from rustic to luxurious. The cottages have fully equipped kitchens with dishes, glassware, pots and pans, coffee makers and toasters. The living rooms have fireplaces and cable television. Each home features separate bedrooms and baths, some with jetted whirlpool hot tubs. Each vacation home has its own private deck or patio with a barbecue and exterior furniture.

In the summer, enjoy the swimming pool, while year-round you can soak in the private hot tub or play in the activity center. There is an on-site Laundromat and gift shop. Bring your sweetie for one of the exclusive LoveScapes® vacations, a private Love Retreat with an abundant deli tray, flowers, champagne and other surprises. In addition to the many activities available in the outdoor wonderland of Rocky Mountain National Park and among the numerous shops and events in Estes Park, Valhalla provides shuffleboard, miniature golf, horseshoes and ping-pong. Other area activities include golfing, horseback riding and sailing. Everything you desire in a vacation, from fine dining and museums to whitewater raft trips and sleigh rides are all within a short drive from Valhalla. Bring hiking boots for the trails, a swimming suit for the pool, and warm sweaters for the cool, crisp mountain evenings.

Valhalla offers senior discounts and special rates during the off-peak season. Ask about the snowshoe packages.

Location: One third of a mile off Highway 66, near milepost marker 1, off Highway 36 West (also known as Moraine Avenue).

15 Cabins with Kitchen	Pay Phone Available	Lynette & Mike Lott & Jeannine & Matt
9 Vacation Homes	Recreation Room	Swatzki, Owners
5 Rooms with Hot Tubs	Elevation: 7700	2185 Eagle Cliff Rd - PO Box 1439
24 Rooms with Fireplaces	Credit Cards: VMAD	Estes Park CO 80517-1439
Central Hot Tub	Rates: $72-$225	800/522-3284
	Open: All Year	970/586-3284
		Fax: 970/586-6361
		E-mail: ValhalaRes@aol.com
		www.coloradodirectory.com/valhallaresort

At the resort:

At resort or within 15 minutes:

Glenwood Springs

Including New Castle — Map: G-7 & F-7

Soaking in the large, brick-lined hot springs pool (it's 615' by 75'), gazing up at pine-covered mountain peaks, you'll understand why first the Ute Indians and then wealthy miners and European aristocrats treasured **Glenwood Springs**. When the Utes were relocated in 1882, the town sprang up, catering to the rich from around the world. With money came trouble: by 1887 there were 22 bars in a two-block area! Doc Holliday, who was wanted in Arizona for killings at the OK Corral shoot-out, is buried here. The Hotel Colorado opened in the early 1890s and was the summer White House for Teddy Roosevelt. A total of seven U.S. presidents vacationed here. Today, people come for the history and hot springs as much as the rugged and beautiful surroundings. Glenwood Canyon has a 9-mile bike path and rafters enjoy the white waters of the Colorado River flowing through the canyon. This area is also popular with spelunkers (cave explorers) because of the number of caves and one of the largest underground rivers in the country. The White River and Gunnison National Forests as well as four wilderness areas can be easily reached for day hikes or cross-country skiing.

Fun Things to Do

- Adventure Bound River Expeditions (800) 423-4668 - See page 128
- Frontier Historical Society & Museum (970) 945-4448
- Glenwood Springs Golf Course (970) 945-7086
- Glenwood Springs Hot Springs Pool (970) 945-7131
- Johnson Park Miniature Golf (970) 945-9608
- Rifle Creek Golf Course, Rifle (800) 958-6737
- Rock Gardens Rafting (970) 945-6737
- Silt Historical Park (970) 876-2668
- Sunlight Mountain Resort (800) 445-7931
- Westbank Ranch Golf Course (970) 945-7032
- White River National Forest Headquarters (970) 945-2521
- Whitewater Rafting, LLC (970) 954-8477 - See page 128
- Yampa Hot Springs Spa & Vapor Cave (970) 945-0667

Adventure Bound River Expeditions

Since 1963 Adventure Bound has been offering professionally guided whitewater trips down the Colorado, Green and Yampa Rivers. See the magnificent beauty of Dinosaur National Monument, Desolation and Westwater Canyons, and Canyonlands National Park all from the vantage point of the rivers that flow through them.

Float trips through Westwater Canyon offer a full day of adventure for the whole family. As the Colorado River begins the last leg of its journey through Colorado, the first part of the Westwater trip begins with a leisurely float through Ruby and Horsethief Canyons. As this hidden stretch of the Colorado River unwinds the beauty and solitude of the dessert canyon sweeps worries and the modern world away. Side canyon stops allow for a tasty riverside lunch (provided) and short hikes to explore hidden splendors including Indian pictographs. As the Colorado River enters Utah the water current becomes swifter as it is forced into the descending and narrowing channel featuring some of the best whitewater rapids in the region. This full day trip leaves Grand Junction at 8 a.m. each Tuesday from May 18th through September 28th and returns that evening at 5 p.m.

Two to seven day trips are also offered. Cataract Canyon offers multi day trips that start southwest of Moab and run through the rugged and beautiful canyons of CanyonLands National Park with class III-V rapids. Desolation Canyon's 4 and 5 day trips are in Eastern Utah's remote wilderness with class II-III rapids, pristine beaches and cool cottonwood glens. Three and four day trips on the Green and Yampa Rivers explore the heart of Dinosaur National Monument with class II-iV rapids.

Since 1963

All trips offer oars rafts and inflatable kayaks. Special group trips can be arranged.

Location: Trips leave from Grand Junction and Steamboat Springs.

Tom & Robin Kleinschnitz, Owners
2392 H Road
Grand Junction   CO   81505
800/423-4668
970/245-5428
Fax: 970/241-5633
E-mail: ab@raft-colorado.com
www.coloradodirectory.com/adventurebound/

Whitewater Rafting, LLC

While visiting Glenwood Springs make sure to raft through Glenwood Canyon one of the most beautiful canyon's in all of Colorado. Whitewater Rafting, LLC has 5 different trips to choose from ranging from a one and a half hour trip to a full-day (6 hour) adventure. Raft down Crystal River, Roaring Fork River or the Colorado River which include rapids named Tuttle's Tumble, Tombstone, and Man-Eater. Each has their own special points of interest all have a variety of scenery, serenity, and excitement.

Half day Kayak adventure: suitable for beginners. Before or after your raft trip enjoy the grassy picnic area with BBQ grills. Also on site are coin operated hot showers. The gift shop offer t-shirts, sweatshirts, postcards, and some river equipment.

When rafting make sure to wear shorts or a swimsuit, tennis or sandals, a windbreaker and light clothing. Also recommended are sunscreen, sunglasses, a hat, towel and change of clothes.

Licensed by the State of Colorado, permitted by US Forest service and Bureau of Land Management. In business since 1974, with certified guides and high quality equipment.

Reservations are recommended. Wetsuits and rain gear available. Ask about overnight and group rates.

Location: I-70 to exit 114, turn south and cross bridge over river, take the next left at the end of the bridge on Devereux Road, drive 1/2 mile up the road.

Since 1974

Ken, Monica & Susi Larson, & Sondra
PO Box 2462
Glenwood Springs CO 81602-2462
970/945-8477
Fax: 970/928-8909
E-mail: whitewaterrafting@juno.com
www.coloradodirectory.com/whitewaterrafting

Hideout Cabins & Campground

Vacation in rustic, yet modernized cabins at Hideout Cabins. These secluded, housekeeping cabins are on nine wooded acres in the shade near Glenwood Hot Springs and the Roaring Fork River. The oldest cabin at Hideout was built in 1888. The cabins have kitchens with dishes, cable television with HBO, linens and fireplaces in some rooms. At night, you'll be lulled to sleep by the gurgling Three Mile Creek — the only sound to break the mountain quiet.

Hideout offers a Laundromat on-site for your convenience. The trees of White River National Forest surround this resort on the bike path to town. Kids will like the video game room and playground on-site. The outdoor pavilion overlooking the creek is perfect for large family gatherings. Recreation here is endless. Ski nearby slopes such as Sunlight, Snowmass and Aspen. Snowmobile on the 120-mile long Sunlight to Powerhorn groomed snowmobile trails. Shorter trails are also available. Hike to Hanging Lake or horseback ride in the Flat Tops Wilderness. Fish the Colorado, Roaring Fork and Frying Pan rivers. Raft the Colorado River and visit Doc Holliday's grave. Explore the historic towns of Marble, Redstone, the ghost town of Ashcroft and Crystal City Mill — one of the most photographed sites in Colorado. A stop at the world's largest thermal pool is a must in Glenwood Springs. Dine in any of the town's fine restaurants after a day of mountain golf.

Streamside RV sites and group sites are also available.

Location: From I-70 take Glenwood Springs Exit 114, go south on by-pass across railroad bridge, continue south on Midland Avenue(County Road 117), turn tight at 3rd stop sign (27th Street) and proceed one and a quarter miles, across from Texaco turn right into property.

11 Cabins with Kitchen	Pay Phone Available	Ric Tanberg & Patricia Tanberg, Owners
1 Cabin without Kitchen	All Units Nonsmoking	1293 Rd 117 - Midland Ave
4 Rooms with Fireplaces	Recreation Room	Glenwood Springs CO 81601
	Elevation: 6000	800/987-0779
	Credit Cards: VMD	970/945-5621
	Rates: $45-$145	Fax: 970/928-0665
	Open: All Year	E-mail: hideoutco@aol.com
		www.coloradodirectory.com/hideoutcabins

At the resort:

At resort or within 15 minutes:

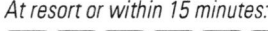

Riverside Cottages

Located in a heavily wooded 7.7-acre site, Riverside Cottages boasts a spectacular 1,200-foot frontage on the Roaring Fork River — Glenwood Springs' only river front resort. The cottages accommodate up to 10 people, and have furnished modern kitchens, cable television with HBO, private bedrooms and linens with maid service daily! Cabins range from one bedroom to three bedrooms with queen size beds in most. Some cottages have fireplaces with furnished wood. For those who like barbecuing, there are plenty of grills, picnic tables and lawn chairs.

The Gold Medal waters of the Roaring Fork River are fishable year-round and is heavily populated with trophy-sized trout. Your hosts can arrange rafting, hunting trips and sightseeing trips for the whole family. Year-round activities include visiting the world famous Glenwood Springs hot mineral and swimming pools and Vapor Caves. In season, go hiking, biking, river tubing and rafting, kayaking, miniature and regulation golfing, and horseback riding. During the winter, enjoy skiing, sledding, snowmobiling and ice skating. For something a little different, enjoy four-wheel driving, the nearby waterslide or take a hot air balloon ride.

Groups and reunions are welcomed at Riverside. Although reservations are encouraged, drive-in visitors are welcomed when space is available. Deposits for reservation are required, be sure to check about their cancellation policy.

Location: At the southern city limits of Glenwood Springs off of Highway 82, turn right at Buffalo Valley Restaurant. Double back on County Road 154 about three-quarters of a mile.

15 Cabins with Kitchen	Elevation: 5800	Stan & Jo George, Managers
6 Rooms with Fireplaces	Credit Cards: VM	1287 CR 154
Central Campfire Area	Rates:	Glenwood Springs CO 81601
	Open: All Year	800/945-5509 Reserve
		970/945-5509
		Fax: 970/945-0247
		E-mail: stajog@glenwood.net
		www.coloradodirectory.com/riversidecottages

At the resort:

At resort or within 15 minutes:

Spruce Tree Ranch

Along the beautiful, wooded banks of the East Elk Creek in New Castle, you'll discover modern log cabins in a magnificent, quiet setting, with views of high mountain peaks. A beautiful creek flows past the roomy cabins which have private baths, linens, two double beds and a hide-a-bed in the main room. Although you can't cook in the cabins, you can barbecue that freshly caught trout on the outside grills by one of the three ponds. Store your supplies in the social/game room's community refrigerator/freezer.

Kids will love the ranch's playground. Ranch activities include horseshoes, volleyball, croquet while nearby activities are playing golf, rock climbing and bird watching. This photographer's paradise features wildlife, birds, flowers and snow-capped mountains. Visit the Rifle Gap Reservoir and the unusual Rifle Falls. Hike in the Flat Tops Wilderness area and fish in streams and reservoirs. Hunt, horseback ride, mountain bike, whitewater raft the Colorado River, or just relax by the stream. And don't forget to visit the famous Glenwood Springs Hot Springs pool to ease the sore muscles after a day of adventure.

Children under 3 are free and a minimum deposit is required.

Location: Two miles northwest of New Castle, I-70 Exit 105. Eight miles west of Glenwood Springs.

5 Cabins without Kitchens	Phone in Lobby	Howard & Kim Johnson, Hosts
Central Campfire Area	All Units Nonsmoking	2026 Road 245
	Recreation Room	New Castle CO 81647
	Elevation: 5900	970/984-2144
	Credit Cards: None	E-mail: hjohnson@rifle.net
	Rates: $45-$50	www.coloradodirectory.com/sprucetreeranch
	Open: 5/1 to 11/15	

At the resort:

At resort or within 15 minutes:

Sunlight Mountain Inn Bed & Breakfast

Sunlight Mountain Inn offers superior personal service, outstanding quality and an excellent value for the price. Each of the inn's 20 guest rooms are cozy and comfortable with private baths, in-room phones, complimentary ski and sports equipment storage and daily maid service. The Romance Suite has a king bed, mountain view, fireplace, wet bar and jetted tub. Family size rooms have little touches that make traveling with young children easier. Guests are pampered with quality linens, in room coffee and tea, and a delicious full breakfast every morning.

Located near Glenwood Springs at the base of the ski resort, this bed and breakfast in is in the heart of countless outdoor adventures. Enjoy dinner at the inn's Apple Ranch restaurant (winter season) which specializes in apple dishes and an American country western style cuisine. In the summer and fall, you can white water raft on the Colorado or Roaring Fork rivers, mountain bike, hike, fish, golf, shop and explore. In the winter, snowboard, alpine and cross-country ski at Sunlight Mountain Ski Resort as well as snowmobile and snow shoe in the surrounding area. Other special amenities include an outdoor hot tub, outdoor ice skating rink, and horseback rides through White River National Forest. Year-round, you can swim in the hot springs and take a soothing break in the Yampa Vapor Caves. Glenwood Canyon offers many activities the whole family will enjoy.

The inn is a great location for special events and business meetings. Smoking is permitted in the bar, and outside of the inn. Children are warmly welcomed, but pets are not allowed.

Location: From I-70 take exit 116. Follow signs to Highway 82 (Aspen), at 23rd St, the road make a "Y" stay right to the stop sign, turn right, cross over bridge. Follow signs to Sunlight Ski Area, 10 miles on 4-Mile Rd (County Rd 117). Crossing a steel bridge.

20 Lodging Rooms	Phone in Rooms	Pierre & Gretchenn DuBois, Owners
1 Room with Hot Tub	Bed & Breakfast Available	10252 CR 117
1 Room with Fireplace	All Units Nonsmoking	Glenwood Springs CO 81601
Central Hot Tub	Recreation Room	800/733-4757
Central Fireplace	Elevation: 8000	970/945-5225
Central Campfire Area	Credit Cards: VMAD	Fax: 970/947-1900
	Rates: $60-$125	E-mail: gddubois@aol.com
	Open: All Year	www.coloradodirectory.com/sunlightinn/

At the resort:

At resort or within 15 minutes:

Grand Lake & Granby Area

Map: D-13

These mountain towns, at the western entrance to Rocky Mountain National Park, sit on great fishing lakes with beautiful, unspoiled views. Anglers will find rainbow, brook, mackinaw and cutthroat trout in abundance and large kokanee salmon as well. From **Granby**, Lake Granby, Shadow Mountain Reservoir and Willow Creek Reservoir are all close at hand. Resting on the shores of the largest natural lake in Colorado, **Grand Lake** is an alpine village with board sidewalks, log-front stores and the modern amenities of dining and shopping. At 8,369', this rustic town is enveloped by peaks, especially the impressive, bald Mt. Craig. Grand Lake has access to two reservoirs, two national forests, the national park and the Never Summer Wilderness Area which is accessible only by hiking trails. You can horseback ride, boat, hike, golf and river raft in this beautiful area. When the snow starts, Grand Lake and Granby become a winter playground, with groomed trails for snowmobiling, cross-country skiing, snowshoeing and close by slopes for downhill skiing. Ute, Arapaho and Cheyenne tribes used to hunt and fish in this Middle Park area and when you visit you'll see why this was land worth fighting over.

Fun Things to Do

- Arapaho National Forest (970) 887-4100
- Grand Lake Golf Course (970) 627-8008
- Kaufman House (970) 627-3351
- Raven Rafting & Adventures (800)332-3381
- Rocky Mountain National Park (970) 627-3471

Circle H Lodge Bed & Breakfast

On the shores of majestic Lake Granby and overlooking the Continental Divide, Circle H Lodge Bed & Breakfast boasts a million dollar view from your lodge room as well as the great room, restaurant and lounge. The six individually decorated, non-smoking guest rooms have their own baths, televisions and have either one or two double beds. Two of the lodge rooms can be made into a suite with an equipped kitchen, living room and private deck, perfect for families. Breakfast — homemade muffins, cereals, warm beverages, juice and fruit, included with your room, is served in the restaurant.

Fish year-round right in front of the 8,000-square foot lodge. The lodge's restaurant specializes in deli sandwiches, soups, salad plates and mouth-watering desserts. Bring your own boat and use their courtesy dock for boating on Lake Granby or rent a boat at one of the nearby marinas. Hiking, horseback riding and golfing are within easy reach. Fall and winter activities include hunting, skiing, ice fishing and snowmobiling. Your hosts live here all year and strive to offer close and personal attention to every guest.

Circle H Lodge has a private meeting room available. Elk and deer hunters welcome (area 18). Roll-away beds are available. Children under 12 stay free.

Location: Six miles north of Granby and nine miles south of Rocky Mountain National Park. On Highway 34 between milepost marker 6-7.

6 Lodging Rooms	Phone in Lobby	Paul & Tricia Navarre, Owners
1 Room with Woodstove	Bed & Breakfast Available	6732 US Hwy 34
Central Fireplace	All Units Nonsmoking	Granby CO 80446
	Recreation Room	888/535-6343
	Elevation: 8300	970/887-3955
	Credit Cards: VMAD	Fax: 970/887-1770
	Rates: $79-$89	www.coloradodirectory.com/circlehlodge
	Open: All Year	

At the resort:

At resort or within 15 minutes:

Daven Haven Lodge

Near the west entrance to Rocky Mountain National Park, and only two blocks from downtown, Daven Haven Lodge features 16 cabins. Six of the units have fireplaces and all have cable television. Daven Haven is in a scenic setting just a half block from Grand Lake. At night, have the entire family gather around the campfire ring and outdoor barbecue area.

The main lodge has a lounge, dining room and banquet facilities. The dining room specializes in casual, affordable family meals. The resort also offers a heated swimming pool, open from June to Labor Day, horseshoes and volleyball. Grand Lake is famous for all the outdoor activities it offers, including four wheel drive tours, horseback riding, river rafting, golfing, miniature golfing, mountain biking and, of course, boating on lovely Grand Lake. Winter time features many things to do as well, including downhill and cross-country skiing, sleigh riding, snowmobiling, ice fishing and hunting. Come to Grand Lake in time for the Winter Carnival and dog sled races.

Daven Haven is ideal for family reunions, wedding receptions and business retreats.

Location: At entrance of Grand Lake go down the hill and take the first right onto Center Road to the first stop sign, then turn left onto Marina Drive, go two blocks.

4 Cabins with Kitchen	Pay Phone Available	Greg & Carey Barnes, Owners
12 Cabins without Kitchens	Elevation: 8369	PO Box 1528
6 Rooms with Fireplaces	Credit Cards: VMD	Grand Lake CO 80447-1528
Central Fireplace	Rates: $78-$110	970/627-8144
Central Campfire Area	Open: All Year	Fax: 970/627-5098
		E-mail: davenhaven@rkymtnhi.com
		www.coloradodirectory.com/davenhavenlodge/

At the resort:

At resort or within 15 minutes:

House on the Hill, The Stable Cabin

Enjoy a warm and comfy rustic log cabin, set snugly on a secluded, wooded acre complete with a wood burning fireplace when you stay at the House on the Hill. You'll sleep in comfort in one of three bedrooms, including one called the Sunroom for obvious reasons. The cabin sleeps up to 10 and amenities include color cable television.

Prepare your daily catch from the local streams in the 1940s vintage kitchen which has all the modern amenities, including a microwave and an automatic coffee maker. Take a break in front of the fireplace in the sun drenched living room, or wander outside to breath the mountain-fresh air on the patio. Area activities include exquisite fishing by fly, lure or bait in the waterway outside your door that runs between Shadow Mountain Reservoir and Lake Grandby. Just four miles away is Grand Lake where you can fish some more, boat, whitewater raft, water ski or just simply relax. Other ways to spend your day include horseback riding, skiing, snowshoeing, snowmobiling, sleigh riding, golfing, mountain biking and taking nature hikes. Try strolling through Grand Lake and exploring the interesting shops and eating in mountain restaurants.

Your dog is welcomed to accompany you to the House on the Hill. Rent by the night, week or year!

Location: South of Grand Lake on Highway 34.

1 Cabin with Kitchen	Phone in Rooms	Edith & Bob Harris, Owners
1 Vacation Home	Recreation Room	47 CR 4107
1 Room with Fireplace	Elevation: 8300	Granby CO 80446
	Credit Cards: VM	888/556-2097
	Rates: $150	970/887-1125
	Open: All Year	Fax: 970/887-0786
		E-mail: emharris@rkymtnhi.com
		www.coloradodirectory.com/stablecabin

At the resort:

At resort or within 15 minutes:

Lake View Bed & Breakfast

Lake View is located in Grand Lake, the gem of the Rocky Mountains so all its rooms are named after gems and decorated in deep greens, blues and purples. Choose between Sapphire, Emerald, Amethyst and the Blue Topaz. Enjoy a view of Shadow Mountain Lake from each guest room. The spacious rooms have color cable television, phones, queen beds, private baths and sitting areas. Your breakfast will include seasonal fruit, homemade baked good and hearty entrées. Light snacks and beverages are served in the afternoon.

Lake View also offers three great rooms with large rock fireplaces, a wet bar service area, library and games for maximum relaxing. The historic village of Grand Lake is just two miles away, while the west gate of Rocky Mountain National Park is a mere three miles away. The inn is surrounded by Arapaho National Forest and is near three lakes, so the hiking, mountain biking, fishing, hunting and other outdoor activities abound. This area is known as the snowmobile capital of the world with over 150 miles of maintained trails and another 150 miles of marked trails in deep powder. Downhill skiing is no more than 30 minutes away.

Mini-seminars and conferences are welcomed with an electric media center available. No smoking or pets, and adults only please. Minimum nights stays are required during holidays and special events.

Location: Two miles from Grand Lake, three miles to the west gate of Rocky Mountain National Park. From Highway 34 turn onto County Road 4650.

---

4 Lodging Rooms
Central Fireplace

Phone in Rooms
Bed & Breakfast Available
All Units Nonsmoking
Recreation Room
Elevation: 8400
Credit Cards: VMAD
Rates: $110-$140
Open: All Year

Evelyn & Delmar Schnittker, Owners
PO Box 1260
Grand Lake CO 80447-1260
970/627-1200
www.coloradodirectory.com/lakeviewbb/

At the resort:

At resort or within 15 minutes:

Mountain Lakes Lodge & Log Furnishings

Mountain Lakes Lodge is a nature enthusiast's dream where the only thing you'll overlook is the spectacular Continental Divide. Located on the waterway that joins Lake Granby with Shadow Mountain Lake and Grand Lake, the resort offers cozy housekeeping cabins with color cable television for your accommodations. Lofted ceilings and wood beams gives these cabins a true rustic flare. All have fully equipped kitchens with dishes, cookware, and microwave ovens. Larger cabins have gas or log fireplaces, french doors with decks, and cooking stoves.

The western entrance to Rocky Mountain National Park and the quaint village of Grand Lake with shopping and restaurants are only minutes away. In warm weather you can enjoy hiking, fishing in lakes or the canal, boating, horseback riding and golf. When the weather cools off the area becomes a winter wonderland with ice fishing, cross-country and downhill skiing and snowmobiling at nearby Winter Park and Silver Creek. Bring along a camera to capture the abundant small wildlife, from chipmunks and squirrels to hummingbirds. There is also beautiful, hand-crafted, log furniture, aspen log beds, night stands, tables, chairs and speical order items, for sale on site.

Reservations are recommended. The Lodge welcomes pets and various sized groups, receptions, reunions and weddings.

Location: Highway 34, near milepost marker 10.

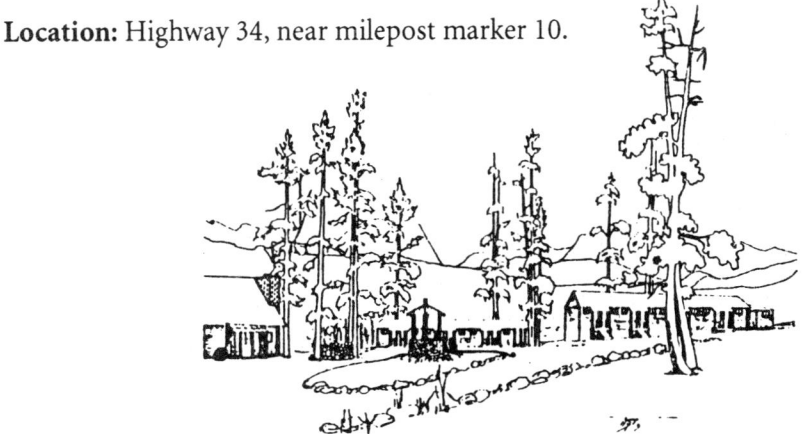

10 Cabins with Kitchen	Pay Phone Available	Dave & Karen Mawhorter, Hosts
1 Vacation Home	Elevation: 8300	PO Box 160
5 Rooms with Fireplaces	Credit Cards: VM	Grand Lake CO 80447-0160
5 Rooms with Wood Stoves	Rates: $45-$100	970/627-8448
Central Fireplace	Open: All Year	www.coloradodirectory.com/mountainlakeslodge
Central Campfire Area		

At the resort:

At resort or within 15 minutes:

Nonehshe Cabins

Named after the Ute Indian word for dream, and pronounced "no-neh-she", Nonehshe Cabins offer peace, quiet and sweet Nonehshe amid lodge pole pines and aspen trees. The cabins are cozy and comfortable with warm, natural pine interiors. Each has a living room, a kitchenette, a shower bathroom and a private picnic area with a barbecue grill. Choose between one-bedroom and two-bedroom cabins. Two units have full kitchens. Some of the cabins have wood burning stoves or fireplaces. The cabins, which sleep up to 10, are fully furnished with linens, dishes, cooking utensils and color cable television.

Located in the quaint village of Grand Lake, Nonehshe is a short walk from many unique shops and restaurants. Summer activities in town include bingo, bowling, live theater and miniature golf. In the area, enjoy swimming, boating, golfing, hiking and mountain biking. Grand Lake, Colorado's deepest natural lake, is a one block stroll away. Winter activities include downhill skiing, cross country skiing and snowmobiling. Relaxing is a year-round pleasure at Nonehshe. Fishing is great any season, from the spring run-off through the glorious fall and into snowy winter with ice fishing on the lake.

Location: 450 Broadway, a half block south of Grand Avenue, behind Grand Co. Lumber.

5 Cabins with Kitchen	Phone in Lobby	Richard & Pat Farmer, Owners
3 Rooms with Fireplaces	Elevation: 8500	PO Box 1696
	Credit Cards: VMD	Grand Lake CO 80447-1696
	Rates: $60-$140	970/627-8012
	Open: All Year	E-mail: NONEHSHE@rkymtnhi.com
		www.coloradodirectory.com/nonehshecabins

At the resort:

At resort or within 15 minutes:

River Pines Cottages

A beautiful setting with towering, lodgepole pines along the boulder-strewn, north fork of the Colorado River is yours for the taking at River Pines. Built between 1900-1940s, River Pines offers the experience of staying in an historic, log cabin reminiscent of the old west. Bordered by national forest with lovely Shadow Mountain Lake a short walk downsteam, the cabins sleep up to six people. All cabins have fireplaces and shower bathrooms, kitchens, gas furnace, and cable television.

Hiking, biking and snowmobile trails begin at your cabin. Catch a rainbow trout in the river behind your cabin or take a soothing soak in the hot tub. Near the river bank are picnic tables and barbecue grills for your convenience. A volleyball net and horseshoes are provided in the large play area. Let your hosts arrange horseback rides, hayrides, snowmobile rentals or ice fishing for you. Just to the north of River Pines is Rocky Mountain National Park where scheduled programs include nature hikes, lectures and tours conducted by the Park Service Rangers. Sight-seeing boat cruises on the two lakes are available as are charter boats for the serious anglers. At River Pines the winter is as pretty as the summer.

A reservation deposit of 50% is required. A two night minimum stay is required; three night minimum on holidays.

Location: On Highway 34 at milepost marker12.

14 Cabins with Kitchen	Pay Phone Available	Mark & Becky Johnson, Owners
14 Rooms with Fireplaces	Some Units Nonsmoking	12082 US Hwy 34
Central Hot Tub	Elevation: 8350	Grand Lake CO 80447
Central Campfire Area	Credit Cards: VM	970/627-3632
	Rates: $69-$158	Fax: 970/627-3482
	Open: All Year	E-mail: RiverPinesCottages@coweblink.net
		www.coloradodirectory.com/riverpinescottages/

At the resort:

At resort or within 15 minutes:

Rock Creek Cabins & Snowmobile Rentals

The historic village of Grand Lake borders the largest natural lake in Colorado, forming the western gateway to Rocky Mountain National Park. Rock Creek Cabins are warm and cozy with gas stove fireplaces with visible flames. The remodeled, spacious cabins have a bedroom, living room and dining room area. Set apart to insure comfortable vacation living and privacy, the modern units have bathrooms with shower, fully equipped kitchens with cooking utensils - dishes, pots and pans, linens, bedding and towels.

Rock Creek caters to families with its children's playground, outdoor barbecue, and lawns edged with towering spruce trees. Located at the west end of Grand Lake Village, the cabins are walking distance from the main part of the town with its varied activities and shopping in quaint shops. Here you'll be a stone's throw from Grand Lake and Shadow Mountain Lake. Granby Reservoir is only a short drive. Water sports abound, from boating and water skiing to fishing for rainbow, German brown and mackinaw trout and kokanee salmon. If you prefer stream fishing, there are plenty of mountain creeks in the area. Warm weather activities include golfing, hiking, sightseeing, horseback riding and mountain biking. As the 'Official Snowmobiling Capital of Colorado", the area has nearly 300 miles of trails, more than 150 are groomed. Rent a snowmobile on-site or ride your own right from your cabin. Other winter activities include cross-country skiing, alpine

skiing (ski areas are within 35 miles), ice fishing, ice skating and romantic sleigh rides.

Snowmobile package includes lodging and snowmobile rental.

Location: In downtown Grand Lake on Grand Avenue.

8 Cabins with Kitchen	Phone in Lobby	Sharon Fagen & Ken Reynolds
8 Rooms with Fireplaces	Elevation: 8500	PO Box 589
Central Hot Tub	Credit Cards: VMAD	Grand Lake CO 80447-0501
	Rates: $78-$125	970/627-8019
	Open: All Year	Fax: 970/627-8121
		E-mail: rockcreek@rkymtnhi.com
		www.coloradodirectory.com/rockcreek

At the resort:

At resort or within 15 minutes:

Rocky Mountain Cabins

Ideally situated between the north fork of the Colorado River and the western entrance to Rocky Mountain National Park, this new resort features luxury cabins with porches. The cabins come with every amenity, including rock fireplaces, washer/dryer, cable television, full kitchens and baths and much more. You'll find plenty of privacy and quiet on these six acres enveloped by stunning mountain scenery. Imagine fishing right off your porch into the river and then dining on your catch while watching a colorful sunset.

From Rocky Mountain Cabins, you can cross-country ski or snowmobile on 130 miles of groomed trails as well as across Shadow Mountain Lake. Great downhill skiing is 15 to 45 minutes away at Winter Park and Silver Creek. Take a romantic sleigh ride over crisp, pure white snow. Summer activities abound here, from mountain biking, horseback riding and hiking to golfing and wildlife watching. Boat and fish on the lake or cast into any number of crystal mountain streams. The small town of Grand Lake offers gourmet dining, melodrama, bingo and shopping.

Reservations are required and there is a two night stay minimum. Rocky Mountain Cabins are great for honeymoons or just a quiet get-a-way. Cabins sleep 2 to 8 people and no pets are allowed.

Location: Just north of River Pines on east side of Highway 34.

3 Cabins with Kitchen	Phone in Lobby	Chris & Kathy Lorens, Owners
3 Vacation Homes	Elevation: 8500	PO Box 835
3 Rooms with Fireplaces	Credit Cards: None	Grand Lake CO 80447-0835
Central Campfire Area	Rates: $115-$185	970/627-3061
	Open: All Year	www.coloradodirectory.com/rockymtncabins

At the resort: *At resort or within 15 minutes:*

Shadow Mountain Guest Ranch

The best of the mountain area's ambiance will be right at your doorstep at Shadow Mountain Guest Ranch. Among aspen and pine trees, all of the cabins are private, some with wood burning stove or fireplaces. Each cabin has a gas barbecue grill, kitchenette or full kitchen. The School House is perfect for large family vacations with 3 bedrooms (some with private entrances), a full kitchen and large living area with a stone fireplace. For a romantic vacation for two the Trapper cabin offers a large room with a sitting area, kitchenette, queen size bed and large bathroom. All of the cabins are without a telephone and television for a true getaway.

The central, historic, log lodge has two large, stone fireplaces and a comfortable living room for conversation, satellite television, card games and socializing. Enjoy the hot tub for the ultimate in relaxation. Anglers will like casting for trout in Willow Creek which runs through the Ranch. Located near Rocky Mountain National Park and Lake Granby, you can hunt, fish, boat and hike to your heart's content. Summer trail rides are a great way to explore the picturesque area. In the evening join in telling your favorite tale around the campfire with marshmallows and song. Winter snow makes an ideal playground for for the sports minded or snuggle by the fire and keep warm with your sweetheart.

Small dogs are allowed for a moderate fee. The lodge is a good place for groups, workshops, entertainment or just plain chat in a homey atmosphere. Take advantage of the licensed massage therapist on-call.

Location: Five and a half miles north of Highway 40 on Highway 125.

7 Cabins with Kitchen	Phone in Lobby	Jim & Dale White, Owners
1 Room with Fireplace	Bed & Breakfast Available	PO Box 963
3 Rooms with Wood Stoves	Recreation Room	Granby CO 80446-0963
Central Hot Tub	Elevation: 8600	800/64-Shadow(647-4236)
Central Fireplace	Credit Cards: VMD	970/887-9524
Central Woodstove	Rates: $105-$165	Fax: 970/887-3059
Central Campfire Area	Open: All Year	E-mail: thebest@coweblink.net
		www.coloradodirectory.com/shadowmtnranch

At the resort:

At resort or within 15 minutes:

SpiritsPlay at Grand Lake

Come relax in front of a crackling fire at this cozy 1930s log home located on the historic Main Street between Grand Lake and Shadow Mountain Lake. SpiritsPlay will sleep up to 12 people in three bedrooms with queen beds, twin beds, double futons and a sleeper couch. There are two bathrooms, one with a shower and one with a claw foot tub. The house has a fully equipped kitchen, large dining room that seats 10, television, VCR, CD player, games, extensive library and puzzles. SpiritsPlay is beautifully decorated with antiques throughout.

Open all year, SpiritsPlay is near areas for boating, golfing, horseback riding, cross country skiing, snowshoeing, snowmobiling and, of course, relaxing in the nearby hot sulphur springs. The house is within walking distance from downtown Grand Lake where you can attend live theater, play miniature golf, or shop.

Small groups and family reunions are welcomed. Sorry, no pets or smoking allowed. A three night minimum is required in the summer and two nights in the winter. A $200 damage deposit is due 10 days after the reservation is made while the total rate plus tax is due before arrival.

Location: From Highway 34, near milepost marker 15, take the first right off Grand Avenue past the post office and school.

1 Vacation Home	Phone in Rooms	Sue & Jim Sell, Owners
Central Fireplace	All Units Nonsmoking	1737 Norwood Lane
	Recreation Room	Ft Collins CO 80525
	Elevation: 8369	970/223-3176
	Credit Cards: VM	www.coloradodirectory.com/spiritsplay
	Rates: $200-$250	
	Open: All Year	

At the resort:

At resort or within 15 minutes:

Western Riviera Cabins & Motel

Located right in the quaint village of Grand Lake, Western Riviera offers a varied choice of accommodations. Relax in the comfort of one of the motel's units featuring one or two double beds or one king bed. Each has a full bathroom and telephone. The suites sleep up to 6 with two queen beds, a queen sofa bed, televisions and telephones in each room, a refrigerator and private bath. The cabins accommodate up to five people and have new kitchenettes with microwave ovens, televisions in each room and a full bath. There are no telephones in the cabins. Enjoy wonderful views of the lake and beach front park from the wooden decks, picnic tables and grills.

Grand Lake, the oldest tourist town in Colorado, had maintained the image of the "Old West". Wooden boardwalks, 4th of July celebration with fireworks, Western Weekend with gun fights and buffalo barbecues — it's all found in Grand Lake. Nearby are over 100s of miles of groomed snowmobile trails, huge mountain snow bowls and meadows. In the summer, these same trails can be explored on foot or by mountain bike. Gather the family for a picnic on the beach area and uses the gas grills available. Soak away your worries in the outdoor spa with a magnificent view of the lake and snow-capped mountains.

Location: On Highway 34 at milepost marker15.

6 Cabins with Kitchen	Phone in Rooms	Darrell & Casey Herk, Owners
4 Cabins without Kitchens	Some Units Nonsmoking	PO Box 1286
15 Motel Rooms	Recreation Room	Grand Lake CO 80447-1286
Central Hot Tub	Elevation: 8400	970/627-3580
	Credit Cards: VMA	Fax: 970/627-3320
	Rates: $65-$100	E-mail: motel@westernriv.com
	Open: All Year	www.coloradodirectory.com/westernrivieracabins

At the resort:

At resort or within 15 minutes:

Winding River Resort Village

You'll have plenty of room to romp in on this 160-acre wooded, family-run ranch resort bordering Rocky Mountain National Park. Hidden among the pines in this mountainous region, the quaint, one-bedroom cabins, the cabin with a loft and the lodge rooms are all non-smoking. The lodge rooms, named Trapper and Larkspur, are bed and continental breakfast accommodations. Adjacent to Rocky Mountain National Park, Arapaho Forest and the North Fork of the Colorado River, Winding River is a family-oriented, great-for-kids resort. A camper cabin that sleeps four is also available.

The Winding River Resort sponsors numerous activities, such as horseback rides, pony rides, hayride steak dinners, sleigh rides, snowmobile rental, a Frisbee golf course, chuckwagon breakfasts, ice cream socials, fishing on-site and an animal farm for the kids. Bring along your horse for high country riding and spend the evening around a campfire. Nearby sports includes mountain biking, hiking, fishing, golfing and cross-country skiing. Rent a mountain bike here or play baseball, basketball, horseshoes and volleyball. The hayride and "steak frys" are great for family reunions. You'll be hard put to not find something for the entire family at Winding River Resort.

Spacious, shaded RV sites and group camping sites for family reunions are also available. Ask about the indoor and outdoor group meeting areas. Winding River has two seasons: from May 15 to October 1 and December 15 to April 1. Advanced reservations are recommended.

Location: Take Highway 34 to Kawuneeche Visitor Center one and a half miles north of Grand Lake. Turn west on 491 and go one and a half miles northwest.

3 Cabins with Kitchen	Pay Phone Available	Wes & Marcia House, Owners
1 Vacation Home	All Units Nonsmoking	PO Box 629
2 Lodging Rooms	Recreation Room	Grand Lake CO 80447-0629
1 Camper Cabin	Elevation: 8700	800/282-5121
3 Rooms with Wood Stoves	Credit Cards: VMAD	303/623-1121 Denver
	Rates: $70-$130	Fax: 970/627-5003
	Open: All Year	E-mail: trailboss@rkymtnhi.com
		www.coloradodirectory.com/windingriverresort/

At the resort:

At resort or within 15 minutes:

Grand Mesa Area

Including Cedaredge, Collbran, Mesa, Paonia & Somerset —
Map: I-5, H-5, H-4, I-6 & I-7

At 10,000', **Grand Mesa,** the largest flat-top mountain in the world, rises more than a mile above the valley floor. Discover aspen and spruce groves, flowered meadows and over 200 cool clear lakes offering fantastic fishing for rainbow, brook and brown trout. Some lakes have boat launches and you can reach many of them from the highway. For the more adventurous, visit the lakes only accessible by four-wheel drive, foot or horseback. Utes called this the "Home of the Departed Spirits" and they brought hostages here after the 1879 Meeker Massacre. Almost entirely within the Grand Mesa National Forest, Grand Mesa has abundant wildlife, making this a popular area for fall hunting. Elk, deer and many smaller mammals roam the alpine forest. Drive the Grand Mesa Scenic and Historic Byway and tour the changing aspen in the fall. Visit Surface Creek Valley Historical Society's Pioneer Town in **Cedaredge** where you can experience the American West at the turn of the century. Hikers will want to trek along the Crag Crest National Recreation Trail, a 10-mile circular trail rising from east and west trail heads. The 6.5 mile long path stretching across the top of Crag Crest is open to foot traffic only. Escape the summer heat and relax in Grand Mesa's cool mountain air. Few places offer such a delightful combination of climate, scenery and recreation as the **Somerset** area just south of Paonia Reservoir State Park. The natural beauty of the countryside, the clean air and the surrounding majestic mountains are the ideal vacation ingredients. The close by West Elk Wilderness is a magnificent place for hiking and hunting. The entire area is a focal point of back roads and trails leading into the wilderness. Take a drive along the West Elk Loop Scenic Byway and record some of this area's uniqueness with your camera. Nearby, in **Paonia,** you'll find abundant orchards filled with sweet and sour cherries, apricots, peaches, plums, pears, nectarines and a large variety of apples. The town of Paonia was founded by Samuel Wade in 1882 when he brought the first fruit trees into the valley. In addition to Paonia's farmers, the area's economy is based on coal mines and ranching. Outside the town of **Collbran** is Vega Reservoir State Park, north of Grand Mesa.

Fun Things to Do

- Deercreek Village Golf Course, Cedaredge (970) 856-7781
- Grand Mesa Lodge Store(800) 551-6372
- Mesa lakes Resort Restaurant, Snowmobile Tours & Horses (888) 420-6372
- Surface Creek Historic & Pioneer Town, Cedaredge (970) 856-7554
- Vega Restaurant, Bar & Boat Rentals (970) 487-3733

Braham's Inn Bed & Breakfast

Braham's Inn is located in the heart of fantastic fruit country. Surrounded by orchards that produce excellent fruit such as apples, peaches, pears, cherries, grapes, apricots and plums, the inn has five non-smoking rooms available. Each of the big, beautiful rooms has its own entrance off the eight-foot covered deck. The rooms are tastefully decorated with antiques and a fruit theme. The enormous rooms have private baths, two queen size beds, cable color television and private phones. The full breakfast, choice of three meals, is served in the large dining room or may be enjoyed in the privacy of your own room.

This cozy and large bed and breakfast inn was remodeled from a fruit packing shed that was built in the 1920s. History of the fruit harvesting is displayed in the large dining area. Braham's is on 10 acres with walking trails for your enjoyment. Roaming the grounds are a pet pot belly pig, and numerous peacocks and pheasants that live here. The inn is conveniently located near Grand Mesa which offers fishing, snowmobiling, hiking, downhill and cross country skiing, and hunting. Also nearby is Deer Creek Golf Course, an historical pioneer town, art galleries, antique shops, tennis courts, rodeo grounds, art and photography exhibits, craft shows, an annual apple festival, wineries and the Gunnison River and much more!

The inn is handicap accessible. Ask about the group and senior citizen discounts. Small pets and guest horses are allowed. All units are non-smoking.

Location: East on Highway 30.

5 Lodging Rooms	Phone in Rooms	Frank & Judy Braham, Owners
	Bed & Breakfast Available	1258 Hwy 65
	All Units Nonsmoking	Eckert CO 81418
	Recreation Room	970/835-3357
	Elevation: 5280	www.coloradodirectory.com/brahamsinn/
	Credit Cards: VM	
	Rates: $58	
	Open: All Year	

At the resort:

At resort or within 15 minutes:

Crystal Meadows Ranch, Cabins & Campground

Tucked between two mountain ranges, in a scenic river valley, Crystal Meadows has accommodations varying from a two-bedroom log house with a full kitchen and a small bath, to a one-room log cabin with three beds and a shared bathroom. The ranch is nestled serenely in the mountains where Anthracite, Coal and Muddy creeks join to form the North Fork of the Gunnison River. At Crystal Meadows, you're surrounded by the sound of cool rushing alpine-fed water and vistas of pine covered peaks.

The restaurant serves tasty breakfasts on weekends, hearty lunches and delectable dinners. The outdoor pavilion and indoor meeting room will be great for your conference or family reunion. Fish in the privately stocked lake, or in the snow-fed Anthracite Creek. Rent horses nearby, or bring your own, to ride. Horseback ride, mountain bike, or hike in the nearby West Elk Mountains and the Raggeds, two vast and scenic wilderness areas. Hunters will find abundant deer and elk here in season. Enjoy West Elk Loop Scenic and Historic Byway as you drive over the picturesque Kebler Pass Road to Crested Butte. For your convenience, there is an on-site grocery store with RV supplies, ice, limited groceries and firewood.

Full hookup RV sites are also available.

Location: Paonia, go 16 miles NE on Hwy 133. Carbondale go SW 47 miles. Near milepost 24, on County Road 12 Crested Butte-Kebler Pass Rd. 30 miles from Crested Butte.

2 Cabins with Kitchen	Pay Phone Available	Bill & Kay Tennison, Owners
3 Cabins without Kitchens	Recreation Room	30682 CR 12
1 Vacation Home	Elevation: 6200	Somerset CO 81434-9625
1 Camper Cabin	Credit Cards: VMD	970/929-5656
1 Room with Woodstove	Rates: $45-$150	Fax: 970/929-5657
Central Fireplace	Open: 5/28 to 11/15	E-mail: wtennison@aol.com
		www.coloradodirectory.com/crystalmeadowsranch/

At the resort:

At resort or within 15 minutes:

G R Bar Ranch Cabins

If you've dreamed about an exciting vacation, high in the spectacular Rocky Mountains, this is it! The secluded G R Bar Ranch cabins are at 9,200 9,600-feet in elevation, adjoining both the Gunnison and Grand Mesa National Forests. These completely furnished ranch houses rent by the week, so you can really settle into a vacation away from it all. Arrowhead Cabin, at 9,200-feet, sleeps 5 and is completely modern. Red Springs Cabin, a half mile from the national forest at 9,600-feet, sleeps 8 and features a fireplace, propane furnace and gas range. Many Penny Cabin, at 9,500-feet, accommodates 8 people and has a spectacular view of lakes and mountains. The rustic, log Kokopelli Cabin is at 9,450 feet, readily accommodates 8 and has a cathedral, beamed ceiling, open stairway with loft, downstairs bedroom and fireplaces. This cabin is modern in all respects with a complete kitchen, full bath, propane stove and refrigerator. Kokopelli also has gorgeous views of the mountain range and Lake Beaver. All cabins have complete kitchens, full bath, hot and cold running water, propane barbecues and linens. To insure privacy, the closest building, the ranch house, is at least a quarter of a mile away.

If you want to get away from it all, spend time in an incredible setting, love nature, peace and quiet, and crave a different experience from the traditional cabin resorts and dude ranches, G R Bar Ranch is what you've been looking for! Take advantage of unlimited fishing in 9 private lakes — no license required, no fee. Angler's will love the variety of fish, from rainbow, brook and cutthroat to the German brown and cutbow trout up to seven pounds. Explore thousands of acres by horseback, jeep or on hiking trails which offer views of the local wildlife. Each cabin has its own corral and furnished tack room to keep the horses happy. You're in the center of nature's wonderland, with scenic views, myriad's of wildflowers & wildlife - a photographer's delight.

Cabins are rented on a weekly basis. Rates are for a couple & their unmarried, dependent children. Price includes 2 horses & unlimited fishing. No pets allowed.

Location: Twelve miles north of Paonia.

4 Cabins with Kitchen	All Units Nonsmoking	N.W. & Barbara Grosse-Rhode, Owners
2 Rooms with Fireplaces	Elevation: 9400	4149 N 80 Lane
2 Rooms with Wood Stoves	Credit Cards: None	Paonia CO 81428-9639
	Rates:	970/527-6434
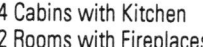	Open: 5/15 to 11/15	E-mail: Grbarranch@aol.com
		www.coloradodirectory.com/grbarranch/

At the resort: *At resort or within 15 minutes:*

Grand Mesa Lodge

In the Grand Mesa National Forest, 55 miles from Grand Junction, this resort features cozy housekeeping cabins and a motel above beautiful Island Lake. These attractively furnished log cabins have fully equipped kitchens, gas heat and bathrooms with showers. One cabin features a fireplace, sauna, and lake view. All cabins are furnished with bedding, towels and barbecue. The motel units, which are non-smoking, are available for those not requiring kitchen facilities. The comfortable lodge lobby has a scenic view for relaxation, conversation and coffee. Settle back in a comfortable cabin and cook somres at your campfire while shooting stars fill the sky.

Shop in the on-site store for groceries, gifts, and fishing and hunting supplies, including licenses. Island Lake, the largest lake on Grand Mesa, is an outstanding mile long and surrounded by evergreens and aspen trees. Rent boats at the lodge for memorable fishing. Deer and elk abound for hunting in season or simply viewing. In winter explore the great outdoors on a snowmobile tour on groomed trails, open meadows, and hidden valleys. The Lodge offers half-day and full-day guided trips for beginners and experts. Cross country ski until your hearts content. The national Craig Crest Trail, a 10-mile loop, is just 0.25 miles from the lodge. Mountain bike trails abound here.

A meeting room with kitchen, deck and barbeque grill is available for groups of up to 25. A deposit equal to 50% of the total is due within 10 days of booking. Balance is due 21 days prior to arrival. Ask about the cancellation policy. Well mannered pets are permitted in the cabins, but must be on a leash at all times.

Location: Highway 65, near milepost marker 28.

14 Cabins with Kitchen	Pay Phone Available	Ken & Conne Simpson, Owners
3 Motel Rooms	Some Units Nonsmoking	PO Box 49
1 Room with Fireplace	Elevation: 10500	Cedaredge CO 81413-0049
1 Room with Woodstove	Credit Cards: VM	800/551-6372
Central Woodstove	Rates: $35-$90	970/856-3250
Central Campfire Area	Open: All Year	Fax: 970/856-6700
		E-mail: gmlodge@aol.com
		www.coloradodirectory.com/grandmesalodge/

At the resort:

At resort or within 15 minutes:

Mesa Lakes Resort

Breathe the cleanest air around! High on fabulous Grand Mesa, surrounded by forests and lakes, Mesa Lakes Resort offers various rustic to modern vacation cabins. Cabins rent by the day or week. The 11 two-bedroom modern cabins have double beds, fireplaces, kitchen/living room and baths. The 3 modern motel units have 1 or 2 bedrooms, double beds and baths; however there are no cooking facilities. For small reunions or groups, ask about the 12-person vacation home with its 6 double beds, a fireplace and a kitchen. Two rustic cabins have two double beds, a small gas cooking stove, table and chairs with a central bath for these units. In all cases, bedding is furnished, but you must bring your own cooking utensils.

A small, on-site grocery store sells hunting and fishing licenses. Enjoy the delicious homemade bread, pies, soups and cinnamon rolls (sometimes gigantic) in the lodge's restaurant which also serves breakfast, lunch and dinner daily. The resort's recreation room is ideal for groups, meetings and weddings. At 9,800 feet in elevation in the Grand Mesa National Forest, Mesa Lake Resort resides near 7 of the finest mountain top lakes, all within walking distance from the cabins. Three of the lakes have rowboat rentals. More than 250 lakes here provide great fishing and boating opportunities. Boat rentals are also on site at the resort. Other summer activities include hiking, mountain biking, and guided horseback riding for all levels offered Mesa Lakes Resort. In the fall, hunt deer and elk, or photograph the wondrous scenery and wildlife. In winter and spring, enjoy miles of groomed cross country ski trails. Try renting snowshoes or taking a snowmobile tour. In addition, the downhill slopes of Powderhorn are only 10 minutes away.

Some non-smoking units. Pets are allowed for a fee & advanced arrangements. Guest horses welcomed.

Location: Fourteen miles south of Mesa, off Highway 65, near milepost marker 36.

11 Cabins with Kitchen	Pay Phone Available	Harold, Judy & Mike Harvey, Owners
1 Vacation Home	Some Units Nonsmoking	PO Box 230
2 Camper Cabins	Elevation: 9800	Mesa CO 81643-0230
3 Motel Rooms	Credit Cards: VMD	888/420-6372
5 Rooms with Fireplaces	Rates: $30-$150	970/268-5467
Central Fireplace	Open: All Year	Fax: 970/268-5467
Central Campfire Area		E-mail: MHARVEY155@aol.com
		www.coloradodirectory.com/mesalakesresort/

At the resort:

At resort or within 15 minutes:

Minnesota Creek Bed & Breakfast

Nestled in the Paonia hills, Minnesota Creek Bed & Breakfast is a unique, century old farm house settled on four acres of lawn, rose gardens, stream and pastures. This historic house, decorated in Arts and Crafts style, offers six elegant bedrooms, three shared bathrooms and pastoral views. Room rates include a hearty breakfast and refreshments.

The inn also offers guests three spacious sitting rooms and a covered patio. Catering and family style dinners are available. Your hostess, a professional quilt maker, has a studio on the premises. Expansive lawns provide an excellent area for croquet or simply lounging on a hammock beneath the towering cottonwood trees. Situated just outside of Paonia, and flanked by the Gunnison National Forest, the inn has splendid access to a variety of activities, including hiking, horseback riding, mountain biking, fishing, hunting and cross country skiing.

This is an ideal, pastoral setting for weddings, private parties and small group retreats. This is a non-smoking resort. Ask about the special rates for family groups, art/quilt retreats and hunters.

Location: Exit Highway 133 into Paonia. From Grand Avenue turn east on 2nd take it till it ends, right or south on Paonia for 2/10 mile. Turn left just past Care Center onto 050 Lane.

1 Cabin without Kitchen	Phone in Lobby	Lynn D. Mattingly, Hostess
7 Lodging Rooms	Bed & Breakfast Available	4175 050 Lane
1 Room with Woodstove	All Units Nonsmoking	Paonia CO 81428
	Recreation Room	970/527-4414
	Elevation: 5700	www.coloradodirectory.com/minnesotacreekbb/
	Credit Cards: None	
	Rates: $55-$70	
	Open: All Year	

At the resort:

At resort or within 15 minutes:

Pomotawh Naantam Ranch

Both a fully functioning cattle ranch and a recreational ranch all in one, Pomotawh Naantam Ranch is on 3,500 acres adjacent to BLM and national forest near Somerset. The ranch's name originates from the Indian words for mountain (pomotawh) and wolf (naantam). The Basic Cabin has a double and two twin beds and can sleep up to 6 comfortably. The Anthracite Cabin is next to a creek of the same name and has double, twin and sofa sleeper beds with a kitchenette and full bathroom. The Layton Cabin is tucked away behind a cedar fence and walk way for extra privacy. Inside are a rustic, queen-size log bed, queen sofa bed, a kitchenette and full bathroom. All three log cabins are fully furnished with rustic, homemade log beds, country comforters and fresh ground coffee. Sit on your front porch and enjoy the view of Muncy Basin and the entrance to the Dark Canyon.

The ranch offers guided and unguided creek and lake fishing, hiking in summer and fall, snowmobiling and cross-country skiing in winter and spring. Take one of the ranch's experienced, well-mannered horses over spectacular mountain trails on rides that range from one hour to pack trips of several days. Bring along a camera to capture bull elk bugling in the fall and newly born calf elk and fawn deer in the spring. Keep a look out for the occasional bear and mountain goat amid fields of wildflowers as well. Only a half mile from the Raggeds Wilderness in Gunnison National Forest and 9 miles from West Elk Wilderness, you'll have plenty of the great outdoors to explore.

Location: On County Road 12, near milepost marker 27, to Kebler Pass.

3 Cabins with Kitchen	Pay Phone Available	Jon & Dori Lee, Owners
	All Units Nonsmoking	26767 CR 12
	Elevation: 6700	Somerset CO 81434
	Credit Cards: VM	970/929-6575
	Rates: $70-$150	Fax: 970/929-6585
	Open: All Year	E-mail: pomotawh@aol.com
		www.coloradodirectory.com/pomotawhranch

At the resort: *At resort or within 15 minutes:*

Vega Lodge & RV Park

Located in the scenic mountain splendor near 1,830-acre Vega State Park is the Vega Lodge & RV Park. The rustic, A-frame lodge is a short drive from Grand Junction. Choose between new, full hookup RV sites with cement pads or cabins. Twelve cabins do not have cooking facilities, while two of them do. A five bedroom cabin that sleeps fifteen is also available. One unit is available with a fireplace. Fourteen of the 23 RV sites are 45 feet or longer. All sites and cabins overlook nearby Vega Lake and the surrounding Grand Mesa National Forest.

On site, the lodge offers a restaurant and full bar, fireplace, laundry room and a game room with coin, board and card games. The on-site store has a bait shop with fishing and hunting licenses for sale. Hot showers and LPG propane are available for those staying in RVs. Try wind surfing, water skiing and jet skiing on Vega Lake. Step out your front door and experience some of the best fishing and big game hunting on Colorado's western slope. Other activities include boating and mountain biking. Within an hour's drive are white water rafting trips, a museum and a golf course.

Ask about the very reasonable daily, weekly, monthly and seasonal rates. Groups are catered to with a live band available for dancing parties. With advanced arrangements, pets may be allowed in the private rental units and at the campsites, as long as they are well-behaved and leashed outdoors. Guests may bring their own horses.

Location: Inside Vega State Recreation Area, 12 miles east of Collbran.

2 Cabins with Kitchen	Phone in Lobby	Robert & Lou Gil, Owners
12 Cabins without Kitchens	Recreation Room	PO Box 166
1 Vacation Home	Elevation: 8000	Collbran CO 81624-0166
1 Room with Fireplace	Credit Cards: VM	970/487-3733
Central Fireplace	Rates: $35	www.coloradodirectory.com/vega/
	Open: 5/1 to 11/1	

At the resort:

At resort or within 15 minutes:

Gunnison Area

Including Almont, Ohio City, Parlin, Sapinero & Sargents — Map: K-9, J-9, I-9, J-10, K-10, K-7 & K-11

Named for a topographer who was mapping a railroad route to the Pacific in 1853, **Gunnison** is surrounded by over 1.7 million acres of public land. The Gunnison River Territory stretches from one spectacular naturescape to another with plunging canyon walls, emerald lakes, imposing peaks and wildflower meadows. Ute Indians, miners, ranchers and the railroads all contributed to the western character of this area. Today, Gunnison prides itself on having some of the best outdoor recreation in the state. Blue Mesa Reservoir in the Curecanti National Recreation Area, 9 miles west, is the largest man-made lake in Colorado with 96 miles of shoreline — an angler's paradise. Gunnison National Forest has more than 750 miles of teeming trout streams and reservoirs. Nearby, the Aberdeen Quarry was in operation from 1889 to 1892 and supplied the stone for Denver's capitol. The Alpine Tunnel is 30 miles east of Gunnison and northeast of **Ohio City** and **Sargents**. The tunnel is now abandoned and only accessible by off-road vehicle, bore through the Continental Divide at 11,523', making it the highest railroad station in the country. Drive along the West Elk Scenic Byway through **Almont**, 30 miles north to Crested Butte.

Fun Things to Do

- 7-11 Ranch Fishing, Hunting & Horses (970)641-0666
- Curecanti National Recreational Area (970) 641-2337
- Dos Rios Golf Course, Gunnison (970) 641-1482
- Gunnison National Forest (970) 641-0471
- Morrow Point Boat Tour, Gunnison, Summer (970) 641-0402
- Taylor Reservoir (970) 641-0471
- Tenderfoot Outfitters & Guide Services (800) 641-0504
- Tenderfoot Rafting (800) 723-8987
- Three Rivers Outfitting, Rafting & Fly Fishing Shop, Almont (888) 761-3474

7-11 Ranch

The Rudibaugh family has hosted outdoor adventures at their ranch, situated on Quartz Creek and surrounded by majestic mountains, since 1958. The semi-rustic cabins have fully equipped kitchenettes with a stove and a central bathhouse.

Fish for dinner in one of the many native trout streams right outside your cabin door or in the ranch's stocked private lake. Home-cooked, ranch-style, meals are available with advanced notice, remember this is a working ranch. Join in their cattle drive, where you can be a cowhand, guiding 800 head of cattle over a 12,000-foot pass to their summer pasture. Camp under the stars and eat meals served by the camp cook with the other cowhands. Back at the ranch, choose from a myriad of horseback trips, such as day-long outings or five- to seven-day pack trips in some of the most beautiful scenery in Colorado. Your hosts also can help outfit your hunting trip for big horn sheep, elk and mule deer in season.

For weddings, ask about the carriage with the fringe on top for a memorable addition to your special day. We specialize in western weddings and family reunions. We plan your activities to make your reunion a true outdoor, western experience.

Location: Take Highway 50 to Parlin, then 5 miles north on County Road 76.

5 Cabins with Kitchen	Phone in Lobby	Rudy & Deborah Rudibaugh, Owners
1 Cabin without Kitchen	Recreation Room	5291 CR 76
8 Beds in Bunkhouse	Elevation: 8500	Parlin CO 81239
4 Rooms with Wood Stoves	Credit Cards: None	970/641-0666 & fax ph 1st
Central Campfire Area	Rates: $35	E-mail: ranch711@gunnison.com
	Open: 5/1 to 11/30	www.coloradodirectory.com/711ranch/

At the resort:

At resort or within 15 minutes:

Almont Resort

The Taylor and East Rivers meet at Almont Resort to form the champion of trout rivers, the Gunnison. The resort features a newly remodeled "Riverhouse" vacation home directly on the river. The vacation home has seven bedrooms, three and a half baths, and two kitchens, perfect for a small family reunion. The resort also has 16 modernized, authentic log cabins, some of which are on the river. All the cabins have baths and many have kitchenettes or full kitchens. Most of the smaller cabins have coffee makers and refrigerators. The largest cabin, with six double beds, one single and a hide-a-way, features two bedrooms, a loft, a full bathroom and kitchen and a wood burning stove.

A restaurant, open for breakfast, lunch and dinner, and lounge resides on Almont's 100 acres. Sunday brunch is offered 7am-2pm. Once an important stop on the railroad and a famous summer resort since 1893 has historical significance. Take the family on a whitewater raft or float trip right from the Resort. Horseback riding is nearby. Many old ghost towns await your 4-wheel drive vehicle. Excellent hunting and fishing are what have brought people to this resort for nearly 100 years. In the winter, ski at Crested Butte and Monarch, take a guided snowmobile tour and explore the endless cross-country trails nearby.

Almont specializes in family and business gatherings, from barbecues to gourmet, sit-down dinners Money-saving ski packages available.

Location: Near Gunnison & Crested Butte on Hwy 135, near milepost marker 10.

9 Cabins with Kitchen	Pay Phone Available	Harold & Susan Seiff, Owners
7 Cabins without Kitchens	Recreation Room	PO Box 306
1 Vacation Home	Elevation: 8026	Almont CO 81210-0306
1 Room with Hot Tub	Credit Cards: VM	970/641-4009 & Fx ph 1st
2 Rooms with Fireplaces	Rates: $80-$300	E-mail: almontr@rmi.net
Central Fireplace	Open: All Year	www.coloradodirectory.com/almontresort/
Central Campfire Area		

At the resort:

At resort or within 15 minutes:

Ferro's Blue Mesa Trading Post & Outfitters

Spend your summer vacation in a relaxing atmosphere amid a natural setting of forest, lakes and streams. Overlooking Blue Mesa Reservoir in the Curecanti Recreation Area, these cabins, which accommodate up to six people, have complete kitchens with all utensils and linens. The four cabins are large, furnished and homey. One unit has a wood stove.

For your convenience, there's a coin Laundromat on-site. The trading post sells groceries, liquor, propane, tackle and fishing and hunting licenses. Experienced hunters will appreciate the guided hunting trips while photographers will get their chance at the wildlife wherever they go. This area is known as a haven for elk and deer and many trophies have been taken by our hunters. Anglers will enjoy the guided fishing trips on wilderness streams in the back country, accessible by four wheel drive or horses only. Bring your horse to ride the trials and board it on the premises. With a marina nearby, boaters can access the lake easily. The whole family will enjoy the occasional barbecues, group entertainment and the annual Western Luau every August. Ferro's Blue Mesa Trading Post is surrounded by the Gunnison National Forest and is a doorway to the West Elk Wilderness, providing ample opportunities for hiking, fishing, four wheel driving and horseback riding.

Worship services are held weekly in the campground from June to Labor Day. Groups and special events are welcomed. Group discounts are available for

horseback rides. Two on-site RVs are also available. Ask about 15 percent off weekly lodging rates. Reservations are strongly recommended.

Location: From Highway 50, near milepost marker 131 take exit Lake Fork Entrance (Highway 92). Go north past the dam, turn right on Soap Creek Road.

4 Cabins with Kitchen	Pay Phone Available	Kay & John Ferro, Owners
1 Room with Woodstove	Elevation: 7800	PO Box 853
Central Hot Tub	Credit Cards: VMD	Gunnison CO 81230-0853
Central Campfire Area	Rates: $25-$65	800/617-4671
	Open: 5/1 to 11/30	970/641-4671 & Fax
		www.coloradodirectory.com/ferrosbluemesa/

At the resort:

At resort or within 15 minutes:

Island Acres Motel & Log Lodges

Make Island Acres Motel and Log Lodges your base for exploring beautiful Gunnison County. Stay in one of the 20 motel rooms or pick one of the two log lodges for your vacation. Most units are equipped with kitchenettes and all have dial-out phones, HBO and cable television. One- and two-bedroom units are available with double or queen beds. The motel and lodges are located between two bridges on an island formed by the Gunnison River. The four acres of grounds provide ample room for children to play safely on the beautiful tree lined lawn.

Step right outside your door to fish on the Gunnison River. Blue Mesa Reservoir, a short drive away, is another popular fishing hole for anglers of all ages. This area has become a mecca for mountain bikers and with good reason as there are many spectacular trails to explore. Other activities include golfing, four-wheel driving, river rafting, and horseback riding. If vacationing during the winter, ask about the ski packages and Crested Butte Mountain Resort which is only 40 minutes away. Come back after your day of fun for a pleasant walk along shaded country roads that begin at the motel. Or barbecue your day's catch under the shade of mature cottonwood and pine trees.

Small dogs are welcomed to accompany you if arrangements are made in advance. Some non-smoking units are available.

Location: West of Gunnison on Highway 50.

16 Cabins with Kitchen	Phone in Rooms	Gwyn & Jaena Howells, Owner
6 Motel Rooms	Some Units Nonsmoking	38339 W Hwy 50
	Elevation: 7800	Gunnison CO 81230
	Credit Cards: VMD	970/641-1442
	Rates: $35-$52	www.coloradodirectory.com/islandacreslodge/
	Open: All Year	

At the resort:

At resort or within 15 minutes:

Lake Fork Resort

Lake Fork Resort rests on the Blue Mesa Reservoir between Gunnison and Montrose. The six new housekeeping cabins are on 35 acres overlooking the impressive lake. The beautiful, one bedroom cabins have queen log beds, and are equipped with full kitchens with utensils and appliances, living areas and private bathrooms. Children or additional guests will be comfortable on the queen pull-down bed in the main living area. Also included are daily maid service and linens. Continental breakfast is served to all guests. Relax on your front porch and enjoy views of the Blue Mesa Lake and Black Mesa.

The new social area with a patio overlooking the lake also has a meeting room with a fireplace and television, and a convenience grocery store. A volleyball court, horseshoes, croquet field and a children's playground are located on site for your enjoyment. Free videos, fax, copy machine and modem service are available. The resort is surrounded by Gunnison National Forest and Curecanti National Recreation Center. With so much open space to enjoy, the activities are limitless — from hiking, mountain biking and fishing to water skiing, sailing, river rafting and horseback riding. Come in the fall to hunt or the winter to downhill and cross country ski, ice fish and snowmobile.

Vacation fun packages for horseback riding, mountain biking, fishing, water skiing, boating and snowmobiling are available for all seasons. Ask about the

group discounts. This is a non-smoking resort and kennels can be arranged for pets.

Location: West of Gunnison on Highway 50 about 22 miles, turn left after Lake Fork bridge onto Cove Road, take first right.

6 Cabins with Kitchen	Phone in Lobby	Carla & David Alley, Owners
Central Fireplace	Bed & Breakfast Available	PO Box 1807
Central Campfire Area	All Units Nonsmoking	Gunnison CO 81230
	Recreation Room	800/368-9421
	Elevation: 7300	970/641-3564
	Credit Cards: VMAD	Fax: 970/641-0623
	Rates: $75-$125	www.coloradodirectory.com/lakeforkresort/
	Open: All Year	

At the resort:

At resort or within 15 minutes:

Ley-Z-B at Sapinero

Located 25 miles off the highway west of Gunnison, Ley-Z-B is on the Blue Mesa Reservoir. The six rental cabins offer rustic charm. A shower house is available. Linens are not supplied unless requested so bring your pillows, towels and sleeping bags for those cold nights, also bring your cookware and eating utensils. The cabins are heated. The two-bedroom cabin has a kitchen and sleeps up to six.

Ley-Z-B has a cafe serving all meals, bar and gas station with groceries, fishing tackle, and licenses for sale. They're famous for their "All You Can Eat" western barbecues on Saturday nights from Memorial Day to Labor Day. The Blue Mesa Reservoir has over 70 miles of shoreline, more than 30 streams, and is one of Colorado's largest lakes. Stocked with hundreds of thousands of trout and salmon, Blue Mesa is a favorite fishing hole from both bank and boat. Fish for kokanee, brook, lake, rainbow, cutthroat and brown trout. Many come to the reservoir to windsurf, water-ski and ice fish as well. Minutes away from Ley-Z-B are boat and jetski rentals, horseback riding stables, boat tours of the stunning Black Canyon and many breath-taking sights. Hunters also favor this area because nearby West Elk Wilderness, Gunnison National Forest and the Uncompahgre forest offer abundant trophy elk and deer. The same barbecue special is offered during the rifle season on Wednesday nights.

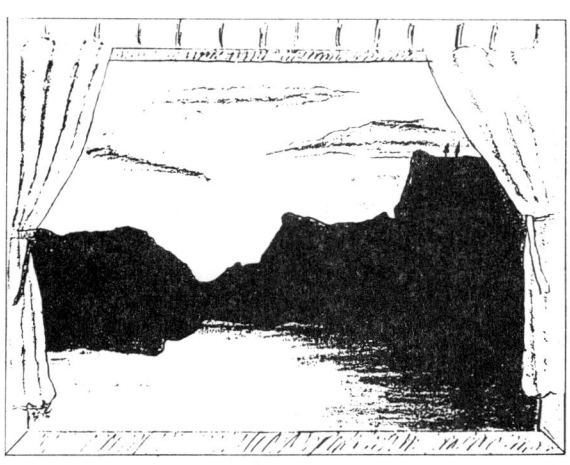

RV sites are also available. Pets are allowed. Formerly known as Sapinero Trading Post.

Location: East of the junction of Highway 92 and Highway 50. On Highway 50 near milepost marker 133.

6 Cabins with Kitchen	Pay Phone Available	Leysa & Alan Brown, & Natalie & Ken
1 Room with Woodstove	Recreation Room	Zaelit, Owners
Central Woodstove	Elevation: 7300	16020 Hwy 50 West
	Credit Cards: VM	Sapinero CO 81247
	Rates: $25-$50	970/641-2340
	Open: All to Year	E-mail: leysab@westelk.com
		www.coloradodirectory.com/leyzb/

At the resort:

At resort or within 15 minutes:

Lost Canyon Resort

Lost Canyon Resort is on a beautiful 10 acres, in a peaceful and grassy setting, with a quarter mile of frontage on the Gunnison River. The log cabins are modern and fully equipped with private bathrooms and kitchens with ranges, refrigerators, dishes and cookware. The accommodations can sleep up to eight people. All bed linens, blankets, soap and towels are supplied. Many cabins feature fireplaces or wood stoves. A fishing and hunting camp environment, come here to really get away from the hustle and bustle of the city; the old style resort's cabins have no televisions or telephones!

Central Gunnison country is ideal for hunting, skiing and fishing. Lost Canyon Resort is the only resort located on the Gold Medal Regulation sectoin of the Upper Gunnison River and is close to three reservoirs, as well as many other smaller rivers and streams. Downhill or cross-country ski at Crested Butte ski area, only 20 miles away.

Open all year Lost Canyon Resort really lets you get away from it all. There is no RV parking or store to disturb the quiet. Pets are allowed here. Ask about the attractive ski packages at Crested Butte ski area.

Location: Eight miles north of Gunnison, just east of Highway 135, near milepost marker 8.

17 Cabins with Kitchen	Phone in Lobby	Max & Michelle & Bob & Catherine
5 Rooms with Fireplaces	Elevation: 8000	Reinhardt
4 Rooms with Wood Stoves	Credit Cards: VM	8264 Hwy 135
Central Campfire Area	Rates: $64-$89	Gunnison CO 81230-9620
	Open: All Year	970/641-0181
		www.coloradodirectory.com/lostcanyonresort/

At the resort:

At resort or within 15 minutes:

Rainbow Lake Lodge & Outfitters

Accessible only by horse or four wheel drive, Rainbow Lake Lodge offers a unique vacation opportunity and is specially tailored for hunters. The three cabins have no kitchen, but are equipped with wood burning stoves.

Hike right from your cabin into the West Elk Wilderness area. New riders are welcomed and learn on gentle, mountain horses. Day horseback riding trips range from an hour to all day — take your pick. After a day of mountain fun, gather around the campfire to share your stories. Pack trips of two or more days include horseback riding, fishing, camping, sightseeing and photography of the unforgettable vistas. Rainbow Lake Lodge specializes in big game hunting. Guided hunts from the lodge in the fall include archery and muzzleloader for deer and elk. Unguided hunts also include deer, elk, bighorn sheep and goats. Call the lodge for more details.

Rates include horse, three meals daily and lodging. Guests may bring their own horses.

Location: Nine miles west of Gunnison at the edge of West Elk Wilderness Area. 100 yards west of the junction of Highways 50 & 149 . North on County Road 20 (Steuban Creek Road) after 1mile take righ fork, then 2 hours on horse or four wheel Drive.

3 Cabins without Kitchens	Phone in Lobby	Don Steenbergen & Aetna Goodner,
3 Rooms with Wood Stoves	Elevation: 10000	Managers
Central Campfire Area	Credit Cards: None	1708 CR 20
	Rates: $200	Gunnison CO 81230
	Open: 7/1 to 11/15	970/641-0057
		www.coloradodirectory.com/rainbowlakelodge

At the resort:

At resort or within 15 minutes:

Rockey River Resort

Homesteaded in 1892, Rockey River Resort features old and new log cabins among cottonwood trees along the steady flow of the Gunnison River. The cabins have fully equipped kitchens and bathrooms. All blankets, bed linens, towels, cooking utensils, dishes and flatware are provided. You'll find modern comfort in a rustic atmosphere here.

The abundant beauty of this country is unmatched. All of nature's colors in rocks and mountain flowers are displayed throughout the many scenic circle trips designed for your enjoyment. Check out a bit of history in the numerous ghost towns, old mines and relics of a by-gone era. If you're more interested in sports, the resort is within easy access to hunting, lake fishing, skiing, whitewater rafting and horseback riding. Fish along almost a half-mile of privately owned river front-age of the churning Gunnison or try lake fishing at nearby Taylor, Spring Creek and Blue Mesa Reservoirs. The playground, with volleyball, basketball, horseshoes, and badminton will keep the children entertained while you prepare a meal of freshly caught trout. The library has books for all ages.

RV sites near the Gunnison River are also available.

Location: Six miles north of town, a half miles east of Highway 135, near milepost marker 6.

14 Cabins with Kitchen	Pay Phone Available	Rob & Dani Wattles, Owners
5 Rooms with Fireplaces	Recreation Room	4359 CR 10
3 Rooms with Wood Stoves	Elevation: 7860	Gunnison CO 81230-9606
Central Woodstove	Credit Cards: VMA	970/641-0174
	Rates: $59-$97	www.coloradodirectory.com/rockeyriverresort/
	Open: All Year	

At the resort:

At resort or within 15 minutes:

Shady Island Resort, Cabins & RV Park

Stay mere feet from the banks of the Gunnison River at Shady Island Resort. The housekeeping cabins range in size from one-room cabins to a large three-bedroom vacation home, with a living room, dining room and kitchen. All cabins have a shower or tub and a kitchen or kitchenette. Some include free standing wood burning stoves. At night, the only sounds you'll hear are the steady gurgle of the river and the wind in the trees. In the morning watch the trout jump for breakfast on the river.

Send the kids off to play badminton, horseshoes and volleyball while you relax in the shade. Ask your hosts about organized raft trips leaving from the resort and tubing on the Gunnison River. Shady Island Resort is conveniently close to Gunnison, within 2 miles of a shopping center, service station and laundromat. Enjoy fishing the Gunnison River or on many of the other nearby lakes and streams. Guest horses are permitted or rent one at local stables. Area activities include four-wheel driving, hiking and mountain biking.

RV sites are also available.

Location: Highway 135, two and a half miles north of Gunnison, near milepost marker 3.

10 Cabins with Kitchen	Pay Phone Available	Jerry & Becky Griffith, Managers
1 Vacation Home	Recreation Room	2776 N Hwy 135
3 Rooms with Wood Stoves	Elevation: 7700	Gunnison CO 81230-9705
	Credit Cards: VMAD	970/641-0416
	Rates: $40-$95	Fax: 970/641-1570
	Open: 5/1 to 11/15	E-mail: siresort@youngminds.com
		www.coloradodirectory.com/shadyislandresort/

At the resort:

At resort or within 15 minutes:

Silent Spring Resort

Silent Springs Resort is a small, unique, yet quaint resort close to all the outdoor activities in the Gunnison area. Choose from two rustic-style, fully modern log cabins with fireplaces or woodstoves, new log-sided cabins with bright interiors and redwood decks. The cabins are located in beautiful Spring Creek Canyon and are surrounded by national forest. Discover quiet, peace and privacy in this secluded but comfortable setting. Both restored log cabins sleeps four, one has a large stone fireplace, while the other includes a wood burning stove. Firewood is provided at no extra cost. The two new cabins sleep four to six with a queen bed, a queen sofa sleeper and a sleeping loft for the kids. Recent improvements include newly remodeled cabin interiors, new paint, and some have satellite television. All cabins come with bedding, towels, well equipped kitchens with cooking and eating utensils, new refrigerators, gas stoves, bathtubs and showers.

A laundromat is conveniently on-site. Try the excellent fishing on Spring Creek, the Taylor River and other reservoirs and streams close by. Take raft trips, horseback or bike rides, hayrides and pack trips from nearby Harmel's ranch. Golf on two 18-hole courses just 30 minutes away. Shop in nearby Crested Butte or Gunnison.

Small pets are accepted. The hosts prefers to rent by the week or month, but require at least a two night stay.

Location: Eighteen miles north of Gunnison on Highway 135, near milepost marker10. Turn east at Almont on Taylor River Road (County Road 742) to Harmel's; then go 1 mile up Spring Creek Road (County Road 744).

4 Cabins with Kitchen	All Units Nonsmoking	Ron Watson, Owner
1 Room with Fireplace	Elevation: 8453	905 CR 744
1 Room with Woodstove	Credit Cards: None	Almont CO 81210
Central Campfire Area	Rates: $50-$90	800/920-1995 code 01
	Open: 4/15 to 11/15	970/641-0583
		Fax: 970/641-5524
		E-mail: rwatson@youngminds.com
		www.coloradodirectory.com/silentspgresort/

At the resort:

At resort or within 15 minutes:

Three Rivers Resort & Outfitting

Named for the Taylor, East and Gunnison rivers in the heart of Gunnison National Forest, Three Rivers Resort features private, rustic and modern riverfront cabins with fully equipped kitchens, bathrooms, and showers. All cabins have a stove, refrigerator, dishes, utensils, linens, bedding, pots and pans for light housekeeping. Some cabins have fireplaces, woodstoves, and full baths. Sit next to the Taylor River and exchange tales about the one that *didn't* get away!

The indoor pavilion can accommodate up to 100 people and has a pool table, foosball and many other table games. It's perfect for large family reunions. Other on-site facilities include a general store, laundromat, professional fly, tackle, kayak, and paddle shop. Sample the grill and deli at the outdoor dining patio. In the summer, participate in resort-sponsored activities such as square dances, bingo and potlucks. The resort also offers mild or wild raft trips and inflatable kayak trips. Raft down scenic Taylor Canyon or combine a raft trip with fishing to access those deep pools only accessible by boat. Hike in the national forest where you'll discover bubbling streams, clear alpine lakes, delicate wildflowers, colorful geologic formations, dense forests and a variety of wildlife in abundance.

Full hookups RV and tenet sites with campfire pits, concrete patios, picnic tables, and dump station are also available. Pets must be declared and registered when making your reservation.

Location: Ten miles north of Gunnison in Almont, take Highway 135 to milepost marker 10, turn right up Taylor Canyon Road (County Road 742) 0.20 mile.

27 Cabins with Kitchen	Pay Phone Available	Mark & Mary Jo Schumacher, Owners
6 Rooms with Fireplaces	Recreation Room	PO Box 339
8 Rooms with Wood Stoves	Elevation: 8000	Almont CO 81210-0339
Central Campfire Area	Credit Cards: VMAD	888/761-FISH (3474)
	Rates: $35-$120	970/641-1303
	Open: All Year	Fax: 970/641-1317
		E-mail: email@3riversresort.com
		www.coloradodirectory.com/3riverresort/

At the resort:

At resort or within 15 minutes:

White Pine Guest Ranch and B&B

Set on 938 acres of rolling meadows, White Pines Guest Ranch is surrounded by aspen groves, timbered forests and spring-fed brooks. Within in view of the picturesque ranch house is the pristine beauty of the remote Gunnison National Forest. Enjoy clean air and mountain living from four large, luxuriously appointed guest rooms with stunning views. Each room has a private entrance, bath, deck, and color cable television with VCRs available. All rooms are non-smoking. Because the ranch accommodates only up to 14 people, White Pine offers an intimate atmosphere and personalized service. Here you'll discover the feel of a New England country inn with all the amenities of a Rocky Mountain guest ranch.

White Pine Ranch offers a choice between bed and breakfast or the full American plan, with all gourmet country meals provided. Other amenities include a bar, meeting room, recreation room and a hot springs. Before dinner, be sure to spend a few minutes relaxing in front of the ranch's huge stone fireplace. And what better way to end your day of outdoor fun than a relaxing soak in the Jacuzzi? The ranch offers four wheel drive tours and horseback rides. In addition to fishing in the numerous ponds and brooks, and the meadows waiting to be explored, you can bike, cross-country ski, snowshoe and snowmobile on nearby trails. In the winter, guests may ice skate on the ranch's frozen ponds. Downhill skiing is only 30 minutes away. In the summer, try white water rafting, golfing or visiting the local museum — all within a short drive.

Ask about the special, downhill ski packages and honeymoon specials. Catered meals are available with advance arrangements. Both wedding planning services and area activity planning services are available on site.

Location: Twenty-seven miles east of Gunnison, till milepost marker 176, then north on Country Road 887 for 8 miles on the right.

4 Lodging Rooms	Phone in Lobby	Kyle & Cheryl Penn, Managers
Central Hot Tub	Bed & Breakfast Available	7500 CR 887
Central Fireplace	All Units Nonsmoking	Gunnison CO 81230
Central Campfire Area	Recreation Room	888/700-PINE (7463)
	Elevation: 9200	970/641-6410
	Credit Cards: VMA	Fax: 970/641-3876
	Rates: $95	E-mail: WHITEPINERANCH@youngminds.com
	Open: All Year	www.coloradodirectory.com/whitepineranch

At the resort:

At resort or within 15 minutes:

Hot Sulphur Springs

Including Parshall — Map: D-12, E-12

Hot Sulphur Springs derived its names from the hot mineral waters that seep from the hillside above the Colorado River. The town site was first platted in early 1860 by a Cherry Creek entrepreneur to develop as a vacation spa. A vacation at Hot Sulphur Springs is a step into the past. Grand County is encompassed by the Continental Divide and syncopated mountain peaks. Wide, sheltered meadows and forested hills brought Ute and Arapaho tribes here 9,000 years ago, followed by French trappers. Come see for yourself why this area remains a mecca for outdoor lovers and home to some of Colorado's oldest cattle ranches. Angler's will enjoy trout fishing along the five miles of public access on the Colorado River. Hot Sulphur Springs boasts a newly refurbished hot springs that is sure to soothe your spirit after a day of fun in the sun. Within an easy drive is the ski resorts of Berthoud Pass, Silver Creek and Winter Park and the charming town of Grand Lake, near the western entrance to Rocky Mountain National Park.

Fun Things to Do

- Grand County Museum (970) 725-3939
- Hot Sulphur Springs Spa (800) 332-3381
- Sulphur Ranger District (970) 887-4100

Bridges' Stagecoach Country Inn

This historic country inn was established in 1874 and offers mountain views to soothe your soul. Bridges' Stagecoach Country Inn has 14 bedrooms, most with private baths. The rooms are decorated with antique style beds and furniture to match the inn's turn-of-the-century charm. Each room has a 30-channel color television. You'll start each day with a specially prepared, full course breakfast.

The inn is on the banks of the Colorado River where fishing opportunities abound for anglers. Area activities include cross country skiing, snowshoeing, horseback riding, fishing, hiking, biking and golfing. Soaking in the hot mineral springs in town. Winter Park and Silver Creek ski resorts are within a 30 minute drive. In addition to skiing, these resorts offer year-round activities such as concerts and hot air balloon festivals. Wildlife abounds here and you might see deer, elk or a red fox strolling past the inn. Be sure to end your day with a soak in the inn's outdoor hot tub before relaxing in the inn's spacious parlor.

Inquire about the group rates for family reunions and conferences. Singles, couples and families are all welcome. All units are non-smoking.

Location: Ten miles west of Grand Lake. Take US Highway 40 into Hot Sulphur Springs, turn right on Aspen Street, drive two blocks, on the corner of Aspen and Nevava Street.

14 Lodging Rooms	Phone in Lobby	Kathy & Lou Bridges, Owners
Central Hot Tub	Bed & Breakfast Available	PO Box 71
Central Fireplace	All Units Nonsmoking	Hot Sulphur Springs CO 80451-0071
	Recreation Room	800/725-3919
	Elevation: 7680	970/725-3910
	Credit Cards: VM	Fax: 970/725-0141
	Rates: $59-$74	E-mail: stagecoach@rkymtnhi.com
	Open: All Year	www.coloradodirectory.com/bridgesbb

At the resort:

At resort or within 15 minutes:

Casa Milagro Bed & Breakfast

Escape your fast-paced life and discover relaxation at this hideaway by the river among the pine trees. Casa Milagro Bed & Breakfast has three rooms, each with queen beds, down pillows and comforters, private baths and TV with VCR (a 300 movie collection is available). Stephanie's Mountain Room on the main floor has log walls, eclectic furniture, southwest art, a gas fireplace, and views of the trees. The reading chairs are perfect for an afternoon of relaxing. You may catch sight of the many varieties of birds and an occasional fox outside the window. Dorothy's River Room on the lower deck level has a screened in porchoverlooking the river. Lounge on the deck or curl up in one of the comfortable chairs. Log, rattan furnishings and southwestern arts give this room a special mountain flavor. Anthony & Kris' Suite has a private enterance, large outdoor living room on the deck, a full kitchen, queen bed, fireplace, private bath and large comfortable leather chairs. Included with all the rooms are robes, slippers, coffee makers, a large variety if tea, coca, a tape player with a selection of tapes.

Breakfast consists of delicious southwestern style food. With advance notice, a dinner may be prepared for you (extra charge). Restaurants in town just a short drive away. Situated on the Williams Fork River, Casa Milagro is just 26 miles northeast of Silverthorne on Ute Pass Road and 45 minutes from Grand Lake, Winter Park, and Keystone — all great places to snowmobile, alpine and cross-country ski. In the summer, hike, fish, bike, golf, horseback ride and explore.

This is a non-smoking resort. The host has two cats, so no pets are allowed. Well supervised, older children are welcome. Horses are welcomed in the stables. Ask about the numerous special packages offered.

Location: 13 miles south of Parshall on Highway 40.

3 Lodging Rooms	Phone in Lobby	Lynn & Paul Schmaltz, Owners
3 Rooms with Fireplaces	Bed & Breakfast Available	13628 CR 3
Central Hot Tub	All Units Nonsmoking	Parshall CO 80468
Central Fireplace	Recreation Room	888/632-8955
	Elevation: 8400	970/725-3640
	Credit Cards: VMAD	Fax: 970/725-3617
	Rates: $115-$185	E-mail: casamilagro@rkymtnhi.com
	Open: All Year	www.coloradodirectory.com/casabb/

At the resort:

At resort or within 15 minutes:

Hot Sulphur Springs Resort and Spa

This resort has just been renovated and offers 17 hot mineral spring pools and baths, a 17 rooms motel and a complete 12 room spa. Decor is western log furniture. This is a quiet, relaxing, health-oriented facility which will leave you feeling relaxed, renewed and invigorated.

While staying here, you can enjoy all the natural hot mineral springs, pools and private baths including outdoor pools and a solarium pool. ,Massages, facials and body wraps are offered by appointment. Take a dip in the new jet spa and the outdoor oriental bath. Relax on the several sun decks after enjoying a swim in the summer pool which is open May through October. There are pools for adults and kids as well as adult-only pools. A conference room and snack bar serving gourmet pizza, soups and fresh fruit smoothies are also located here. Hot Sulphur Springs Resort is near skiing, snowmobiling, hunting, fishing, mountain biking and hiking. Or you can stay here and explore the 60 scenic acres, watch the trains or just relax.

This is a non-smoking, drinking and drug facility. No pets, please. Kids under six are free. RV parking is one minute away on the Colorado River

Location: Two hours northwest of Denver on Highway 40.

The All New

HOT SULPHUR SPRINGS

RESORT and SPA

...SINCE 1864

17 Motel Rooms	Pay Phone Available	Charles Nash, Owner
Central Hot Tub	All Units Nonsmoking	PO Box 275
Central Fireplace	Elevation: 7670	Hot Sulphur Springs CO 80451-0275
	Credit Cards: VM	800/510-6235
	Rates: $82-$105	970/725-3306
	Open: All Year	Fax: 970/725-3206
		E-mail: HotSprings@rkymtnhi.com
		www.coloradodirectory.com/hotsulphurspringsresort

At the resort:

At resort or within 15 minutes:

Lake City

Map: M-7

Lake City is home to several 14,000' mountain peaks: Uncompahgre, Sunshine, Handies, Red Cloud and Wetterhorn. Tucked into the grassy canyon where Henson Creek and the Lake Fork of the Gunnison River meet, Lake City is a state secret. Hike in any of the four national forests (600,000 acres) that surround this small town. The Alpine Scenic Loop Backcountry Byway begins in town and runs through Ouray and then on to Silverton on 65 miles of dirt and gravel roads. The backcountry byway has some of the most stunning four wheel driving in the world! The Silver Thread Historic Byway (Highway 149) ribbons through the communities of South Fork, Creede and Lake City in the San Juan Mountains, once a toll road and stage route for miners, is a 75 mile paved highway. Try boating on spectacular Lake San Cristobal, Colorado's 2nd largest natural lake — approximately 350 acres. Fish for rainbow trout in the swirling Lake Fork River or explore the Victorian charm of downtown with over 75 buildings from the late 1800s — one of Colorado's largest historical districts. Lake City's history is pretty mild compared to the more notorious mining towns. But one story just won't die: Alferd Packer. In 1874, Packer convinced some prospectors to let him guide them through the snow-covered mountains. Six weeks later, he appeared 76 miles to the northeast alone with a beard and long hair. He claimed to have survived on roots and berries but the truth soon came out and Packer was accused of murder and cannibalism. He was sentenced to hang in 1883 at Lake City's courthouse but Packer got off on a legality and ended up only serving 14 years. Every September, Lake City remembers its famous cannibal with the Annual Alferd Packer Jeep Tour and Barbecue!

Fun Things to Do

- Hinsdale County Museum (970) 944-9515
- Lakeview Boat Rentals & Outfitters (800) 456-0170
- National Historic District (970) 944-2527
- Rocky Mountain Jeep Rental (970) 944-2262

Lake City Resort

Let Lake City Resort be your "home away from home" in the middle of the majestic San Juan Mountains. The six modern, housekeeping cottages sleep two to five people. The two efficiency suites accommodate two people. All units are carpeted and have queen sized beds, color cable television, a kitchen and a tub-shower bath. Towels and linens are provided.

Located on the quiet, south end of town, Lake City Resort is close to everything. Restaurants, evening entertainment, four wheel drive rentals and tours, fishing, whitewater raft trips, museums and mountain bike trails are all within five minutes of the resort. Within 10 minutes are horseback rides, hunting guides and the lake where you can fish to your heart's content.

Ask about the 10 percent discounts for stays longer than 10 days, and the 15 percent discount for stays longer than 21 days. All units are non-smoking. Pets are allowed for a fee with advanced arrangements.

Location: Three blocks south of downtown Lake City, between Hall Realty and Cannibal Outdoors on South Gunnison Avenue.

8 Cabins with Kitchen	Phone in Lobby	Dave & Joan Roberts, Owners
Central Campfire Area	All Units Nonsmoking	PO Box 699
	Elevation: 8600	Lake City CO 81235-0699
	Credit Cards: VMD	970/944-2866
	Rates: $54-$84	www.coloradodirectory.com/lakecityresort
	Open: 5/15 to 10/1	

At the resort:

At resort or within 15 minutes:

Lakeview Resort, Cabins, Suites, Lodge Rooms & Outfitters

Lakeview resort offers what Colorado used to be — few people, deep blue lakes, bubbling streams, mountain peaks, dusty ghost towns and high mountain passes. A family resort on the shores of Colorado's second largest and one of the most beautiful natural lakes, the park has mountain cabins in the pine trees adjacent to a lodge and marina on Lake San Cristobal. The cabins have kitchenettes, living areas, woodburning stoves or fireplaces, private baths and one to three bedrooms. The cabins sleep from three to nine people depending upon the accommodation. The lodge suites have kitchenettes, living areas, private baths and an extra-large bedroom with a queen and double bed. Lodge rooms sleeping up to four people are also available. All rooms are non-smoking.

The resort boasts fishing and pontoon boats for rent, guided fishing trips, horseback riding, and sunset supper rides. The resort's outfitting service offers a variety of hunts in Colorado (CO Lic #939) and Montana (MT Lic #6299). Combine horses and fishing on high mountain rides to alpine lakes and streams where the trout are the freshest! In one of the last real wildernesses Colorado has to offer, you'll likely see elk, deer, coyotes, rabbits and numerous other wildlife. Here bald eagles soar over towering peaks and bright wildflowers dot lush meadows where babbling brooks hide rainbow trout.

RV sites are available. Ask about the complete facilities for groups, seminars and family reunions. If you're over 55 ask about their Elderhostel. Pets on a leash are allowed with a per day fee.

Location: On Highway 149, near milepost marker 70, Turn south on County Road 33 and drive half a mile.

10 Cabins with Kitchen	Pay Phone Available	Tom & Midge & Dan & Michelle Murphy
10 Lodging Rooms	All Units Nonsmoking	PO Box 1000
10 Motel Rooms	Recreation Room	Lake City CO 81235-1000
3 Rooms with Fireplaces	Elevation: 9000	800/456-0170
7 Rooms with Wood	Credit Cards: VM	970/944-2401
Stoveswith Wood Stoves	Rates: $55-$125	Fax: 970/944-2925
Central Campfire Area	Open: 5/1 to 10/1	E-mail: murphy@lakeview-inc.com
		www.coloradodirectory.com/lakeviewresort/

At the resort:

At resort or within 15 minutes:

Matterhorn Mountain Lodge & Cabins

You'll enjoy the views from the Matterhorn Mountain Lodge & Cabins in its quiet, mountainside location, yet only two blocks from the heart of historic Lake City. This "40s lodge" has undergone extensive renovation and redecoration for your comfort and convenience. Yet the Matterhorn Mountain Lodge & Cabins retains the elegance, charm and hospitality of an era past. Two housekeeping cabins and 12 motel rooms are available. The accommodations are clean and comfortable. Most units have fully furnished kitchenettes and cable television.

Scenic mountain tours are available and leave right from the lodge to take you on unforgettable high mountain adventures on the Alpine Loop Back Country Byway. You'll travel up to 12,800 feet over Cinnamon and Engineer passes to follow the footsteps of settlers and miners who once traversed the mountains. A knowledgeable guide will share the fascinating history of bygone days of the mining boom in this area. Be sure to bring your camera along for the panoramic views. Within minutes of the resort, anglers of all expertise levels will find plenty of cold, clear, flowing streams, beaver ponds and high alpine lakes. Hike into the San Juan Mountains to experience unspoiled, back country scenery. To catch a

glimpse of Lake City's past, visit the Hindsdale Country Museum or take a walking tour among the Victorian homes dating from the 1800s.

The Lodge is a non-smoking facility.

Location: Two blocks from the Lake City Historic District.

2 Cabins with Kitchen	Pay Phone Available	Candy & David Beebe, Hosts
6 Lodging Rooms	All Units Nonsmoking	PO Box 603
6 Motel Rooms	Elevation: 8684	Lake City CO 81235-0603
	Credit Cards: VMD	800/779-8028
	Rates: $55-$65	970/944-2210
	Open: All Year	Fax: 970/944-2267
		www.coloradodirectory.com/matterhorncabins/

At the resort:

At resort or within 15 minutes:

Ox-Yoke Riverside Resort-The River Runs Through It

This resort of 12 housekeeping cabins is in a picturesque mountain setting with cabins nestled along the crystal waters of Lake Fork/Gunnison River. The one- and two-bedroom cabins are spacious, comfortable and clean. Each is fully equipped with cable television, picnic tables, grills and campfires. All cabins face the river.

Located on the recreational and scenic Alpine Loop. From Ox-Yoke, walk to town and explore the intriguing history of Lake City. You can both fish and river raft right from the resort. Area activities include lake and river fly fishing, four wheel driving to ghost towns, hiking, climbing and mountain biking to scenic vistas. You can also go on four wheel drive tours, horseback riding tours or rent boats to take on the lake's pristine waters. Ox-Yoke is open from May through September. The opportunities for photography and observing wildlife are unlimited no matter the activity you undertake.

This is a non-smoking facility. No pets.

Location: On Highway 149, near milepost marker marker 71.

12 Cabins with Kitchen
Central Campfire Area

Phone in Lobby
All Units Nonsmoking
Elevation: 9000
Credit Cards: VM
Rates: $65-$80
Open: 5/15 to 10/1

Sam & Sherry Elrod, Owners
PO Box 97
Lake City CO 81235-0097
970/944-2252
www.coloradodirectory.com/oxyokeresort/

At the resort: *At resort or within 15 minutes:*

Pleasant View Resort & Rocky Mountain Jeep Rental

Come discover a stress-free, laid back environment with the wide open spaces of Pleasant View Resort. Owned by the same hosts since 1971, the completely modern and fully equipped housekeeping cabins with queen sized beds and color cable television (Disney and assorted movie and sports channels) are at the south end of town. The wood paneled walls and cowboy furniture will remind you of days gone by. Nine of the cabins have cooking facilities. Barbecue supper on the grills provided and watch the spectacular sunsets over the mountains from your front porch. Large groups are welcomed to congregate for campfires at the community firepit where firewood is provided.

There is a large playground for children with swings, a playhouse, tether ball, horseshoes and more. The large lawn is perfect for a friendly game of tag or an impromptu baseball game. Pleasant View is within easy walking distance of shops and restaurants. Explore the hiking trails staring at your doorstep or climb any of the five 14,000-foot mountains in the area: Uncompahgre, Sunshine, Handies, Red Cloud and Wetterhorn. Rent a new jeep on-site for a scenic ride through the beautiful San Juan Mountains. Be sure to check out the Alpine Scenic Back Country Byway. For those who want the scenery, but not the four wheel drive, try a trip down the paved Silver Thread Historic Byway for a picturesque, 75-mile tour. Minute away are rivers to fish and whitewater raft, horses to ride, museums to

explore, and lakes to boat upon. Visit Silverton, Ouray or the old abandoned mining town of Carson.

No pets are allowed.

Location: On South Gunnison.

9 Cabins with Kitchen	Phone in Lobby	Juanell & Jim Skinner, Owner
Central Campfire Area	Some Units Nonsmoking	PO Box 174
	Elevation: 8671	Lake City CO 81235-0174
	Credit Cards: VMD	970/944-2262
	Rates: $75	Fax: 970/944-2275
	Open: 5/1 to 10/31	www.coloradodirectory.com/pleasantviewresort

At the resort:

At resort or within 15 minutes:

Texan Resort Cabins

Established in 1946 on the banks of the Lake Fork of the Gunnison River, this resort features a 65-foot waterfall and a landscaped river's edge. The comfortable log cabins are set in a wooded hollow among tall spruce, fir, aspen and cottonwood trees. Surrounded by large green lawns, all of the cabins have modern plumbing with showers or tubs and completely equipped kitchens. Some have fireplaces. You might enjoy requesting their large, Scandinavian style log cabin. Your hosts supply all linens and towels. There are several barbecue areas to grill your favorite meal.

Enjoy the traditional, resort-sponsored Thursday night cookouts. By mid summer the many flower beds are a riot of color. Fishing is a year round sport here. Four-wheeling on hundreds of miles of old 1890s mining trails takes you to exciting new vistas and remote fishing locations. Lake San Cristobal is just 2.5 miles from your door, while dozens of other smaller lakes are nearby.

Texan Resort Cabins has many loyal, repeat customers so reserve early for your vacation.

Location: Highway 149, near milepost marker 71. South of Lake City on County Road 142.

16 Cabins with Kitchen	Pay Phone Available	Steve & Gayle Meredith, Owners
3 Vacation Homes	All Units Nonsmoking	PO Box 156
5 Rooms with Fireplaces	Elevation: 8671	Lake City CO 81235-0156
Central Woodstove	Credit Cards: None	970/944-2246
Central Campfire Area	Rates: $48-$110	www.coloradodirectory.com/texanresort/
	Open: All Year	

At the resort:

At resort or within 15 minutes:

Woodlake Park Cabins & Campground

Near the Alpine Loop Scenic Backcountry Byway, on the Silver Thread Scenic Byway and at the foot of beautiful Slumgullion Pass, Woodlake Park is adjacent to the river and far enough from town for quiet, but close enough for convenience. It has two camper cabins with a double bed and bunk bed. An outdoor grill and picnic table are provided, but you supply bedding, lantern and cooking utensils. The luxury vacation home facing the Lake Fork of the Gunnison River sleeps up to 10 in its two bedrooms and on sleeper sofas. It also boasts a full bath downstairs, a half bath upstairs, a kitchen with new appliances and a dining area. Woodlake Park is surrounded by river and mountain vistas and shaded by tall pine trees. You'll only hear the babble of the Lake Fork of the Gunnison River as it runs its course.

Get the whole family involved in the fun, organized pavilion activities such as line dancing (instruction given). There's no end to the exciting adventures this mountainous area has to offer: bird watching, fishing, hiking, hunting, mountain biking, horseback riding, Jeeping, ATVing and exploring areas of geological interest and old ghost towns. Check out historic Colorado lore at the Alferd Packer massacre site nearby.

RV camping with uncrowded, spacious sites is also available.

Location: Two and a half miles south of Lake City on Highway 149, between milepost markers 69-70.

1 Vacation Home	Pay Phone Available	Latellya Smith, Owner
2 Camper Cabins	Elevation: 9000	PO Box 400
Central Campfire Area	Credit Cards: None	Lake City CO 81235-0400
	Rates: $25-$60	800/201-2694
	Open: 6/1 to 10/1	970/944-2283
		www.coloradodirectory.com/woodlakeparkcamp/

At the resort:

At resort or within 15 minutes:

Meeker

Map: E-5

Meeker, gateway to the White River National Forest and the Flattops Wilderness (accessible only by foot or on horseback), attracts many visitors who come for the excellent fishing and hunting. The White River Forest, with one of the largest elk herds in Colorado, has 111 miles of fishable streams and 780 acres of lakes. Named for Nathan C. Meeker who arrived in 1878 to head White River Indian Agency, the town sits amidst hidden valleys, hot springs and quiet retreats which prompted Utes to call it the land of shining mountains. Meeker is still a ranching community with old brick buildings and relaxed, small-town atmosphere. In 1919, Arthur Carhart, a Forest Service landscape architect working east of Meeker, wanted to create wilderness preserves which would be conserved forever, untouched by man and civilization. His idea was the core of the 1964 Wilderness Act which was fought by most Colorado politicians. Today, however, it's the designated wilderness areas that bring a steady stream of tourists. Wildlife in Piceance Basin includes thousands of animals that pick their way through sagebrush, cedar, piñon-juniper, and douglas fir. The basin has some 1,200 elk, 350 species of wildlife, 22 species of raptors, ranging from owls to eagles, and even a wild horse herd.

Fun Things to Do

- Buford Store & Museum (970) 878-4745
- Dinosaur National Monument (970) 374-3000
- Flattops Wilderness Area (970) 878-4039
- Pollard's Outfitting & Horseback Riding (888) 414-2022
- White River Museum (970) 878-9982

Buford Hunting & Fishing Lodge and Store

On the Scenic Flat Tops Byway, Buford Lodge is adjacent to the beautiful White River in the center of the White River National Forest. Some of the rustic and modern housekeeping cabins have fireplaces or wood stoves and televisions. The cabins date back to 1908 and the new Buford White River Historical Museum, filled with a growing number of artifacts of every kind, is on the property in an 85-year-old log building. Wander among old agricultural equipment, cream separators and antique slot machines while proprietor Harry Tucker relates tales of friendly Utes and the last of the mountain men in the time honored traditional of oral history.

The on-site grocery store, which is on the National Registry of Historic Places, is stocked with sporting goods, gifts and gas. Excellent fishing and hunting abounds in White River National Forest. Buford Lodge will help arrange hunt/drop camps and provide guides to those interested in a real wilderness experience. The resort also offers women's clinics in fly fishing. Dine at the nearby restaurant, then rent a horse from the local stables and trek through the backcountry's magnificence.

Location: Twenty-two miles east of Meeker on Trappers Lake Road (County Road 8) at Buford, near milepost marker 20.

11 Cabins with Kitchen	Pay Phone Available	Harry Tucker, Owner & Betty Morlen, Manager
1 Room with Fireplace	Some Units Nonsmoking	20474 CR 8
10 Rooms with Wood Stoves	Elevation: 7000	Meeker CO 81641
	Credit Cards: VMAD	970/878-4745
	Rates: $45-$65	Fax: 970/878-4745
	Open: 5/15 to 11/15	www.coloradodirectory.com/bufordlodge/

At the resort:

At resort or within 15 minutes:

Pollard's Ute Lodge Cabins

At the quiet end of the road up the White River Valley near the Scenic Flat Tops Byway, Pollard's Ute Lodge has cabins in a secluded forest of pine and spruce trees. Prepare your favorite evening meal in a modern kitchen, then listen to the crackling fire while you relax and watch the stars. Cabins range from one to three bedroom cabins. The Spruce Cabin is a two-story, three bedroom cabin which sleeps 9 people ideal for large family or small groups. The Oak and Wild Rose Cabins are one bedroom with a bathhouse near by for the more adventuresome. Picnic during the day outside under azure skies. Some cabins and bathhouse are equipped with handicap facilities.

Pollard's has unlicensed fishing on their private, snow-fed mountain lake. Ask your hosts, licensed outfitters #502, about the experienced guides and top-quality horses that will take you to drop camps for superb fishing and hunting trips in the back country. You can mountain bike, horseback ride or hike through the Flat Tops Wilderness area and the White River National Forest. There are mountain bike trails accessible from the property. Ride your horse or take a guided horseback tour to the world's largest aspen tree grove where, in the fall, the shades of ruby red, brilliant yellow and soft amber will amaze you.

RV sites are also available. Ask about the discounts for seniors, firemen and policemen. They also offer an weekly and monthly rate. There is an additional charge for more than 2 people.

Location: Twenty-eight miles east of Meeker on County Road 8 and follow the signs.

6 Cabins with Kitchen	Phone in Lobby	Buck & Gloria Pollard, Owners
2 Cabins without Kitchens	Elevation: 8000	393 CR 75
5 Rooms with Wood Stoves	Credit Cards: VM	Meeker CO 81641
Central Campfire Area	Rates: $25-$60	888/414-2022
	Open: 5/15 to 11/15	970/878-4669
		www.coloradodirectory.com/pollardsutelodge

At the resort:

At resort or within 15 minutes:

Mesa Verde Area
Including Cortez, Dolores & Mancos — Map: O-2, O-3 & O-4

The ruins of the Anasazi, a Navajo word meaning "Ancient Ones," are what bring people to this quiet, sun-drenched area. At **Mesa Verde** National Park visitors walk among the incredible cliff dwellings of these prehistoric Pueblo people. The Anasazi culture flourished here from approximately A.D. 1 to 1300, leaving behind a priceless legacy of their achievements in the famous cliff houses and mesa top villages. The reasons the Ancient Ones abandoned the area remains an enigma, despite decades of research. At one point, more than 40,000 Anasazi lived here. A short distance south of the town of **Mancos** enroute to Weber Canyon (the eastern boundry of Mesa Verde National Park) is a new old-fashioned horse drawn stage line for your enjoyment run by the Bartels Family. Ten miles west of the park is **Cortez**, once called by the Navajo "Tsaya-toh" (rock-water) for its spring. Lowry Indian Ruins, 26 miles north of Cortez, contain the largest and best preserved painted Anasazi kivas in world. Hovenweep National Monument, 40 miles west, has its unique Anasazi ruins. Nearby is Four Corners Area Monument, located on Ute Mountain Ute and Navajo Indian reservations, the only place in the United States where four states meet. **Dolores** boasts the second largest lake in Colorado, McPhee Lake. Fish from a boat for large and small-mouth bass, blue gills and crappies. Or try the Dolores River, named by two Spanish friars in honor of "Our Lady of Sorrows," where the nutrient-rich waters are teaming with rainbow, brown, cutthroat and brook trout. This area also has excellent hunting, with an abundance of wildlife and big game. See the area's beautiful archeology in the nearby Anasazi Heritage Center which has over 2 millions artifacts, educational and participatory exhibits. Hike, jeep, or horseback ride in the San Juan National Forest, from the Dolores River Valley to 14,000-foot peaks in the Mount Wilson Primitive Area. Or take the scenic byway that goes northeast to Telluride on Highway 145 or southeast to Durango. The drive from Dolores to Telluride is especially magnificent.

Fun Things To Do
- Anasazi Heritage Center, Dolores (970) 882-4811
- Bartels' Mancos Valley Stage Line (800) 365-3530
- Conquistador Golf Course, Cortez (970) 565-9208
- Cortez/University of Colorado Center & Cultural Park (970) 565-1151
- Crow Canyon Archeological Center (800) 422-8975, (970) 565-8975
- Echo Basin Horse Rides, Rodeo Events, Snowmobiling & Restaraunt (800) 426-1890
- Galloping Goose Museum (970) 882-4018
- Hovenweep National Monument (970) 529-4465
- Lowry Indian Ruins (970) 247-4874
- Mesa Verde National Park (970) 529-4465
- San Juan National Forest, Dolores District (970) 882-7296
- Ute Mountain Casino (800)258-8007
- Ute Mountain Tribal Park (970) 565-3751

A Bed & Breakfast on Maple Street

Located in downtown Cortez, A Bed & Breakfast on Maple Street is a log and rock house where you will find a warm western welcome. The main house is decorated in a country style with plenty of antiques adding to the atmosphere. The large, airy Spruce Room has a private balcony and outside stairway access, a queen bed/daybed with popup, and shower bath. The room sleeps up to four. The Pine Room, also upstairs, is an attic-style room with a sloping ceiling, an adjoining child's room with twin bed, toys and an autograph wall. The Pine Room has a queen bed, and a romantic king size shower with a seat and two shower heads. This room takes up to three. The Aspen Room downstairs is great for a couple with its queen bed. Because there is no window, you'll have lots of peace, quiet and privacy. The dining room and parlor are just a step away and the bath is large and spacious. The Aspen Room sleeps 2 and is limited handicap accessible. The Loft, at the top of a spiral staircase, is a cozy hideaway overlooking the parlor. Great for a family, it has a queen bed, 1 twin bed, and a bath with a tub/shower lit by a skylight. The Loft sleeps up to 3 people. All rooms are air conditioned.

On the walls and around the house are momentos to recreate an earlier, more tranquil era. The garden and patio areas are perfect for weddings, anniversaries, reunions and private parties. The parlor is always available for relaxation and socializing. Enjoy evening refreshments, read a book, play games or relax in the gazebo-enclosed hot tub near the water garden. Nonnie's "Deluxe Brown Bag Lunches" are available upon request as well as a "to go breakfast". This cozy home is within walking distance to Cortez's restaurants, shops & theaters. The Native Indian Dancing is not to be missed! With spectacular Mesa Verde only 9 miles away, you'll want to include a trip to these ruins in your plans.

Ask about the romance packages. The B&B does not allow pets or smoking.

Location: In Cortez on South Maple St.

A BED & BREAKFAST on MAPLE

---

4 Lodging Rooms	Phone in Lobby	Roy & Nonnie Fahsholtz, Owners
Central Hot Tub	Bed & Breakfast Available	PO Box 327
Central Fireplace	All Units Nonsmoking	Cortez CO 81321-0327
	Recreation Room	800/665-3906
	Elevation: 6200	970/565-3906
	Credit Cards: VMAD	Fax: 970/565-2090
	Rates: $79-$99	E-mail: maple@fone.net
	Open: All Year	www.coloradodirectory.com/maple

At the resort:

At resort or within 15 minutes:

Dolores River Cabins & RV Park

In the beautiful Dolores River Valley, this park features camper cabins and house-keeping cabins. Along the Dolores River in a valley, the accommodations have bar-becue grills and firewood is available. Some cabins are shaded by trees along the tumbling river. Hot showers, clean restrooms and a coin laundry are available. Come here to simply relax.

Fish right on the river, at the pond or down the road at McPhee Reservoir. The playground is great for the kids while the adults can enjoy the game room with exercise equipment, card tables and color TV. The lounge and commercial kitchen are ideal for family reunions. Exercise your best friend at the pet walk and then exercise yourself along the picturesque river walk. Nearby, you can horseback ride, whitewater raft, golf and mountain bike. End the day with a visit to the soda fountain for a refreshing drink and snack.

Weekly and month rates are available. Groups are welcomed. Ask about the wooded and open RV and tent sites.

Location: One and a half miles east of Dolores on Highway 145 in route to Telluride.

4 Cabins with Kitchen	Pay Phone Available	Tomas & Sharon Kurpius, Owners
6 Camper Cabins	All Units Nonsmoking	18680 Hwy 145
Central Campfire Area	Recreation Room	Dolores CO 81323
	Elevation: 7000	800/200-3299
	Credit Cards: VM	970/882-7761
	Rates: $25-$69	Fax: 970/882-4829
	Open: 4/1 to 10/31	www.coloradodirectory.com/doloresriverrvparkcabins

At the resort:

At resort or within 15 minutes:

Echo Basin Dude Ranch Resort & RV Park

Formerly a working ranch on more than 600 acres, Echo Basin is lush with meadows, streams and high timber forests. The deluxe A-frame cabins with fireplaces are nestled in the forest next to the dude ranch and resort's bunk house rooms. Gather your own firewood to toss on the campfire during the cool nights. Rent cabins by the night or the week, meals included.

The Ranch has everything you need — a laundromat, a rustic, family-style restaurant, a swimming pool, hot tub and store. In between the ranch-sponsored activities like horseback rides, hayrides, weekend rodeo events and western cookouts, you can fish on the two stocked lakes or in the swift Mancos River which runs deep and fresh through the ranch. Hunting and changing colors are both wonderful in the fall. In winter snowmobile or strap on your cross-country skis and discover the snowing back country. In spring and summer, volleyball, basketball and baseball are popular activities. Venture into the San Juan National Forest on foot or by mountain bike on some spectacular trails. Be sure to see the many southwest Colorado landmarks, including Mesa Verde National Park, the Silverton/Durango rail road, the mountains around Durango and the southwestern desert.

Full hookup sites in the forest are also available. Ask about the lodge for family reunions, weddings, youth camps and company picnics.

Location: Three miles north of Highway 160, near milepost marker 59, on County Roads 44 and M (marked Echo Basin Road).

3 Cabins with Kitchen	Pay Phone Available	Dan & Kathi Bjorkman, Owners
20 Cabins without Kitchens	All Units Nonsmoking	43747 Rd M
3 Vacation Homes	Recreation Room	Mancos CO 81328-9214
40 Beds in Bunkhouse	Elevation: 7800	800/426-1890 Reserv only
Central Hot Tub	Credit Cards: VMAD	970/533-7000
Central Fireplace	Rates: $89-$169	Fax: 970/533-7800
Central Campfire Area	Open: All Year	E-mail: info@echobasin.com
		www.coloradodirectory.com/echobasinranch/

At the resort:

At resort or within 15 minutes:

Green Snow Oasis Cabins & Shop

In the heart of the San Juan Skyway, about 6 miles south of Rico on the Dolores River, you'll find log cabins that sleep four to six, with full baths, kitchens, wood-burning stoves and outdoor barbecue areas. Complete housekeeping, so bring only your own food.

Green Snow Oasis' gift shop has homemade quilts of all sizes, local crafts, Indian jewelry and antiques. Other items in stock are nostalgic prints, Mexican items, dolls, clowns, yard sale treasures, miniatures, books, cast iron bells and chimes. The Green Snow Oasis is near Telluride, Cortez, Mancos and Durango. Enjoy the excellent trout fishing nearby. Hike, mountain bike and four-wheel drive in the surrounding forests. Come visit during the hunting season! Ask your hosts about hunting trips with meals. Explore Mesa Verde National Park, the Anasazi Heritage Center, the San Juan Scenic Highway and the historic Galloping Goose Train in Dolores. Walk back in time when you visit the turn-of-the-century mining camps of Rico, Ophir, Dunton and, of course, Telluride.

Daily, weekly, monthly and seasonal rates are all available

Location: Highway 145, near milepost marker marker 40.

5 Cabins with Kitchen	Phone in Lobby	Ouida North
5 Rooms with Wood Stoves	All Units Nonsmoking	28434 Hwy 145
Central Campfire Area	Elevation: 8300	Dolores CO 81323-9715
	Credit Cards: None	970/562-3829
	Rates: $65-$75	www.coloradodirectory.com/greensnowoasiscabins
	Open: 5/15 to 11/15	

At the resort:

At resort or within 15 minutes:

Kelly Place B&B and Archæological Preserve

Kelly Place offers a unique bed and breakfast experience at Four Corners, in the heart of Anasazi (ancient Indian) country on 100 acres of red-rock canyons that includes over 25 archaeological sites! The lodge is an adobe-style building dating from the 1960s. The ten private, carpeted guest rooms have queen beds and private baths. Three cabins with kitchens are also available. All cabins are non-smoking. A satisfying hot breakfast is served daily in the guest house.

Take advantage of a chance to explore ancient history while vacationing at Kelly Place. Half and full day tours of the Anasazi ruins on the property are available. Other unique activities includes archaeological programs, Anasazi pottery reproduction, guided botany, ethno-botany and rock art hikes in addition to horseback riding. The B&B also hosts weddings, family reunions, covered wagon trips and Elder hostel programs. The whole family will enjoy the free movies in the Adobe Lodge. Come be a part of living history at Kelly Place.

Kelly Place can accommodate groups of up to 24 people. Ask about their week long educational programs.

Location: Ten miles west of Highway 160 at milepost marker 35, on County Road G.

2 Cabins with Kitchen	Pay Phone Available	Kristie & Rodney Carriker, Owners
1 Cabin without Kitchen	Bed & Breakfast Available	14663 CR G
8 Lodging Rooms	All Units Nonsmoking	Cortez CO 81321
1 Room with Hot Tub	Recreation Room	800/745-4885
1 Room with Fireplace	Elevation: 5500	970/565-3125
Central Fireplace	Credit Cards: VMD	E-mail: kellypl@fone.net
Central Woodstove	Rates: $69-$110	www.coloradodirectory.com/kellyplacebb
Central Campfire Area	Open: All Year	

At the resort:

At resort or within 15 minutes:

Laughing Coyote Lodge

Retreat to your own private, two story, seven bedroom wilderness vacation home at Laughing Coyote Lodge. The large, log cabin-type lodge accommodates up to 24 people with shared baths and kitchen privileges in a fully equipped kitchen with a microwave. Some of the lodge rooms have private baths. Individual rooms may be rented, or you can use the entire lodge for your family reunion. Also available are three new modern cabins with kitchens and shower baths. The log cabins sleep six to eight people, have handmade log queen beds and sleeping lofts with twin beds. Linens are provided in all rentals.

Near Groundhog Lake, the lodge is in the heart of the San Juan Mountains and near the Lizard Head Wilderness Area. The lodge rents horses, mountain bikes and snowmobiles on-site for your convenience. You'll be close to excellent, high county fishing. Horseback trail rides and guided hunting/fishing trips can be arranged with local outfitters with advance notice. In the winter, snowmobile to the property — if you don't have your own snowmobile, rentals can be arranged. Winter activities in the miles of open meadows and roads include snowmobiling, snowshoeing and cross country skiing. Telluride, Norwood and Dunton are popular destinations. Summer brings an abundance of recreational opportunities: hiking, mountain biking and four wheel driving. In the fall, bring your own horse for hunting in the national forest. The lodge's sauna offers the perfect way to relax after a day of fun.

Laughing Coyote Lodge specializes in group and family reunions. All units are smoke-free. No pets are allowed in the lodge. Reservations are required.

Location: Thirty-five miles northwest of Dolores & 1.7 miles east of Groundhog Reservoir on County Road 32

3 Cabins with Kitchen	Phone in Lobby	Kevin & Paulette Barlow, Owners
1 Vacation Home	All Units Nonsmoking	PO Box 893
7 Lodging Rooms	Recreation Room	Dolores CO 81323-0021
2 Rooms with Wood Stoves	Elevation: 9200	800/373-7321
Central Woodstove	Credit Cards: VMD	970/882-7321
Central Campfire Area	Rates: $65-$105	E-mail: lcoyote@fone.net
	Open: All Year	www.coloradodirectory.com/laughingcoyotelodge/

At the resort:

At resort or within 15 minutes:

Outpost Cabins, Motel & RV Park

Breathe in cool mountain air at the Outpost resort along the sparkling Dolores River. Surrounded by tall shade trees, these rustic, cozy cabins come equipped with everything including cooking utensils — housekeepers even clean daily. Motel rooms with kitchens are available and the on-site laundromat is convenient. Relax on the grassy lawn during your barbecue picnic.

Fish right from Outpost's spacious deck overlooking the Dolores River. Or try for some of the best bass and trout in Colorado at McPhee Reservoir. If fishing isn't your game, try water skiing, boating, sailing or jet skiing on the reservoir. In the surrounding national forest you can hike, hunt and four-wheel drive. For those who like to get wet, try a river rafting trip or inner tubing down the Dolores. After a day of Colorado fun, guests can sit on the deck overlooking the Dolores River. The restaurants in town are walking distance away.

RV sites and seasonal rentals are also available.

Location: In Dolores, 10 miles north of Cortez on Highway 145.

3 Cabins with Kitchen	Pay Phone Available	Ray & Darlene LeBlanc, Owners
4 Lodging Rooms	Elevation: 6900	PO Box 295
6 Motel Rooms	Credit Cards: VMAD	Dolores CO 81323-0295
Central Campfire Area	Rates: $48-$93	800/382-4892
	Open: All Year	970/882-7271
		www.coloradodirectory.com/outpostcabinsrvpark

At the resort:

At resort or within 15 minutes:

Ponderosa Cabins

A short drive from either Mancos or Dolores, Ponderosa Cabins are near Summit Lake's eastern side. The cabins are on eight acres snug under tall ponderosa pine trees and a short distance from the main road — ideal for families with children and pets. The cabins have modern electric ranges, wood burning stoves, cooking utensils and dishes, refrigerators, hot and cold running water, full size baths and gas heat. Cabin 1 sleeps up to four people, while Cabin 2 sleeps up to seven. Both cabins are non-smoking.

Near the San Juan National Forest and next to Summit Lake, Ponderosa Cabins are great for fishing and big game hunting. This resort is great for hunters, with deer passing near the property. Elk are plentiful in this part of the high country. Hunt famous "Lost Canyon" area with easy access to the vast national forest's miles of roads and trails, only 30 minutes from your cabin. If lake fishing doesn't appeal, try casting your line into the Dolores River. McPhee Reservoir, a short drive away, offers water skiing, boating, pontoon excursions and more lake fishing. Visit nearby Mesa Verde National Park, just 20 minutes away.

A 50 percent deposit is required when making reservations.

Location: From US Highway 160, turn north on Highway184 and drive 8 miles. Near milepost marker 18, turn south on County Road 37 for 0.2 miles.

2 Cabins with Kitchen	Elevation: 7500	Jack & Ressa Muller, Owners
2 Rooms with Wood Stoves	Credit Cards: None	PO Box 457
All Units Nonsmoking	Rates: $55-$60	Mancos CO 81328
	Open: 4/1 to 12/1	970/882-7396
		E-mail: jr_muller@juno.com
		www.coloradodirectory.com/ponderosacabins

At the resort:

At resort or within 15 minutes:

Riversbend Bed & Breakfast

Riversbend is a newly constructed two-story log inn where the charm of yesteryear welcomes you with the soft glow of overhead hurricane lamps and the warmth of log walls and antiques. Conveniently located on the scenic San Juan Skyway just seven miles east of Mesa Verde National Park, the inn has four guest rooms with private baths, plus a mini-suite with a private bath and a fireplace. All rooms are comfortably furnished with antiques and quilts. Set among tall cottonwood trees, the inn is on six acres where you're free to wander. Two common areas are available to guests at all times for reading or joining in conversations with other guests.

Guests begin each day with a scrumptious, gourmet breakfast, such as walnut caramel French toast stuffed with fresh peaches and cream! Walk along the Mancos River beside the inn, visit Mesa Verde National Park or ride the Durango & Silverton Narrow Gauge Railroad. McPhee Reservoir is 18 miles to the north and offers water sports and fishing. Available in the area are snow sleigh rides, cross country skiing trails, deluxe dinners, river rafting trips, stagecoach rides, chuckwagon dinners and shows, fly-fishing spots, and horseback riding stables. When you return to Riversbend, sit on the porch swing or wooden rocker before taking a relaxing dip in their hot tub.

No smoking and no pets are allowed at Riversbend.

Location: North of Highway 160, near milepost marker 58, east of Mancos.

5 Lodging Rooms	Phone in Lobby	Gaye & Jack Curran, Proprietors
1 Room with Fireplace	Bed & Breakfast Available	PO Box 861
Central Hot Tub	All Units Nonsmoking	Mancos CO 81328-0861
Central Woodstove	Recreation Room	800/699-8994
	Elevation: 6900	970/533-7353
	Credit Cards: VMAD	Fax: 970/533-1221
	Rates: $75-$125	E-mail: riversbn@fone.net
	Open: All Year	www.coloradodirectory.com/riversbendbb

At the resort:

At resort or within 15 minutes:

Ryter House Bed & Breakfast

Located in beautiful Mancos Valley between Mesa Verde National Park and the La Plata Mountains, Ryter House is open May through October. The three clean bedrooms have queen beds with quilts made by the host's family and shared baths. A country breakfast is included in the room rate.

Relax in Ryter House's sun room, on the deck, in the Jacuzzi or in the common room. Rock hounds and naturalists will love the rock garden full of native plants and geological specimens. The bed and breakfast is situated in the piñon-juniper forests that blanket rustic hills at 7,000 feet in elevation. The whole family will enjoy the trials in the woods around Ryter House. Area attractions include Mesa Verde National Park, access to the Ute Mountain Indian Tribal Park, fishing, hiking, mountain biking, horseback riding and golfing. You can even try a western stage coach ride nearby.

Good pets and children are welcome. The rooms are non-smoking.

Location: One and a half miles south of town, then drive 1 mile west on County Road H.

3 Lodging Rooms	Phone in Lobby	Bill & Sue Ryter, Owners
Central Hot Tub	Bed & Breakfast Available	40580 CR H
Central Woodstove	All Units Nonsmoking	Mancos CO 81328
Central Campfire Area	Recreation Room	970/533-7661
	Elevation: 7000	E-mail: SueRyter@compuserve.com or
	Credit Cards: None	75403.263@compuserve.com
	Rates: $65	www.coloradodirectory.com/ryterhousebb/
	Open: 5/1 to 9/31	

At the resort:

At resort or within 15 minutes:

Willowtail Springs

Willowtail Springs features log cabins secluded amid the sunwashed landscapes of Montezuma County in the southwestern corner of Colorado just minutes off the San Juan Scenic Skyway Loop. Vacation here on 40 acres of pastures, woods and streams. Choose between two one-bedroom log cabins, a two bedroom log home, each with a fully equipped kitchen and full bath. The charming, comfortable interiors, furnished with antiques, are ideal for romantic get-a-ways, honeymooners, and family vacationers. Accommodations include decks overlooking a bass-filled lake with a canoe available to guests for fishing. Swimming is also allowed.

From here, you'll be mere steps from the wilderness of the La Platta Mountains in the San Juan National Forest. Peacocks, deer, waterbirds, coyotes and other wildlife live at Willowtail Springs. During the summer, spend your vacation hiking, mountain biking, canoeing, fishing and horseback riding. In the winter, go downhill and cross-country skiing, ice skating, fish on the pond or go on a sleigh ride. The resort is 10 minutes from the ancient wonders of Mesa Verde, 60 minutes from Hovenweep National Monument, Four Corners, and the natural beauty of Canyon Lands. Less than 40 minutes from the city amenities of Durango, the Anasazi Heritage Center, and Purgatory ski area. And just 75 minutes from Telluride's ski resort and summer/fall festivals.

No smoking and no pets are allowed at the resort. Senior discounts available. There is studio space which is ideal for artists, writers or group workshops. A full payment is required 30 days prior to your stay.

Location: About 5 miles west of Mancos.

2 Cabins with Kitchen	Phone in Rooms	Peggy Conklin, Owners
1 Vacation Home	All Units Nonsmoking	PO Box 89
3 Rooms with Fireplaces	Elevation: 6500	Mancos CO 81328-0089
	Credit Cards Accepted: VM	800/698-0603
	Rates: $150-$185	970/533-7592
	Open: All Year	Fax: 970/533-7641
		www.coloradodirectory.com/willowtailsprings/

At the resort:

At resort or within 15 minutes:

Pagosa Springs

Map: P-9

Pagosa Springs was named by the Utes who called the hot springs "Pagosah," or "healing waters." This little town, surrounded on three sides by the San Juan National Forest, is a good place to get away from it all. Explore the mystery of the only mountain home of the Anasazi at nearby Chimney Rock Ruins where these ancient farmers lived some 1,000 years ago. The twin pinnacles were once a scared shrine to the "Ancient Ones". Later, the unusual formations were a landmark for prospectors, missionaries and conquistadors who settled this rugged country. While clambering among the ruins, keep an eye out for the endangered peregrine falcon which nests here. Enjoy the town's hot springs, considered to be the hottest in the world. Windsurf, water-ski and sail on Navajo Lake, which extends southward 35 miles into New Mexico. The Weminuche and South San Juan wilderness areas' untouched beauty are only accessible on foot or horseback. The nearby Echo Lake Park and Lake Capote are stocked with rainbow and cutthroat trout, large-mouth bass and yellow perch. (Lake Capote is only open occasionally inquire locally.) Other nearby places to go include hiking to Treasure Falls, prospecting on Treasure Mountain, fishing in Williams Creek and visiting the local museums. Nearby Wolf Creek Ski Area gets "The most snow in Colorado." Let the land of healing waters soothe you and the breath-taking wilderness inspire you.

Fun Things to Do

- Fairfield Pagosa Golf Course: April-November (970) 731-4755
- Fred Harman Art Museum (970) 731-5785
- Navajo State Park (970) 883-2208
- Pagosa Ranger District Office (970) 264-2268
- San Juan National Forest (970) 247-4874
- Wolf Creek Ski Area (970) 264-5629

Be Our Guest Bed & Breakfast

The 5,000 square foot lodge-like home at Be Our Guest Bed & Breakfast is very inviting. It sleeps up to 30 people in five bedrooms and a sleeping loft. Six bathrooms are available and the owner refers to the decor as "poor man's Ralph Lauren." A southwestern flavor carries throughout the house. The house can be divided into upper and lower levels, each having a kitchen, dining room and common areas. The lower level, for example, can sleep up to 16 and has a private entrance. Individual rooms may be rented as well. The Rustic Room has a queen bed with a private bath and hillside view. The Victorian Room is warm and romantic with a shared bath. The Family Room has a queen bed and two twin beds with a shared bath. The Loft has 5 single beds.

In addition to the included breakfast, you may have more meals provided with advanced reservations. Activities abound here, including fishing, skiing, horseback riding, golfing, hiking, hot air ballooning, sleigh riding, elk hunting, skating, white water rafting and relaxing. Among the sites to see are the Chimney Rock an archeological site, Navajo Lake, Vallacito Lake, Cumbres/Toltec Train, the Million Dollar Highway, Wolf Creek Pass and Purgatory Ski Areas for starters!

Allow your hosts to arrange for candy, flowers, dining, massage or a soak in the famous mineral springs. Children and small pets are welcome. Smoking is permitted on the deck only. Ask your host about where you can corral your horse while you stay with them.

Location: Six miles east of Pagosa Springs on the north side of Highway 160 in San Juan River Village right across from milepost marker 150.

1 Vacation Home	Phone in Lobby	Tom & Pam Schoemig, Owners
5 Lodging Rooms	Bed & Breakfast Available	19 Swiss Village Dr
5 Beds in Bunkhouse	All Units Nonsmoking	Pagosa Springs CO 81147
1 Room with Hot Tub	Recreation Room	970/264-6814
Central Fireplace	Elevation: 7500	Fax: 970/264-6953
Central Campfire Area	Credit Cards: None	E-mail: beourguest@pagosa.net
	Rates: $55-$80	www.coloradodirectory.com/beourguestbb/
	Open: 5/15 to 4/15	

At the resort:

At resort or within 15 minutes:

Bruce Spruce Ranch & Faris House Lodge

Surrounded by thousands of acres of national forest, Bruce Spruce Ranch is a wonderful retreat at the base of Wolf Creek Pass. If you're looking for the log cabin atmosphere that Colorado is known for, this is the place for you. Most of the cabins are full log with chinking, wood floors, and furnished with a country flair. The clean, rustic cabins are ideal for groups of up to 10 and have modern half-baths, kitchens with gas stoves, wood stoves for heat and centralized, clean hot showers. All kitchen utensils and bed linens are furnished. You may use the on-site washers and dryers as often as necessary. The Faris House Lodge is great for family reunions, church retreats and workshops. The lodge accommodates up to 31 people and has a large kitchen, dining room and living room areas, 5 bedrooms, 3 baths as well as a washer and dryer.

This scenic ranch offers many activities, including volleyball, horseshoes, horseback rides (License #1138), nature hikes and pack trips for trout fishing in lakes, streams and rivers. The private fishing pond on the ranch requires no state license; there is a fee. During the season, take a hunting pack trip for deer, bear and elk. Rent a horse by the hour or day or bring your own. Close by, enjoy the four-wheel

drive roads, Mesa Verde National Park and other Indian ruins, narrow-gauge railroad trains, hot mineral baths, wilderness hot springs and more.

Ask about the group meeting areas, RV and tent sites also available.

Location: Sixteen miles northeast of Pagosa Springs on Highway 160, near milepost marker 158. Go 0.25 miles northwest on the gravel road.

14 Cabins with Kitchen	Pay Phone Available	Craig & Eugenia Hinger, Owners
1 Vacation Home	Some Units Nonsmoking	PO Box 296
14 Rooms with Wood Stoves	Recreation Room	Pagosa Springs CO 81147-0296
Central Woodstove	Elevation: 8200	970/264-5374
Central Campfire Area	Credit Cards: VM	Fax: 970/264-5059
	Rates: $38-$52	E-mail: genacraig@juno.com
	Open: All Year	www.coloradodirectory.com/brucespruceranch/

At the resort:

At resort or within 15 minutes:

Fireside Inn

Fireside Inn, built in 1996, has 15 modern housekeeping cabins on seven acres beside the San Juan River. A lot of love and care went into designing and decorating the cabins, with a western decor which includes branded walls, old horse tack hanging up, homemade Latilla bedposts and handmade quilts on the walls — its truly the western experience your looking for. Each cabin has a living room, one or two queen-size bedrooms, fully equipped kitchens, gas fireplaces, cable televisions with HBO and phones. The two bedroom cabins sleep up to six people, while the one bedroom cabins sleep four people. All kitchens have a range with oven, refrigerator, pots & pans, dishes, utensils, coffee pot, microwave and toaster. Linens are furnished. Also provided are coffee, sugar, creamer, salt & pepper and dishing washing soap for your convenience.

The Inn offers horse corrals, and guests are welcome to bring their horses with them. The San Juan River offers wonderful trout fishing. In summer the area has something for the entire family with horseback rides, Indian ruins, whitewater rafting, hiking and mountain biking. In fall watch the aspen turn golden or hunt for big game. Winter offers downhill skiing at Wolf Creek Ski Area only 25 minutes away, cross country skiing, sleigh rides, snowmobile trails and tours, and ice fishing. After a day of outdoor adventure enjoy the hot tub. For your convenience there is a community washer and dryer.

Ask about their ski packages. Pets are welcome, for an additional fee.

Location: A quarter mile east of Highway junction 160 and 84 on Highway 160 near milepost marker 145.

---

15 Cabins with Kitchen	Phone in Rooms	Robert L & Deborah Sparks, Owners
15 Rooms with Fireplaces	All Units Nonsmoking	1600 E Hwy 160
Central Hot Tub	Recreation Room	Pagosa Springs CO 81147-9740
Central Campfire Area	Elevation: 7200	888/264-9204
	Credit Cards: VMAD	970/264-9204 & fax
	Rates: $89-$134	E-mail: firesideinn@pagosa.net
	Open: All Year	www.coloradodirectory.com/firesideinncabins/

At the resort:

At resort or within 15 minutes:

Indian Head Lodge

Indian Head Lodge on an acre of land is a little taste of the past locked in by the quiet of San Juan National Forest. The original lodge building still stands and is being refurbished. There are two two-bedroom cabins with Kitchenettes to choose from each sleeps 8 people. The rustic lodge offers a King bedroom with a full bath and a 2-bedroom bunk house with a sitting room which will sleep 12 people. There is also a two bedroom cabin with an adjoining bath.

Enjoy a soda on the front deck picked from the 1050's vintage cold water Coca Cola box. The convenience store on sites has a selection of groceries, gifts, supplies, sporting licenses, gas, diesel and propane. The Lodge is the closest facility to William Creek Reservoir, the Weminuche trailhead, and the best hunting, hiking, fishing and rock collecting in the area.

Tent sites area available. Reservations are important as this is a small facility.

Location: From Highway 160 north turn right on Piedra Road (country Road 631) toward the airport. It is approximately 17 miles to the lodge after entering the National Forest. Turn right at the T of 631 and 640 (Williams Creek Road).

2 Cabins with Kitchen	Phone in Lobby	Jody Thigpen & Ann Roberts, Owners
2 Cabins without Kitchens	All Units Nonsmoking	PO Box 2499
10 Beds in Bunkhouse	Recreation Room	Pagosa Springs CO 81147-2499
2 Rooms with Fireplaces	Elevation: 8250	970/731-2282
1 Room with Woodstove	Credit Cards: VMD	Fax: 970/731-2283
Central Fireplace	Rates: $24-$65	E-mail: 76614.1514@compuserve.com
Central Campfire Area	Open: 5/15 to 11/15	www.coloradodirectory.com/indianheadlodge

At the resort:

At resort or within 15 minutes:

Oso Grande Ranch

Oso Grande Ranch features five unique, comfortable rooms in a large, ranch style log home. A full breakfast each morning is included in your room rate. Complimentary turndown service is offered nightly as are thick bathrobes in each room.

Be prepared for breathtaking mountain top views from the wraparound porch. Relax in front of the ranch's fireplace and play board games with your family. Trail rides for guests are offered by the ranch. Area activities include skiing, both down hill and cross country, horseback riding, hunting, fishing in lakes and rivers, white water rafting and hunting. Oso Grande Ranch is walking distance to 2 million acres of national forest which is home to some of the largest elk and deer herds in Colorado, as well as wild turkey, Canadian geese and water fowl. From here you can access thousands of acres of mountain biking terrain, downtown Pagosa Springs, and Durango and its narrow-gauge railroad. However you spend the day, return to Oso Grande Ranch for a soothing soak in their hot tub.

Smoking is permitted on the deck only. Ask about the daily and weekly rates.

Location: Turn by Shell Station 5 miles north on North Pagosa Boulevard, to Hatcher Circle (.3miles).

1 Vacation Home	Phone in Lobby	Nan & Gary Rowe, Owners
5 Lodging Rooms	Bed & Breakfast Available	PO Box 5110
Central Hot Tub	All Units Nonsmoking	Pagosa Springs CO 81147-5110
Central Fireplace	Recreation Room	970/731-9548
Central Woodstove	Elevation: 7900	www.coloradodirectory.com/osogrande
	Credit Cards: None	
	Rates: $65-$75	
	Open: All Year	

At the resort:

At resort or within 15 minutes:

Piedra River Resort

Snug among tall pines on banks above the Piedra River, and surrounded by the San Juan National Forest, these cozy, secluded log cabins come with linens, dishes and cooking utensils. Pick between housekeeping, with kitchenettes, and non-housekeeping cabins.

The cowboy cookout area is a short horse ride up the trail, where you'll be served delicious food cooked outdoors during the breakfast and supper rides. Fish, ride horses or just relax at Piedra River Resort. The resort offers daily summer horseback rides, longer pack trips, fishing trips, plus hunting and outfitting in season (licenses #102). You'll journey along the river that Anasazi Indians once roamed and cowboys still ride. Your hosts, who have lived here since 1967, can direct you to excellent hiking trails, fishing holes and other "inside" secrets of this Rocky Mountain region. Charter a fishing boat to catch kokanee salmon and northern pike — the resort owns a 20-foot cabin cruiser on Lake Navajo, 30 minutes away on the Colorado-New Mexico border.

Location: Twenty miles west of Pagosa Springs and 35 miles east of Durango, on Highway 160, near milepost marker 121.

6 Cabins with Kitchen	Phone in Lobby	David & Nancy Guilliams, Owners
	Elevation: 6500	PO Box 4190
	Credit Cards: VMD	Pagosa Springs CO 81157-4190
	Rates: $47-$60	800/898-2006
	Open: 4/15 to 11/15	970/731-4630
		Fax: 970/731-4633
		E-mail: backcountry.prr@worldnet.att.net
		www.coloradodirectory.com/piedrariverresort/

At the resort:

At resort or within 15 minutes:

Peak-to-Peak Scenic Highway Area

Including Allenspark, Boulder, Eldora & Nederland
Map: D-14, D-16 & E-14

This highway, which stretches along the Front Range from Central City to Estes Park, highlights Colorado's mountain scenery, history and culture.It is between the two 14,000' peaks of Mt. Evans and Longs Peak. Railroad buffs will want to drive up the grade of the Rollins Pass railroad, or seek out the route of the Switzerland Trail narrow-gauge to the small towns where Colorado's first gold strikes were made. The Central City and Black Hawk mining area boomed during the late 19th century. Its gold helped build the mansions of Denver as well as its own glamorous historic hotels and saloons. Recently, many of the old hotels and saloons have been restored as limited-stakes gambling casinos. To the north, you'll pass through and **Nederland** to **Eldora**, old gold mining towns that produced tungsten through the 1940s. This small mountain town was the supply center to the silver camp of Caribou nearby which is now a ghost town. Down the scenic canyon from Nederland is the university town of **Boulder** featuring the Boulder Reservoir where you can swim, sail and water ski during the summer months. Hiking, mountain biking and cross-country trails abound in and around town. In addition to all the culture and art events this college town offers, Boulder is becoming known for its many coffee shops, bagel bakeries and micro-breweries. Back up the canyon, passing by Boulder Falls and heading north on the highway again, you'll pass by Ward, an old gold camp that now harbors those who crave peace and quiet. **Allenspark** is along the scenic route into Estes Park, where majestic Longs Peak presents its most dramatic face. This highway is particularly popular during the fall when the aspen turn golden under crisp blue skies.

Fun Things to Do

- Boulder Reservoir (303) 441-3468
- Colorado Shakespeare Festival (303) 492-0554
- Eldora Ski Area (303) 440-8700
- Eldorado Artesian Springs (303) 499-1316
- Eldorado Springs State park (303) 494-3943
- Flatirons Golf Course (303) 442-7851
- Leanin' Tree Museum of Western Art (303) 530-1442
- Twin Peaks Municipal Golf Course (303) 651-8401
- University of Colorado Museum (303) 492-6892

Allenspark Lodge

This classic, high-mountain bed and breakfast lodge is set in the flower-starred village of Allenspark. The three-story, hand-hewn log lodge, constructed of native stone and ponderosa pine, offers the time and the place to create sweet memories to last a lifetime. The lodge's spacious front porch welcomes you to step into the golden-hued, log entry, relax before a crackling fire, enjoy the candlelight. Six of the comfortable rooms have private baths with a shower or a big tub. The other 7 rooms, all homey and each different (some with sinks, some not) have access to a large, private shower. All rooms have nice views and some are furnished with original, handmade pine furniture from the 1930s. The Hideaway Room which has decorator linens, lace-edged pillows, a big brass bed and mountain views from windows on three sides has a claw-footed bath and fireplace–prefect for a romantic weekend or honeymoon. Your hosts offer warm hospitality, creating a special magic to make your stay unforgettable.

Relax your muscles in a private hot tub or enjoy the quiet game room and library. The Allenspark Lodge serves delicious hot, family style breakfasts, on winter evenings enjoy home-made soups and fresh bread along with wine and local micro-brewbeer. In nearby Estes Park, explore the wonders of Rocky Mountain National Park.

Ideal for small weddings of 75 people, family gatherings, and conferences. Reservations are strongly recommended.

Location: Off of Route 7 in Allenspark, near milepost marker 15.

13 Lodging Rooms	Pay Phone Available	Bill & Juanita Martin, Owners
1 Room with Fireplace	Bed & Breakfast Available	PO Box 247
Central Hot Tub	All Units Nonsmoking	Allenspark CO 80510-0247
Central Fireplace	Recreation Room	303/747-2552
Central Woodstove	Elevation: 8500	E-mail: APLBNB@aol.com
	Credit Cards: VMAD	www.coloradodirectory.com/allensparklodge/
	Rates: $60-$105	
	Open: All Year	

At the resort:

At resort or within 15 minutes:

Alps Boulder Canyon Inn

The Alps is a historic, luxury country inn located 2 miles from downtown Boulder in scenic Boulder Canyon. Twelve elegant guest rooms are furnished with down comforters, period antiques and include a sitting area, a deluxe bathroom and a Victorian fireplace. Several rooms feature double whirlpool tubs, two even have old-fashioned, claw-foot tubs. All rooms have unforgettable mountain views and many have private porches. Formerly a stagecoach stop, a bordello and a gateway for miners, the inn has played an historical role in the pioneer history of this area. The entire inn is non-smoking.

Enjoy the gourmet breakfasts and afternoon teas and cookies included with your stay in the dining room. Relax in the lounge's social area, furnished in the warm and homey style of the Adirondacks. Venture outside to roam the 25 acres of beautiful forest on the local hiking and bike trails. The property adjoins the Boulder County Parks and Open Space Betasso Preserve, a 715 acre park featuring miles of scenic hiking trails, picnic and camping areas as well as fantastic cross-country skiing. Located at the very edge of the Front Range of the Rocky Mountains, from the inn you can head down the canyon to Boulder or Denver for shopping, cultural events and sight-seeing year round. Take a leisurely drive up the canyon to view the snow-capped peaks of the great divide, visit old mining towns, drive the Peak-to-Peak Scenic Highway, or hike to high mountain passes, glaciers and lakes. If you want to relax, fish in Boulder Creek and bask in the scenic beauty of the high canyon walls.

All reservations require deposit equal to one night's stay.

Location: In Boulder Canyon (Highway 119), near milepost marker 38.

12 Lodging Rooms	Phone in Rooms	John & Jeannine Vanderhart, Owners
7 Rooms with Hot Tubs	Bed & Breakfast Available	PO Box 18298
12 Rooms with Fireplaces	All Units Nonsmoking	Boulder CO 80308-8298
Central Fireplace	Recreation Room	800/414-2577
	Elevation: 5700	303/444-5445
	Credit Cards: VMAD	Fax: 303/444-5522
	Rates: $125-$245	E-mail: alpsinn@aol.com
	Open: All Year	www.coloradodirectory.com/alpsbouldercanyoninn

At the resort:

At resort or within 15 minutes:

Arapaho Ranch Cabins

Pleasantly situated in a valley between Nederland and Eldora, on the Middle Boulder Creek, Arapaho Ranch is in Roosevelt National Forest. The cabins are 0.5 miles inside the gate, away from the highway. Most cabins are along the creek, while others are close by with a panoramic mountain view. Featuring roofed porches and rustic charm, each cabin has two to four bedrooms with double beds and plenty of blankets and pillows, gas heat, a bathroom, refrigerator, stove and equipment for light housekeeping. *Bring or rent sheets, pillowcases and towels.*

Kids will like the playground, while groups can participate in activities in the new recreation hall. Be on the lookout for deer, racoons or beavers that occasionally meander through the ranch. Everyone likes Monday night cookout. Fishing enthusiasts will appreciate the exclusive fishing rights to Middle Boulder Creek. Also, on the private, stocked pond. Hike or drive to the many high mountain lakes for more alpine casting. While hiking up to the Continental Divide, notice the many beautiful and unfrequented pine dells, meadows and scenic points. If you're in the mood for old-time casino gambling, Arapaho Ranch is an easy drive from Central City.

Location: Seventeen miles west of Boulder on Highway 119, near milepost marker 25. Turn off on Eldora Road (County Road 130). Go 1 mile to the gate.

6 Cabins with Kitchen	Phone in Lobby	Kayla Evans & Maryanne Flynn, Managers
4 Vacation Homes	All Units Nonsmoking	1250 Eldora Rd
Central Campfire Area	Recreation Room	Nederland CO 80466-9525
	Elevation: 8200	303/258-3405
	Credit Cards: None	www.coloradodirectory.com/arapahoranch/
	Rates: $70	
	Open: 5/1 to 10/1	

At the resort:

At resort or within 15 minutes:

Crystal Springs Cabins

Get a taste of history when you vacation in one of the three cozy, authentic historic 1920s cabins at Crystal Springs. The small cabins are nestled in native wild roses, aspen and pine trees in the tiny village of Allenspark. All the cabins are modern and comfortable inside with kitchenettes, private baths, color television, outdoor grills and picnic tables. Fresh linens are available every third day upon request. Some cabins even have old-fashioned porch swings to spend a few hours on admiring the scenery.

All the outdoor activities Rocky Mountain National Park, Indian Peaks Wilderness Area and Roosevelt National Forest, have to offer, from fishing, hunting, hiking and mountain biking to cross-country skiing and snowmobiling, are nearby. Bird watchers will love taking a picnic along on the many nature trails here. Crystal Springs is close to many gourmet restaurants in town and Estes Park. This is an especially marvelous area for hiking and horseback riding.

All cabins are non-smoking. No pets are allowed in the cabins. Advance reservations are recommended.

Location: Off of Route 7 in Allenspark, near milepost marker 15.

3 Cabins with Kitchen	Phone in Lobby	Mike & Becky Osmun, Owners
	All Units Nonsmoking	PO Box 48
	Elevation: 8451	Allenspark CO 80510-0048
	Credit Cards: VM	303/747-0145
	Rates: $75-$100	Fax: 303/747-0145 Call first
	Open: All Year	www.coloradodirectory.com/crystalspringscabins

At the resort: *At resort or within 15 minutes:*

Goldminer Hotel, Rocky Ledge Cabin & The Nederhaus

The 1897 Goldminer Hotel, a registered National Historic Landmark, is the centerpiece of the Eldora National Historic District. Stay in one of the fully modernized, Gold-Rush style rooms or suites, all room have color cable televisions and VCRs. Two rooms have jetted tubs and most with private bathrooms and some with fireplaces in this historic bed and breakfast. All rooms have direct-dial phones available. Rooms include a delicious breakfast to start your day right. The "Rocky Ledge" cabin sleeps six and has a full kitchen, a fireplace, a patio and an old-fashioned bathtub on legs. The Nederhaus is a modern hotel with suites, kitchens, rooms and conference facilities. Rooms are furnished with antiques and have the modern conveniences of cable television and direct-dial phones.

Depending on the seasons, take back-country jeep, cross-country ski, snow cat and horseback tours. Eldora Mountain Resort is nearby and offers downhill skiing the whole family can afford. Ride the free shuttle to the limited-stakes gambling casinos of Central City and Black Hawk. The Goldminer and Nederhaus are adjacent to the Indian Peaks Wilderness, where you can hike to the Continental Divide. The bustling town of Boulder is only 30 minutes away. At night, soak your road-weary muscles in the communal hot tub.

Location: Off of Highway 119, near milepost marker 25.

1 Cabin with Kitchen	Phone in Rooms	Carol Rinderknecht & Scott Bruntjen
5 Lodging Rooms	Bed & Breakfast Available	601 Klondyke Ave
2 Rooms with Hot Tubs	Some Units Nonsmoking	Eldora CO 80466-9542
1 Room with Fireplace	Recreation Room	800/422-4629
1 Room with Woodstove	Elevation: 8600	303/258-7770
Central Hot Tub	Credit Cards: VMAD	Fax: 303/258-3850
Central Fireplace	Rates: $75-$149	E-mail: bruntjen@bouldernews.infi.net
	Open: All Year	www.coloradodirectory.com/goldminer

At the resort:

At resort or within 15 minutes:

Pine Grove Cabins

Be a part of the quiet serenity at Pine Groves Cabins where the accommodations are comfortably furnished and well-serviced. Choose among four sizes family housekeeping cabins completely equipped for all your needs (you will only need to bring normal suitcase items). Located in a pine grove off the highway with individual privacy, the modern cottages, all are furnished for light housekeeping with dishes, cooking utensils, beds, linens, electricity, heat and shower baths. Most of the cabins have a wood fireplace.

Take time while vacationing here to meander through the aspen, pine and spruce forests, past virgin meadows to higher plateaus where wildlife abounds in nearby Rocky Mountain National Park. Kids will like the large playground area at the resort, while adults will appreciate the economic, family vacation here. The small village of Allenspark offers both a cafe and gormet dining room service near the cabins as well as a gift shop, fishing licenses, square dancing, chuck wagon dinners, buffets and national park ranger programs. Nearby activities include horseback riding on well-marked trails, fishing in lakes and streams, playing volleyball and horseshoes. Just two miles north, Copeland Lake offers plenty of opportunities for scenic, high country fishing, hiking and picnicking. The trail for Longs Peak, a breathtaking 12,255-feet high, starts only six miles from Pine Grove.

Rates by the day, week or month are available. All units are non-smoking. Guests are welcomed to bring their horses and house them in the on-site corral.

Location: Two blocks south of State Highway 7 in Allenspark, near milepost marker 15, half way between Lyons and Estes Park

7 Cabins with Kitchen	Phone in Lobby	Bob & June Wesel, Owners
2 Vacation Homes	All Units Nonsmoking	PO Box 85
8 Rooms with Fireplaces	Elevation: 8500	Allenspark CO 80510-0085
	Credit Cards: None	303/747-2529
	Rates: $62-$145	www.coloradodirectory.com/pinegrovecabins/
	Open: All Year	

At the resort:

At resort or within 15 minutes:

Pikes Peak Area

Including Cascade, Chipeta Park, Colorado Springs, Cripple Creek, Lake George, Manitou Springs & Woodland Park — Map: I-17, I-16, I-17 & I-15

Catch the excitement of Pikes Peak purple mountain majesty and see why Katharine Lee Bates was inspired to write "American the Beautiful" when she stood on the mountains overlooking **Colorado Springs**. From a ride on the Pikes Peak Cog Railway to the dramatic 14,110' summit, to the sunny charm of an afternoon hike through an alpine forest near **Manitou Springs**, the Pikes Peak area offers a myriad of activities. Visit the out-of-this-world natural red rock formations of the Garden of the Gods or tour the U.S. Air Force Academy. Explore Old Colorado City, the original site of Colorado Springs, where restored 1800s architecture made it a registered National Historic District. Fish for Rocky Mountain trout and enjoy the fresh, pine-scented air of this high-country region. One of the most famous towns in this area is **Cripple Creek**, nestled in an extinct volcano crater riddled with gold fields in a remote region on the backside of Pikes Peak. The town and its surroundings eventually produced $600 million in gold. Cripple Creek's limited stakes casino gambling offer the opportunity to strike it rich. **Lake George** was founded in 1887 a few miles from the dam at the mouth of Eleven Mile Canyon. Six miles east, Florissant Fossil Beds National Monument was once a raging volcanic field whose lava and ash preserved insects, leaves and fish. Numerous fossils were discovered in 1874 — the monument was established in 1969, encompassing ancient Lake Florissant which existed some 38 million years ago. At the nearby 7,000-acre Dome Rock State Wildlife Area, see Rocky Mountain bighorn sheep, deer, elk, bobcats, coyotes, eagles and wild turkeys. The fishing is truly excellent on Tarryall Creek and Reservoir, and at Eleven Mile and Spinney Reservoirs, all near Lake George.

Fun Things to Do

- American Adventure Expeditions (800) 288-0675
- Broadmoor Golf Club, Colorado Springs (719) 577-5790
- Cave of the Winds (719) 685-5444
- Cheyenne Mountain Zoo & Will Rogers Shrine (719) 475-9555
- Cripple Creek District Museum (719) 689-2634
- Cripple Creek Mountain Estate Golf Course Summer (719) 689-7850
- Eleven Mile State Park (719) 748-3401
- Florissant Fossil Beds National Monument (719) 748-3253
- Flying W Ranch (800) 232-FLYW See Page 213
- Garden of the Gods (719) 634-6666
- Mueller State Park (719) 687-2366
- Mule Creek Outfitters (800) 289-4868
- Pikes Peak Highway (719) 684-9383
- U.S. Olympic Complex (719) 578-4644/4618
- United States Air Force Academy (719) 333-8723

Flying W Ranch — Chuck Wagon Suppers

Flying W Ranch offers Chuck Wagon Suppers in a western town with 14 restored historical buildings and gift shops. Chuck Wagon Suppers feature tender slices of beef in a mild barbecue sauce or barbecue chicken, and foil wrapped potatoes, Flying W beans, chunky applesauce, old fashioned spice cake and mouthwatering biscuits. If the weather is nice, you can enjoy your chuck wagon supper outside under the stars. A heated, indoor area for dining is available if necessary. In the colder months, the Winter Steak House offers cowboy-size, U.S. choice steaks, smoked beef brisket, smoked pork ribs, flame grilled trout and barbecue chicken. The meal is rounded out with a salad, foil wrapped potato, Flying W beans, coffee and the very best biscuits you have ever eaten.

The town has a Dry Goods Store, a Leather Shop, a log school house, a blacksmith and other buildings to transport you back in time. Browse among the antiques and artifacts in the authentic western town. You won't want to miss the western stage show featuring the famous Flying "W" Wranglers.

During the summer, Flying W Ranch is open seven nights a week. The Winter Steak House is open October through mid-May, Thursday, Friday and Saturday evenings only for two seatings at 5 and 8 p.m.. The ranch is closed for January and February. Private chuckwagon suppers, breakfasts and lunches are available year round by special arrangement. All meals include the great stage show.

Location: Northwest of Garden of the Gods Road (4600 N) & 30th Street.

Russell Wolf, Owner & Vern Thomson
3330 Chuckwagon Rd
Colorado Springs   CO   80919-3501
800/232-3599
719/598-4000
Fax: 719/598-4600
E-mail: flyingw@rmi.net
www.coloradodirectory.com/flyingwsupper/

Carolyn's B&B Cabins At Windmill Meadow Ranch

Discover elegance and the Wild West at Carolyn's B&B Cabins At Windmill Meadow Ranch. Stay in one of two luxury cabins on "Bonanza's" Ponderosa Ranch. The cozy Southwestern motif of the Getaway Cabin and the rustic cowboy setting of the Hideout Cabin allow you to experience romance and the spirit of the pioneer west in fully self-contained log cabin units. Each have a full, modern kitchen, wood stove, satellite television, VCR and CDs. Other amenities include Jacuzzi tubs, barbecues and private decks. Just outside the cabin are the clear sounds of Pettit Creek and wildlife roaming the meadow with livestock. This is a pristine retreat in a unique setting that's sure to create vacation memories for a lifetime.

You can choose to enjoy the seclusion of the ranch's private valley, sitting streamside and hiking aspen lined trails to refresh your spirit or venture out to try any of the numerous nearby recreational activities, including limited stakes gambling in historic Cripple Creek. Arrangements can be made for horseback rides and massages from a professional therapist. Downhill skiing is just over an hour away, while cross country ski and mountain bike are five minutes away. A gold medal trout stream is only 20 minutes away, lake and ice fishing are a 10 minute drive.

Gourmet meals can be arranged at the ranch house with prior arrangements Ask about the Business and Writer's Package.

Location: In Woodland Park on Highway 67 near milepost marker 80. Forty minutes from the Colorado Springs Airport.

2 Cabins with Kitchen	Phone in Rooms	Carolyn & Gary Taylor, Owners
2 Rooms with Wood Stoves	Bed & Breakfast Available	28556 Hwy 67
Central Hot Tub	All Units Nonsmoking	Woodland Park CO 80863
	Elevation: 8400	877/434 CABIN (2224)
	Credit Cards: VMAD	719/687-7385
	Rates: $150-$170	Fax: 719/687-3694
	Open: All Year	E-mail: carolyn@operatorservices.com
		www.coloradodirectory.com/carolyns

At the resort:

At resort or within 15 minutes:

Cascade Hills Motel & Cabins

Tucked away at the base of spectacular Pikes Peak, Cascade Hills Motel & Cabins offers charming facilities in a mountain hideaway. Among the 14 motel rooms are full bedrooms, queen-sized bedrooms, 2 bedrooms and 2 room family suites with kitchens. All rooms have air conditioning and most have microwaves and refrigerators. The secluded Anne's Mountain Cottage is fully-equipped with a kitchen, large stone fireplace, spacious deck and cable TV. The hot tub is just steps away from this cabin which sleeps 1 to 6 people in its 2 bedroom, 1 bath lodging. Connie's Cabin offers beautiful mountain views from its 1,500 square feet and sits on 1.5 acres boarding the national forest. Fully furnished, this cabin has 2 bedrooms, 1 full bath, kitchen, dining room, living room with a stone fireplace, family room, stone front porch and an enclosed back porch. Connie's Cabin sleeps up to 8 people and is ideal for larger groups or reunions. All accommodations have continental breakfast, 50 channel cable TV with remote control, direct dial phones (local calls are free) and Cripple Creek Fun Book coupons.

Just 10 miles west of Colorado Springs and seven miles east of Woodland Park, Cascade Hills borders the Pike National Forest which offers abundant opportunities for hiking, picnics and explorations of nature at its most breathtaking. Nearby outdoor activities include horseback riding, four wheel driving, golf and mountain biking. The resort is just minutes from numerous attractions, including Seven Falls, Cave of the Winds, Historic W Ranch chuckwagon dinners, Pikes Peak Cog Railway, Garden of the Gods, Cripple Creek Gambling and the Cheyenne Mountain Zoo and Will Rogers Shrine. End the day with a soak in the outdoor hot tub and spa surrounded by beautiful mountain views.

Some non-smoking units. Ask about the low weekly rates.

Location: West on Colorado Springs in Cascade on West Highway 24

1 Cabin with Kitchen	Phone in Rooms	Ted & Agatha Palka, Owners
1 Vacation Home	Some Units Nonsmoking	PO Box 125
14 Motel Rooms	Elevation: 7375	Cascade CO 80809
2 Rooms with Fireplaces	Credit Cards: VMD	888/247-8990
Central Hot Tub	Rates: $55-$125	719/684-9977
	Open: All Year	Fax: 719/684-4966
		www.coloradodirectory.com/cascadehillscabins/

At the resort:

At resort or within 15 minutes:

El Colorado Lodge

Enjoy the tranquil mountain beauty and adventure of the Pikes Peak Region in the family-owned and operated Historic El Colorado Lodge. The lodge is the oldest continually-operated business in Manitou Springs. On four acres of rolling lawns dotted with mature Colorado blue spruce trees, the resort has a distinct southwestern flavor. The resort features adobe-style, modernized "casitas" that sleep from one to six people and have one or two bedrooms. All cabins have heat, air-conditioning, color cable television, direct-dial telephones and fireplaces. Some cabins offer kitchens and beamed ceilings.

Picnic with the whole family on the patio after a round of basketball and shuffleboard. Pleasant amenities include the largest outdoor, heated swimming pool in Manitou Springs, a pavilion, outdoor barbecue grills and a children's playground. Historic El Colorado Lodge is centrally located for all Pikes Peak Region attractions and sights such as Garden of the Gods, Pikes Peak Cog Railway, Cliff Dwellings Museum and the Buffalo Bill Museum. A short drive away are Seven Falls, Cripple Creek and the Cheyenne Mountain Zoo.

Your hosts will help you make reservations at area attractions. Family reunions are a specialty.

Location: Off of Highway 24, near milepost marker 299, on Manitou Avenue.

8 Cabins with Kitchen	Phone in Rooms	Grace & Wally Walicki, Owners
17 Cabins without Kitchens	Some Units Nonsmoking	23 Manitou Ave
1 Vacation Home	Elevation: 6035	Manitou Springs CO 80829
21 Rooms with Fireplaces	Credit Cards: VMAD	800/782-2246
	Rates: $54-$120	719/685-5485
	Open: All Year	Fax: 719/685-4645
		www.coloradodirectory.com/elcoloradolodge

At the resort:

At resort or within 15 minutes:

Eleven Mile Motel Cabins

Surrounded by the Pike National Forest, Eleven Mile Motel Cabins are located in the small, rural community of Lake George. Some of these modern, comfortable log cabins have kitchens. Cabins range from one to three bedroom, and have all been recently remodeled. All feature television, carpets, modern bathrooms with showers and great views of the Tarryall Mountain Range. The rustic furnishings in combination living room and bedroom cabins are complete with a modern kitchen. Cabins sleep from 2 to 6 people. Cook up your fresh catch on the grill and dine on the picnic table right outside your door. Enjoy the convenience of private parking beside your cabin.

The Pike National Forest, only 0.25 miles away, is known for its scenic beauty. Possibilities for horseback riding, hiking, biking, stream and lake fishing and rock hunting here are endless. Only 22 miles from Cripple Creek, you make an easy day trip to its historic buildings and casinos. Fish in the South Platte River or in nearby Eleven Mile, Spinny, Tarryall and Antero reservoirs. Visit the famous Royal Gorge and the nearby Florissant Fossil Beds National Monument. Colorado Springs and its many attractions are less than an hour away.

No pets please.

Location: In town on Highway 24, near milepost marker 267.

6 Cabins with Kitchen	Phone in Rooms	Tom & Pat Brown, Owners
4 Cabins without Kitchens	Elevation: 8100	Box 146
	Credit Cards: VMAD	Lake George CO 80827
	Rates: $42-$99	719/748-3931
	Open: All Year	E-mail: tbrown8568@aol.com
		www.coloradodirectory.com/11milecabins

At the resort: *At resort or within 15 minutes:*

Green Mountain Falls Resorts

The individual cottages at Green Mountain Falls Resort are conveniently located within a short drive to 30 Pikes Peaks attractions, including gaming in the Historic Cripple Creek Mining District. The ten cottages have fully furnished kitchenettes and bathrooms. Five cottages have fireplaces. The cottages range from cozy, one-room nests for two to four people, to a three-bedroom, two-bath cottage that can accommodate up to 10 people. Eight cozy lodge rooms have microwaves, refrigerators, coffee makers and continental breakfasts. All units are clean, comfortably furnished with linens and color cable television.

From the resort, you can walk to swimming, tennis courts, biking and hiking trails and local shops. Just across the street, anglers will find a picturesque mountain lake to cast into. In the winter, try ice skating outdoors. Within a short drive are horseback rides, four wheel drive tours, a museum and a golf course. A family style restaurant serving breakfast and dinner is on-site. Additional meals may be available with advance arrangements. After a day of fun, be sure to relax in the hot tub. For reunions and big groups, the indoor meeting room accommodates 100 while the outdoor covered picnic shelter is a great place for cookouts.

Ask about the special rates from October through April. All units are non-smoking.

Location: West of Colorado Springs on Highway 24 near milepost marker 290.

10 Cabins with Kitchen	Bed & Breakfast Available	David Pearlman, Owner
2 Vacation Homes	All Units Nonsmoking	PO Box 298
8 Lodging Rooms	Elevation: 7800	Green Mountain Falls CO 80819-0298
5 Rooms with Fireplaces	Credit Cards: VMAD	888/684-9576
Central Hot Tub	Rates:	719/684-9576
	Open: All Year	Fax: 719/684-8269
		E-mail: gmfresorts@juno.com
		www.coloradodirectory.com/greenmtnfallsresort/

At the resort:

At resort or within 15 minutes:

Green Willow Motel Cottages

Cross the bridge on Fountain Creek and discover clean, rustic-style modern cottages at Green Willow Motel — a family business since 1953. All cottages have color cable television and showers; and refrigerator/mircowave or fully equipped kitchens. All cottages have double beds. Light daily maid service provided. The Heruth's create a welcoming atmosphere with spacious grounds full of flowers and well landscaped lawn areas complete with views of magnificent Pikes Peak. Chairs on each porch allow a relaxing view of the scenery. A stream runs right through the resort. The creekside picnic area has chairs, picnic tables, grills and a swing set. There's even an adult swing for those young at heart. Hot drinks are served for your enjoyment.

Explore the hiking trail that begins at the back of the property through the park and into Garden of the Gods. Royal Gorge and Cripple Creek are only an hour's drive away, or you can take a relaxing, sightseeing bus tour. Walk from your cottage to Manitou Springs city parks or the Olympic-sized pool with kiddie-pool and hot tub. Visit the nearby quaint shops and restaurants. Green Willow offers guests old fashioned, country hospitality and friendship.

Prices vary depending on the time of year. There is a nominal charge for baby beds, cots and roll-aways. There is a campground next door. Tour pickup is available from here.

Location: Within city limits; on a bus and trolley line. Off of Highway 24, on Manitou Avenue (Business Highway 24).

14 Cabins with Kitchen	Pay Phone Available	Ron & Bev Heruth, Owners/Operators
	Elevation: 6450	328 Manitou Ave
	Credit Cards: VMAD	Manitou Springs CO 80829-2506
	Rates: $45-$70	719/685-9997
	Open: 5/1 to 9/30	Fax: 719/685-4760
		E-mail: greenwilow@aol.com
		coloradodirectory.com/greenwillowcottages/

At the resort:

At resort or within 15 minutes:

Lake George Cabins & RV Park

A small creek runs through the property at this inn just minutes away from the historical gold mines of Cripple Creek. Wildhorn Inn offers newly remodeled log cabins with private baths, kitchenettes and color television.

Pike National Forest surrounds Wildhorn and offers the best in hunting, fishing, mountain biking, hiking and cross-country skiing. Wildlife in this area includes elk, deer, bighorn sheep, black bear, bobcat, mountain lions, wild turkey, blue grouse and other small game. The Lake George area is the trophy fishing capital of Colorado with fishing opportunities in the South and Middle Fork of the Platte River, in Tarryall, Antero, Skagway, Spinney and Eleven Mile Reservoirs. The limited stakes gambling casinos of Cripple Creek are 23 miles away. The historic town has maintained the look of the boom days of yesteryear when gold was plentiful and gambling legal.

RV and tent sites along the creek are also available. Ask about the reduced weekly and monthly rates during the winter.

Location: Off Highway 24, near milepost marker 265, on Park County Road 90, across from South Platte River. 40 miles west of Colorado Springs.

9 Cabins with Kitchen	Pay Phone Available	Dave & Rose Sorrentino, Owners
1 Cabin without Kitchen	Elevation: 8000	8966 CR 90
Central Campfire Area	Credit Cards: VM	Lake George CO 80827
	Rates: $60-$90	719/748-3822
	Open: All Year	Fax: 719/748-3822
		www.coloradodirectory.com/lakegcabinsrv/

At the resort:

At resort or within 15 minutes:

Lost Burro Campground

Lost Burro Campground offers a summer home rental on its 17 secluded acres in addition to its RV and tent sites. The rental home, set amid fragrant pine trees and shimmering aspens, has 2 bedrooms and 1 bath. The living room has a hide-a-bed sofa & futon so you can sleep 8 comfortably here. The home comes with all bedding, cooking utensils and dishes supplied. Fifteen RV and 15 tent sites are also available.

A stream running through the valley presents the opportunity to pan for gold just like miners in days gone by. Children will enjoy the playground on site while families can barbecue outdoors at the firepit and picnic site. Just 4 miles from Cripple Creek, Lost Burro is close to all the town's attractions from gambling and a ride on the Narrow Gauge Steam Engine, to an authentic gold mine where you can take a tour from a miner. Be sure to visit the original stage coach, a museum and several shops in town as well. In the evening, take a Ghost Walk around town, while a storyteller recounts the town's history and describes the resident "ghosts". Just 7 miles further down the road is the tiny town of Victor, an authentic mining town from the 1800s. Visit antique stores, a mining museum and an old mine. A short drive in the other direction is Florissant Fossil Beds which offers wonderful hikes for bird watchers and other nature lovers. Some trails are handicap accessible. Anglers will find plenty of opportunities here, from Sagway Reservoir outside of Victor to the wide meandering streams of Happy Meadows and the Eleven Mile reservoir for boating. No matter what you do, watch for the local wildlife, from elk, deer & big horn sheep to fox, antelope, bears, eagles, hawks & prairie dogs.

Pets are welcomed in the summer home & campers can use the 8-foot by 10-foot portable kennels at their site. Guest horses welcomed. A night's deposit is required with reservations.

Location: Four miles northwest of Cripple Creek on County Road 1.

Central Campfire Area	Pay Phone Available	Jim & Mary Eddleman, Owners
	Elevation: 8800	Box 614
	Credit Cards: VM	Cripple Creek CO 80813-6140
	Rates: $60-$60	719/689-2345
	Open: All Year	www.coloradodirectory.com/lostburrocamp

At the resort:

At resort or within 15 minutes:

Mountaindale Cabins & Campground

The new cabins at Mountaindale sit in a secluded mountain setting, offering a great summer or winter getaway. Cozy Cabin has electricity, heater, bunk bed, double bed and sleeps four. A fully furnished RV is also available with a full kitchen and bathroom, queen bed, hid-a-bed in the living room, television and sleeps up to six. Getaway Cabin, which sleeps six, is fully furnished and has a loft with a ladder, kitchenette, bathroom and a pleasant porch. Seclusion Cabin offers fully furnished rooms, a loft with stairs, full kitchen, bathroom, fireplace, screened porch and sleeps six. Hideaway Cabin has a private bedroom, a loft with stairs, full kitchen, bathroom and a fireplace, and sleeps up to six. All cabins and rental RV have barbecue grills, picnic tables and a fire ring. Each unit is supplied with linens, pots and pans and some paper products.

Mountaindale sits on 45 beautiful acres with huge ponderosa pine trees just 14 miles southwest of Colorado Springs. Surrounded by mountains, you'll find plenty of wilderness to explore in addition to day trips to any of the numerous area attractions, including Pikes Peak Cog Railway, Cave of the Winds, Garden of the Gods, Pro Rodeo Hall of Fame, gold mine tours, chuckwagon dinners and much more! Or stay at Mountaindale where the kids can play on the volleyball court or

challenge each other to horseshoes. Other resort amenities include a convenience store, a coin laundry, hot showers for RV and tent guests and plenty of fresh air for all.

Ask about the winter rates. Thirty full hookup RV sites are also available.

Location: From I-25 take exit 135 (Academy Blvd) drive west two miles till Highway 115, go south 14 miles.

3 Cabins with Kitchen	Pay Phone Available	Ron & Ann Heck, Owners
2 Camper Cabins	All Units Nonsmoking	2000 Barrett Rd
2 Rooms with Fireplaces	Recreation Room	Colorado Springs CO 80926
Central Fireplace	Elevation: 6625	719/576-0619
Central Woodstove	Credit Cards: VMD	Fax: 719/576-0619
Central Campfire Area	Rates: $39-$100	E-mail: Mt.dalecamp@juno.com
	Open: All Year	www.coloradodirectory.com/mountaindale/

At the resort:

At resort or within 15 minutes:

Mule Creek Outfitters/M Lazy C Ranch

The M Lazy C Ranch is an actual working cattle ranch, homesteaded in the early 1900s by the Thatcher Family. The original house and out buildings, with a few added modern conveniences, still exist to provide an 'Old West' setting for guests. Stay in individual log cabins, complete with antiques and woodburning stoves. Home cooked meals are served daily, family style in the main ranch house.

The ranch offers a variety of activities including horseback rides, chuck wagon meals, hay rides, carriage rides, fishing, overnight pack trips into the wilderness, cattle drives, cross-country skiing and sleigh rides in the winter. Hunters will want to join in for big game hunting in season. Pack trips venture into the Gore Wilderness Range or the Lost Creek Wilderness. More locally, visit historic Cripple Creek, South Park City Museum, Royal Gorge and Florissant Fossil Beds. Anglers will find plenty of fishing spots to choose from with Eleven Mile, Spinney and Tarryall Reservoirs a short distance away.

Although only sixteen to eighteen overnight guests can be accommodated in the cabins, your hosts can provide for larger groups up to 200 in the authentic Indian teepees and outfitters' wall tents. For large groups, choose from western reenactments, rodeos, picnics and chuck wagon meals as entertainment.

Location: Five miles west of Lake George, on Highway 24 between milepost markers 260-261, on right is a sign M Lazy C Ranch, make a right and go 0.75 miles. Approximately 35 miles west of Colorado Springs.

1 Cabin with Kitchen	Phone in Lobby	Randy & Brenda Myers, Owners
3 Cabins without Kitchens	Bed & Breakfast Available	PO Box 461
3 Rooms with Wood Stoves	All Units Nonsmoking	Lake George CO 80827-0461
Central Hot Tub	Recreation Room	800/289-4868
Central Campfire Area	Elevation: 8300	719/748-3398
	Credit Cards: VMAD	Fax: 719/748-3250
	Rates: $60-$95	E-mail: mlazyc@aol.com
	Open: All Year	www.coloradodirectory.com/mulecreekcabins

At the resort:

At resort or within 15 minutes:

Serenity Pines Guesthouse

Experience a true Colorado getaway amongst pristine acres of whisperings pines at Serenity Pines Guesthouse. Choose from the Guesthouse or the Lower Garden Room both with cable TV/VCR, video library, phone and answering machine. Feel immediately at home inside the Guesthouse with 1200 square feet, it sleep six, and offers the charm and amenities of a bed and breakfast, with the privacy and convenience of a cottage. Grandma's kitchen inside the Guesthouse has new full size appliances (dishwasher/microwave) and comes stocked with milk, juice, lemonade, eggs, sausages, english muffins, butter, home-made jam, condiments, hot and cold cereals, pancake mix, fruit, teas and coffee. Savor a "hot and hearty cook your own" or continental breakfast from the tray delivered the night before. The Lower Garden Room for two, decorated with a country garden theme featuring lattice and bird houses, offers the same amenities, private entrance, bath, and has a refrigerator, microwave, coffee pot, toaster, breakfast bar and continental breakfast. The Lower Garden Room may be reserved by itself or along with the Guesthouse, when another bedroom and bath are desired.

Serenity Pines is nestled among the pine trees of the Black Forest. With a park like setting the only sounds outside your door are singing birds and grazing horses. Enjoy the private sun deck, picnic and barbecue areas. Relax in the secluded private hot tub. Watch the wildlife, stroll through the whispering pines on the 5 acres, or meander down country roads. Most Pikes Peak area attractions are within a scenic half hour drive.

Location: From I-25 take exit 149, drive east on Woodmen 5.2 miles to Black Forest Road and turn left. Turn right onto Vollmer for 4.4 miles, turn right onto Burgess Road. Go 1.4 miles and turn left on Windmill Road. watch for a yellow and green windmill in front number 11910.

1 Cabin with Kitchen	Phone in Rooms	Kathy & Bob Benjamin, Hosts
2 Lodging Rooms	Bed & Breakfast Available	11910 Windmill Road
1 Room with Fireplace	All Units Nonsmoking	Colorado Springs CO 80908
Central Campfire Area	Elevation: 7500	887/737-3674
	Credit Cards: VMA	719/495-7141
	Rates: $129	Fax: 719/495-7141
	Open: All Year	E-mail: serenpines@aol.com
		www.coloradodirectory.com/serenpines

At the resort:

At resort or within 15 minutes:

Town & Country Resort — The Suites

The Suites at Town & County Resort offer a touch of class for those looking for a quiet mountain retreat in a wooded setting. The eight luxurious, two-room private suites offer a special vacation in Woodland Park. The Suites are well adorned with vaulted beamed ceilings and fans in each room. Amenities include a complimentary breakfast bar, satellite television plus VCRs, kitchenettes with microwaves and coffee makers, free local calls and laundry facilities.

Relax by the woodstove in the lodge as the day winds down and dusk settles over this mountain town. Rent mountain bikes at the resort to explore the back country roads. On-site amenities include a new hot tub. Partake in game nights, and poker. Area activities include playing golf and tennis, horseback riding, hiking local trails, cross-country skiing and lake or stream fishing just minutes away. Shuttle vans to the Cripple Creek Casinos are available. In the heart of Pikes Peak country, you'll find the nights cool and quiet, the days sunny, and your vacation perfect.

Ask about the personalized, romantic getaway and golf packages which can be tailored to suit every occasion. Smoking and pets are not allowed in the suites. RV sites are also available.

Location: Eighteen miles west of Colorado Springs on Highway 24, then 2 blocks north on Highway 67 at milepost marker 77.

8 Cabins with Kitchen	Recreation Room	C J & Ginny Solar, Owners
Central Hot Tub	Elevation: 8500	PO Box 368
Central Campfire Area	Credit Cards: VMD	Woodland Park CO 80866
All Units Nonsmoking	Rates: $116-$126	800/600-0399
	Open: All Year	719/687-9518
		Fax: 719/687-9518
		E-mail: suites@citystar.com
		www.coloradodirectory.com/towncountryresort

At the resort:

At resort or within 15 minutes:

Ute Pass Cabins & Motel

Historic Ute Pass Cabins is your gateway to Colorado. Cabins sleep 2 to 11 people with color cable television and air conditioning. The family-sized, equipped kitchen in the cabins feel like home. The motel, originally built in 1895, has been recently expanded and restored decorated with antique furniture. Each room is different and some are connected. Fall asleep to the soothing sounds of the ever-gurgling mountain stream meandering through the resort. You can also enjoy the indoor spa. The outdoor picnic area borders Fountain Creek, where you can dine outdoors amid scenic splendor.

A laundromat is available for your convenience. Explore historic Manitou Springs on a walking tour. Visit many of the sights of the Pikes Peak area nearby. Drive Ute Pass to the gambling casinos at Cripple Creek. Fish in Fountain Creek right on the property or at other nearby mountain streams and lakes. Meals are available one block away.

Your hosts will be happy to help you with local Pikes Peak area attraction tour reservations. Family reunions welcome.

Location: In Manitou Springs on business route 24, one block from downtown.

4 Cabins with Kitchen	Phone in Rooms	Helena & Jerzy Gudel & Zbigniew & Irena
13 Motel Rooms	Some Units Nonsmoking	Konaszewski, Owners
Central Hot Tub	Recreation Room	1132 Manitou Ave
Central Fireplace	Elevation: 6400	Manitou Springs CO 80829
	Credit Cards: VMAD	800/845-9762
	Rates: $35-$55	719/685-5171
	Open: All Year	Fax: 719/685-0529
		E-mail: UTEPASSMOT@aol.com
		www.coloradodirectory.com/utepasscabins

At the resort:

At resort or within 15 minutes:

Ute Trail River Ranch

Escape to the peaceful and relaxing beauty of this restored fly fishing camp tucked into Pike National Forest and the Lost Creek Wilderness. Ute Trail River Ranch has seven charmingly furnished, cozy, hand-hewn log cabins that sit on the Tarryall River beckoning you to settle in for a quiet retreat. The cabins take you back in time with their woodstoves, antique iron beds and western lodge decor. All are fully furnished from snugly flannel bed linens to coffee pots and mugs. The cabins sleep from two to six people; some have private baths while others share a convenient shower house (flannel robes are provided in shared bath cabins). There is also a bed & breakfast suite and lodge room available. Ute Trail River Ranch is a non-smoking facility.

The natural surroundings invite you to slow down and enjoy the tranquil beauty of the forest and the relaxing sounds of the rushing Tarryall River. Private, streamside fishing is a must, especially since the Ranch was featured on the cable network ESPN's "Fly Fishing America" show. Experience the breath-taking scenery exploring the mountain hiking trails or enjoying a trail ride at a local riding stable year- round. Try a little rock hunting or wildlife watching.

Reservations are strongly recommended. A confirmation deposit equal to 50%of the entire stay is required. There is a two night minimum stay requirement; three night minimum on holidays. Be sure to inquire about the Ranch's off-season Bed, Breakfast and Dinner packages.

Location: From Highway 24, go 1 mile west of Lake George. Take Tarryall Road north (County Road 77) for 21 miles. From Highway 285 at Jefferson, take County Road 77 south for 21 miles.

7 Cabins with Kitchen	Phone in Lobby	Debra Baxter & Jim Fagerstrom, Owners
2 Lodging Rooms	Bed & Breakfast Available	21446 CR 77
1 Room with Fireplace	All Units Nonsmoking	Lake George CO 80827-9302
3 Rooms with Wood Stoves	Recreation Room	719/748-3015
Central Fireplace	Elevation: 9000	E-mail: utrr@aol.com
Central Campfire Area	Credit Cards: VMD	www.coloradodirectory.com/utetrailriverranch
	Rates: $50-$95	
	Open: All Year	

At the resort:

At resort or within 15 minutes:

Waltons Mountain Lodge

Waltons Mountain Lodge, in picturesque Manitou Springs, is open year round for your vacation enjoyment. This mountain home may be rented for two to six days and easily sleeps 12 in six bedrooms with 3.5 baths. For larger groups, ask about arrangements for bunkroom use. The lodge has a 23-foot stone fireplace in the great room, a dining room, fully equipped kitchen, family room and outside deck with barbecue grills. Waltons Mountain Lodge is ideal for family vacations, reunions and retreats.

The lodge is situated on privately owned property and adjacent to Pike National Forest. Spend your days hiking, mountain biking and visiting many area attractions. The lodge is a five minute drive from Manitou Springs' restaurants and shops. Nearby attractions include Pikes Peak Railroad Depot, the Cave of the Winds, cliff dwellings and Garden of the Gods.

A four night minimum is required during the high season, and a minimum of two nights is required year-round. The lodge is non-smoking and no pets are allowed.

Location: In manitou Springs, leave US Highway at the Cave of the Winds exit. Drive down the ramp and turn left on Manitou Avenue. Immediately turn right on Minnehaha Avenue. Follow Minnehaha through a sharp left turn and continue

past playground. Turn right on Mesa Avenue and proceed straight ahead through the gate. Turn right at the sign and follow the road a quarter of a mile to the Lodge.

1 Vacation Home	Phone in Rooms	Herald & Naomi & Dave & Teri Walton,
Central Fireplace	All Units Nonsmoking	Owners
Central Campfire Area	Recreation Room	235 Mesa Ave
	Elevation: 6700	Manitou Springs CO 80829
	Credit Cards: None	719/685-4728
	Rates: $150-$250	E-mail: halhcw@aol.com
	Open: All Year	www.coloradodirectory.com/waltonsmtnlodge

At the resort:

At resort or within 15 minutes:

Western Cabins

This resort is a quiet get-a-way in Manitou Springs with scenic red rocks of the Garden of the Gods as your backyard. All of the rustic, western-style cabins are equipped with kitchenettes, private bath and shower, direct dial phones, cable television and air-conditioning. Upper terrace cabins have lovely, unobstructed views of Pikes Peak.

On-site conveniences include a coin laundromat, a beauty and barber shop, a play area, a heated outdoor swimming pool, picnic tables and barbecue area. Your hosts will arrange sightseeing tours and reservations for chuckwagon dinners, melodramas and the Pikes Peak Cog Railway at no extra charge. Just three minutes away in downtown, picturesque Manitou Springs, you can shop for gifts, antiques and western wear. Dine fine restaurants, try the local mineral water or just browse. Walk a few blocks from your cabin to a nightclub, restaurants, churches and horseback riding stables. Western Cabins is an excellent starting point for many Pikes Peak area attractions.

There is a five night minimum stay. Ask about the lower rates from October 5 to April 15. Reservations are required, with a confirmation deposit of $200.00 per cabin.

Location: North of Manitou Avenue on Beakers Lane, off Business 24.

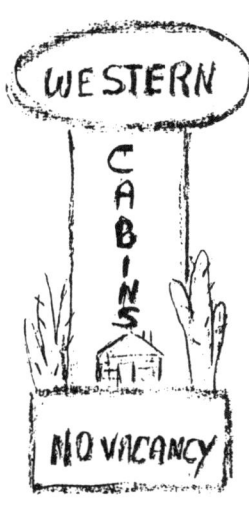

11 Cabins with Kitchen	Phone in Rooms	Lillian Simek, Owner
Central Hot Tub	All Units Nonsmoking	106 Beckers Lane
	Elevation: 6400	Manitou Springs CO 80829
	Credit Cards: None	800/873-4553
	Rates:	719/685-5755 x251
	Open: All Year	Fax: 719/685-9061
		E-mail: Cabinsinq@aol.com
		www.coloradodirectory.com/westerncabinsresort/

At the resort:

At resort or within 15 minutes:

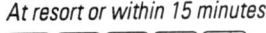

Poudre River Canyon Area

Including Bellvue, Livermore and Red Feather Lakes —
Map: B-16 & B-14

Designated Colorado's first National Wild and Scenic River in 1986, the **Poudre River Canyon**, also known as Cache la Poudre, is in the midst of the Roosevelt National Forest. In 1840, French trappers camped at the mouth of the canyon west of Fort Collins. A heavy snow fell, forcing them to reduce their load, so they buried their gun powder, or "cache la poudre," along the river's banks. In 1879, settlers built a rough road along the river, soon leading to a steady stream of more cabins. With water rushing east from Rocky Mountain National Park, the crashing Poudre River runs along Highway 14 and has brown and rainbow trout. Some areas of the river are Wild Trout sections where bait fishing is not allowed. Where there are rapids, there are white water rafting trips — the river is a hot spot with both rafters and kayakers. Accessible from the canyon, the Cache La Poudre Wilderness Area ranges in altitude from 6,000' to 8,600' and its steep, rugged terrain is seldom traveled. Hiking is popular in the Comanche Peak Wilderness, the Rawah Wilderness, the Neota Flat Tops Wilderness and in Roosevelt National Forest. While fishing is the number one draw here, hiking comes in a close second. In the winter, try one of the many cross-country ski trails in the breathtaking high peaks of the Cameron Pass area at 10,276'. **Red Feather Lakes**, a group of 14 lakes, are about 50 miles northwest of Fort Collins. Six of the lakes are open to the public for trout fishing and boating. The scenic beauty of the San Isabel and Roosevelt National Forests boasts abundant wildflowers and wildlife. Look for elk, antelope, mule deer, bears, quail, grouse, mountain lions, big horn sheep and wild turkey. Wintertime brings cross-country skiers, snowmobilers, snowshoers and ice-fishing enthusiasts to the area.

Fun Things to Do

- Glen Echo General Store, Gift Shop & Restaurant (800) 348-2208,
- Cottonwood Hollow Restaurant & Trail Rides (970) 482-4401
- Rocky Mountain Adventure Rafting, Kayaking & Fly Fishing (800) 858-6808
- Roosevelt National Forest Visitors Center (970) 498-2770

Beaver Meadows Resort Ranch

In a high mountain River Valley, Beaver Meadows Resort Ranch adjoins national forest land. Choose among comfortable accommodations designed to suit your style — from modern cabins complete with fireplaces and full kitchens to luxurious condominiums to new motel rooms. Pick a unit close to the restaurant and lounge or a secluded cabin overlooking the North Fork of the Poudre River. Either way, relax in the community sauna after an exhilarating day of adventures.

Activities include taking a horseback ride, a romantic horse-drawn carriage ride or a memorable sleigh ride in the winter. Hike and mountain bike in the national forest. Fish in the private ponds during the summer and skate on them in the winter. Other nearby winter activities include cross-country skiing on groomed trails, past pine and spruce trees with boughs drooping under the weight of snow. The resort provides skiing lessons. Spring brings melting streams, budding aspen, tiny flowers snuggled in the new grass as well as hungry trout. Summer means songbirds, wildflowers, fresh-washed air after a rain shower and night stars undimmed by city lights. Autumn explodes with color in golden aspen, deep blue skies and the heavy green of the pines — perfect for hiking and picture taking.

If you're planning a wedding contact us for a wedding brochure. The resort offers a large meeting room for business conferences, reunions and retreats.

Location: 50 miles northwest of Fort Collins, 6 miles northwest of Red Feather Lakes on the North Fork of the Poudre River. Take Highway 287 north from Fort Collins 21 miles to Livermore, turn left onto Country Road 74E for 24 miles until it intersects with County Road 73C (gravel road) take for 5 miles.

4 Cabins with Kitchen	Phone in Lobby	The Weixelmans Owners
1 Cabin without Kitchen	Some Units Nonsmoking	100 Marmot Dr, Unit 1
1 Vacation Home	Recreation Room	Red Feather Lakes CO 80545
5 Lodging Rooms	Elevation: 8400	800/462-5870
8 Motel Rooms	Credit Cards: VM	970/881-2450
1 Room with Hot Tub	Rates: $49-$150	Fax: 970/881-2643
9 Rooms with Fireplaces	Open: All Year	E-mail: bmrr@verinet.com
2 Rooms with Wood Stoves		www.coloradodirectory.com/beavermeadowsresortranch

At the resort:

At resort or within 15 minutes:

Glen Echo Resort

In the heart of Roosevelt National Forest, quiet Glen Echo Resort is on the beautiful Poudre River, Colorado's "trout route." Choose among modern cottages with full kitchens and baths, rustic cabins with kitchens and shared bathroom-shower facilities or family mountain homes with large living rooms and everything but food. All cottages have dishes, cooking supplies, bedding and linens. Several cabins have decks overlooking the Cache La Poudre River where you and your family can relax while listening to the water's murmur. Tall pine trees and a lawn with attractive flower beds abound this landscaped resort.

Amenities include a laundromat, picnic pavilion and a general store with fly fishing and tackle, picnic supplies, sporting goods, groceries and gasoline. Enjoy the casual, non-smoking, family restaurant with tasty home cooking with made-from-scratch pies and rolls. Be sure and try the restaurant's peanut butter malts and pies. The upscale gift shop has a wide variety of T-shirts and the largest selection of authentic Native American jewelry and crafts in northern Colorado. While browsing, check out the Native American and African wildlife exhibit. Glen Echo sports a playground, recreational hall and horseshoes. Enjoy fishing on Colorado's

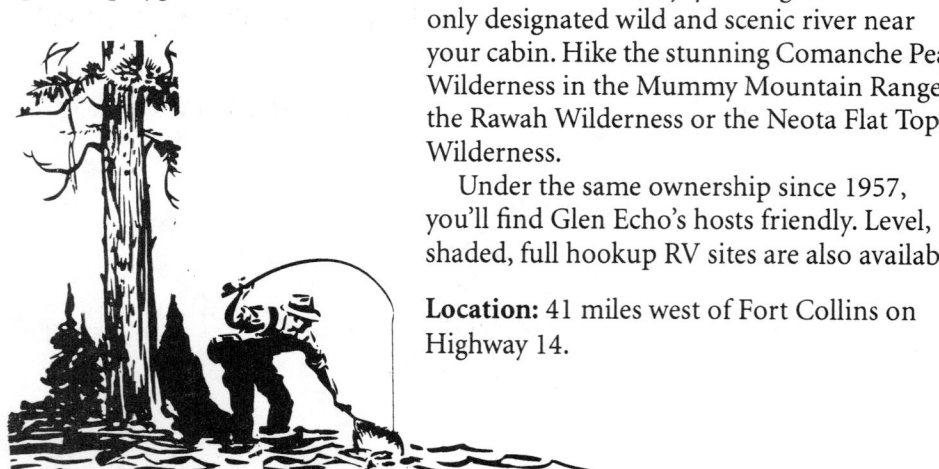

only designated wild and scenic river near your cabin. Hike the stunning Comanche Peak Wilderness in the Mummy Mountain Range, the Rawah Wilderness or the Neota Flat Tops Wilderness.

Under the same ownership since 1957, you'll find Glen Echo's hosts friendly. Level, shaded, full hookup RV sites are also available.

Location: 41 miles west of Fort Collins on Highway 14.

14 Cabins with Kitchen	Pay Phone Available	Sam Shoultz & Ken Matzner, Owners
2 Vacation Homes	Some Units Nonsmoking	31503 Poudre Canyon Dr
6 Rooms with Fireplaces	Recreation Room	Bellvue CO 80512-9312
Central Campfire Area	Elevation: 7200	800/348-2208 Reserv
	Credit Cards: VM	970/881-2208 Resort
	Rates: $40-$125	Fax: 970/881-2066
	Open: 5/1 to 11/10	www.coloradodirectory.com/glenechoresort/

At the resort:

At resort or within 15 minutes:

Indian Meadows Resort

Indian Meadows Resort is open year round. Stay in cabins along the river or have an adventure in a teepee, with a shower house providing the modern amenities. The Lone Star is a single cabin by the river with a double bed, fully equipped kitchen with a propane stove and bathroom with a shower. The Pueblo is a large guest house on the river that can sleep up to seven people. It has a living room with a fireplace, a full bath and a kitchen with a hot plate and small refrigerator. Its many windows provide spectacular views of the Poudre River. The 8-plex is a line of 8 kitchenette units consisting of three rooms: a fully equipped kitchen, a bathroom and a bedroom. The new duplexes have a queen bed, a queen hide-a-way, a small table and chairs and a bathroom with a shower. The teepee is unfurnished– bring your camping gear minus the tent.

Indian Meadows boasts excellent food (authentic Mexican and American), a comfortable, quiet lounge, friendly service and cleanliness. Where beauty and friendship will bring you back again and again. Spend your vacation relaxing and photographing the wildlife. Plenty of fishing spots and hiking trails abound in the Poudre River Canyon.

Under new management. Campsites are available. Pets are allowed for an additional fee per night.

Location: On Highway 14, Poudre Canyon Road, near milepost makrer 92.

10 Cabins with Kitchen	Pay Phone Available	Naomi Betz & John & Colleen Martinez,
2 Cabins without Kitchens	Recreation Room	Owners
1 Room with Woodstove	Elevation: 7400	29839 Poudre Canyon Rd
Central Woodstove	Credit Cards: VM	Bellvue CO 80512
Central Campfire Area	Rates: $45-$125	970/881-2281
	Open: All Year	www.coloradodirectory.com/indianmeadowslodge/

At the resort:

At resort or within 15 minutes:

Mountain Greenery Resort

Mountain Greenery Resort is snuggled on the banks of The Cache La Poudre River, Colorado's first National Wild and Scenic River. The resort offers clean, modern rooms ranging from one bedroom with no cooking facilities to two bedrooms with kitchenettes, living rooms and tub-showers. There are also six mobile homes for rent.

Mountain Greenery's restaurant features home cooking, feast on a hearty breakfast, a quick lunch and a leisurely dinner, be sure to leave room for their home baked pies and mouth watering cinnamon rolls. The small country store offers fishing supplies and gifts. Children will enjoy the large lawn and playground, while all will relish casting a line into the Poudre River. After catching a trout fry it up in the picnic area by the river. There are no televisions at the resort, so family time is spent escaping into the great outdoors. The area offers four-wheel-drive trails, horseback riding, mountain biking and ample hiking trails. Or drive Highway 14 (Poudre Canyon Drive toward Walden and relax as you meander on this scenic and historic byway. The winter offers quieter time in the canyon with snowshoeing, cross country skiing and snowmobiling.

This is a perfect resort for family reunions and weddings. RV sites are available. Pets are allowed for an additional fee per night. When you stay seven nights, the seventh night is free. They offer a Senior's discount on lodging.

Location: Forty-two miles from Ft Collins, on Highway 14, Poudre Canyon Road, near milepost 90.

5 Lodging Rooms	Phone in Lobby	Vic & Sharon McLachlan & Cindy & Al
3 Motel Rooms	Elevation: 7205	Robinson
Central Fireplace	Credit Cards: VM	32595 Poudre Canyon
Central Campfire Area	Rates: $45-$75	Bellvue CO 80512-9415
	Open: 5/1 to 11/15	970/881-2242
		Fax: 970/881-2723
		E-mail: vmclach@aol.com
		www.coloradodirectory.com/mountaingreeneryresort/

At the resort:

At resort or within 15 minutes:

Poudre River Resort

Adjacent to the spectacular Poudre River, high in the Rocky Mountains, the resort has modern cabins with ample bedrooms, linens, bathrooms, showers, towels and fully equipped kitchens with electric or gas ranges. One cabin sleeps up to 10 people and has a fireplace. The comfortable cabins are well spaced for privacy and picnics. Fall asleep in the cool mountain air and wake to birds chirping in the trees along the river. You'll find the Poudre a quiet mountain getaway.

For relaxation, soak outdoors in the community hot tub or rent a movie from the on-site video service. For added convenience, there's a well-stocked store with craft items, groceries, fishing licenses, tackle, books and souvenirs as well as a playground, snack bar and a coin-laundromat. Meander along a path from your cabin to the river. Hike one of the excellent trails and fish in stocked lakes, both at the resort and in the nearby mountains. If you get tired of cabin cooking, dine at one of the local restaurants nearby. In the winter, pristine back country areas are accessible by cross-country skis or snowmobile. Whether you hike it or ski it, Poudre River country is refreshingly un-crowded and the mountainous terrain where pine forests and wildlife abound is Colorado at its best.

Full hookup RV sites are also available. The resort specializes in family reunions, birthday bashes, anniversary celebrations, religious and company retreats and outdoor weddings. A one night deposit is required with reservations. One pet per cabin is allowed for some cabins. There are non pet and non smoking cabins. Children four and under stay free.

Location: 45 miles northwest of Fort Collins, on Highway 14, near milepost marker 89.

9 Cabins with Kitchen	Pay Phone Available	Arlyn & Allyn Atadero, owners
1 Vacation Home	Some Units Nonsmoking	33021 Poudre Canyon Dr
1 Lodging Room	Recreation Room	Bellvue CO 80512-9426
Central Hot Tub	Elevation: 7200	970/881-2139
Central Campfire Area	Credit Cards: VMAD	Fax: 970/881-2129 ph 1st
	Rates: $79-$99	E-mail: allyn@info2000.net
	Open: All Year	www.coloradodirectory.com/poudreriverresort/

At the resort:

At resort or within 15 minutes:

Red Feather Ranch

Experience tranquillity at Red Feather Ranch where you'll vacation amid 40 acres of pine, aspen, rugged hills and grassy meadows. The ranch is both a bed and breakfast and a lodge for those desiring a home in the mountains for their quiet getaway or group gathering. The six bedroom lodge and rustic cabin accommodate up to 20 people in double rooms with shared baths. Prepare your own feasts in the panoramic kitchen or outside on at barbecue facilities.

The ranch has a spacious great room which is ideal for meetings, activities or quiet relaxation. Spend an evening around the secluded fire circle and experience the sights and sounds of native wildlife. Soak in the spa, lounge in a hammock or simply stroll among the ranch's natural beauty. The ranch is just an hour scenic drive north of Fort Collins and is minutes from spectacular lakes, mountain trails and the Cache La Poudre River. Nearby the outdoor activities include cross-country skiing, fishing, rafting, mountain biking and horseback riding. Miles of hiking trails begin in the backyard and lead into Roosevelt National Forest with breathtaking views of the Mummy Range. Within a short drive are white water rafting, golfing, boating, sleigh riding, snowmobiling, ice fishing and hunting.

Red Feather Ranch is perfect for group retreats, corporate and education workshops, family and friends gatherings and celebrations, or a romantic night in the mountains. The lodge and cabin are both non-smoking. Guest horses are welcomed.

Location: In Red Feather Lakes on Country Road 68C.

1 Vacation Home	Phone in Lobby	Clay & Lawton Harper, Owners
6 Lodging Rooms	Bed & Breakfast Available	3613 CR 68C
1 Room with Woodstove	All Units Nonsmoking	Red Feather Lakes CO 80545
Central Hot Tub	Recreation Room	970/881-3715
Central Woodstove	Elevation: 8500	E-mail: rfranch@earthlink.net
Central Campfire Area	Credit Cards: None	www.coloradodirectory.com/redfeatherranch/
	Rates: $75	
	Open: All Year	

At the resort:

At resort or within 15 minutes:

Rustic Resort

Rustic Resort lies on the banks of the Poudre River. Like its name, all cabins are rustic with electricity and cold running water (summer only), but have no cooking facilities. Choose among cabins that sleep up to seven people, or smaller cabins just for couples. Antique wood burning stoves or fireplaces provide heat in all the units. Three cabins overlook the Cache La Poudre — a wild and scenic river. Linens, towels and wood are furnished. The shower and restroom facility is located directly behind the restaurant.

Rustic Resort has a restaurant (breakfast, lunch and dinner daily), lounge, liquor store and small gift shop. You may fish right on the resort in the river. Nearby are horseback riding, lake fishing, mountain biking, cross-country skiing, snowshoeing, snowmobiling, ice fishing and hunting. Within an hour's drive are whitewater rafting tours, a museum, golf course and sleigh rides.

The restaurant serves as an indoor group meeting area and accommodates 60 guest along with catered meals are available with advanced arrangements. Six full hookup RV sites, 12 RV sites with electric and water only, and tent camping are also available.

Location: 41 miles west of Fort Collins on Highway 14.

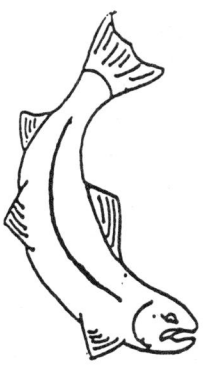

6 Cabins without Kitchens	Pay Phone Available	Bill & Linda Leigh, Owners
2 Rooms with Fireplaces	Recreation Room	31443 Poudre Canyon
6 Rooms with Wood Stoves	Elevation: 7650	Bellvue CO 80512
Central Fireplace	Credit Cards: VM	970/881-2179
Central Campfire Area	Rates: $45-$60	www.coloradodirectory.com/rusticresort/
	Open: All Year	

At the resort:

At resort or within 15 minutes:

Sundance Trail Guest Ranch

Boarding on Roosevelt National Forest, Sundance Trail Guest Ranch is nestled amid the beauty of stately pines and whispering aspen groves in the heart of mountain country. Warm. cozy, family-sized rooms or suites are in either a newly renovated lodge or newly built cabins, Each room/suite is uniquely decorated, and all have refrigerators, coffee-makers, clock radios, private bath, heat control, daily housekeeping, queen beds and twins/bunks for children. Two rooms are wheelchair friendly.

Sundance Trail is famous for family fun, hospitality, lifetime memories and friendship. Riding on endless mountain trails is the principle activity. Experienced wranglers match you with a horse for your skill level, who will be your horse throughout your stay. With an unstructured atmosphere the Ranch offers whitewater rafting, river float trips, off-road jeep trips, hiking, fishing, evening campfires, and hammocks for an afternoon nap. Children programs are available with counselor/wranglers for activities such as gathering eggs from the hen house, singalong, treasure hunts, fishing and crafts. One evening each week the young folks enjoy stories around the campfire and a camp-out in a teepee. On this same night the adults catch their breath with a quiet, candle light dinner in the lodge.

During the summer it is run as a full scale dude ranch, while in the fall, winter and spring it is a bed & breakfast. In Summer rates, based on double occupancy, are all inclusive covering lodging, meals, activities, raft trips, and a horse. The minimum stay at Sundance Trail is seven days between June 21 and August 23. During fall, winter and spring the Ranch is available for seminars and retreats. Cribs are available.

Location: Thirty-five miles north of Fort Collins in Red Feather Lakes.

8 Lodging Rooms	Bed & Breakfast Available	Dan & Ellen Morin, Owners
1 Room with Fireplace	All Units Nonsmoking	17931 Red Feather Lakes Road
Central Hot Tub	Recreation Room	Red Feather Lakes CO 80545
Central Fireplace	Elevation: 8000	800/357-4930 ph/fax
Central Campfire Area	Credit Cards: VM	970/224-1222 ph/fax
	Rates:	E-mail: SundanceTr@aol.com
	Open: All Year	www.coloradodirectory.com/sundancetrail

At the resort:

At resort or within 15 minutes:

Trout Lodge

This lodge wasn't named for nothing! Be sure to bring your fishing rods along when you vacation here. The private, romantic cabins come with fireplaces, bathrooms and fully equipped kitchens. Set in a scenic, quiet atmosphere, the modern, completely furnished cabins feature comfortable rooms for your enjoyment. Choose among nine cabins, some of which have wood stoves and one is a non-smoking unit. Spend an afternoon relaxing on your front porch and an evening of candlelight dinner in the privacy of your own cabin. Or dine out in nearby restaurants.

Trout Lodge is in a wooded area, near meadows and adjoining the national forest, five state lakes and a rustic, mountain-top golf course. A central meeting room can accommodate larger groups or be a sports center for family games. Enjoy endless trout fishing on the lakes and three nearby streams. Try boat fishing on the many lakes. Hikers and photographers alike will appreciate the numerous forest and mountain trails where wildflowers and wildlife flourish. Rent mountain bikes on-site or bring your horse along for some back country riding. In the winter, bring your skis, snowshoes and ice-fishing gear. Historic Red Feathers Lakes village has quaint country stores, restaurants and friendly town folks.

Location: 45 miles northwest of Fort Collins, about 26 miles west of Highway 287. West of Livermore 24± miles to Red Feather Lakes, turn right on Prairie Divide Road, then left on Main Street.

9 Cabins with Kitchen	Phone in Lobby	Steve & Charlotte Schliening
5 Rooms with Fireplaces	Some Units Nonsmoking	PO Box 126
4 Rooms with Wood Stoves	Recreation Room	Red Feather Lakes CO 80545-0126
	Elevation: 8200	970/881-2964
	Credit Cards: VMAD	E-mail: Airstrea95@aol.com
	Rates: $49-$99	www.coloradodirectory.com/troutlodge
	Open: All Year	

At the resort:

At resort or within 15 minutes:

Royal Gorge Area

Including Cañon City, Coaldale, Cotopaxi & Texas Creek —
Map: K-16 & K-14

Considered the climate capital of Colorado, **Cañon City**'s natural setting protects it from harsh weather. Once a favorite camping area of the Ute Indians, both dinosaur bones and oil were discovered here. Five miles north of the city is the Garden Park Monument commemorating the 1877 dinosaur find. The Arkansas River, flows through the city and offers great fishing west of town, formed one of the most spectacular attractions in the state – the Royal Gorge, 8 miles west. The world's highest suspension bridge hangs a dizzying 1,053' above the rushing river, offering unforgettable vistas of the 8 mile canyon in the city's largest park. Beginning in May 1999, for the first time in 30 years, you can now travel through the spectacular Royal Gorge by rail aboard the Cañon City and Royal Gorge Railroad. Next to viewing the bridge, rafting the Arkansas River is the most popular reason for vacationing here, followed by fishing in the spring and fall. **Cotopaxi** and **Coaldale** are also popular launching pads to rafting the Arkansas River. The Colorado Territorial Prison in Cañon City, built in 1868, is the only prison museum located next to a currently operating prison. Several scenic byways lead out of Cañon City, including one through Phantom Canyon where the road passes granite tunnels and between sheer cliff walls on its way to Cripple Creek. **Texas Creek,** located between the Royal Gorge and Cotopaxi, was named by a Texas drover whose heard of longhorns was stampeded by a marauding bear one night.

Fun Things to Do

- American Adventure Expeditions (800)288-0675
- Arkansas River Tours (800) 321-4352
- Arkansas Headwaters Recreation Area (719) 539-7289
- Cañon City & Royal Gorge Railraod (888) RAILS-4U
- Clear Creek Rafting (800) 353-9901
- Dinosaur Depot Museum & Garden Park Fossil Area (800) 987-6379
- Indian Springs Ranch National Natural Landmark (719) 372-3907
- Lazy J Rafting Company (800) 678-4274
- Raft Masters (800)568-7238
- Raven Rafting & Adventure Trips (800) 332-3381
- River Runners Ltd. (800) 525-2081
- Royal Gorge Bridge Park (888) 333-5597 ext 228 see page 241
- Shadow Hills Golf Course (719) 275-0603

Royal Gorge Bridge & Park

Just twelve miles west of Cañon City, Royal Gorge Bridge and Park offers an unforgettable opportunity — the chance to experience the world's highest suspension bridge, a dizzying 1,053 feet above the rushing Arkansas River. The bridge was completed in 1929 and is one of Colorado's most exhilarating attractions. You can walk, drive or ride the trolley across the nearly one-quarter mile span, marveling at the vistas of snow-capped peaks and the blue green river swirling below. Enjoy a breathtaking ride on the aerial tram 1,200 feet above the chasm. Or take a trip on the world's steepest incline railway to the bottom of the incredible canyon where you might catch white water rafters shooting the rapids. Another way to see the sights is to walk along the well maintained nature trail, with a stop at Point Sublime to catch the best views in the park.

Other family activities include a multi-media show at the Plaza Theater, professional talent performing in the Coca-Cola Entertainment Gazebo and special seasonal events such as a fiddler's contestt. The kids will love the Kid's Krazy Korner with its slides, climbing areas and other treats for the little ones. A vintage miniature train delights visitors of all ages. Friendly mule deer roam freely near the park's entrance. And when all the activities make you hungry, be sure to stop at the Cliff Terrace Cafe on the south side, or the Royal Grill Pizza Garden on the north rim. Before leaving, be sure to check out the six unique gift shops throughout the park.

The Royal Gorge Bridge and Park is open all year and a must-see for anyone vacationing in the area.

Location: Twelve miles west of Cañon City on Highway 50 to Royal Gorge Bridge exit, south to County Road 3A, proceed to the entrance gate.

Dorothy Day, Sales & Marketing Dir
PO Box 549
Cañon City   CO   81215-0549
888/333-5597
719/275-7507
Fax: 719/269-3501
E-mail: rgb@ris.net
www.coloradodirectory.com/royalgorgebridge/

Arkansas River KOA & Kamping Kabins™ & Loma Linda Motel

Make the Arkansas River KOA & Loma Linda Motel in Cotopaxi your base camp for family reunions. Bounded by scenic Highway 50 and the Arkansas River, you'll find a whole new world to roam and unwind in. Guest motel rooms with kitchenettes and Kamping Kabins along the river are available. The rustic camping cabin has electricity and sleeps up to four. Bring your own sleeping bag. The clean motel rooms have private showers, television, linens and at least two double beds. The kitchenettes have a stove, refrigerator and dishes. All units have close access to the river as well as picnic tables and campfires. Borrow a grill to cook supper outdoors. Sit back and listen to the roar of the raging river while you gaze at the red rocks and snow-tipped peaks of southern Colorado. Every night you'll have starry, starry skies and wide open spaces filled with fresh air.

The KOA also has clean restrooms and a coin laundry on-site. From here you can fish on the beautiful Arkansas or scramble along its picturesque banks, rock hunting. Summer time activities include miniature golf, nightly movies, shuffleboard and hay rides — all for free! Nearby you can pan for gold, hike, hunt, mountain bike, whitewater raft or horseback ride. After it all, take a dip in the heated swimming pool or challenge your family to a video game in recreation room.

Indoor and outdoor group meeting areas, tent and RV sites are available.

Location: Off Highway 50 at milepost marker 247, between Cañon City and Salida, one mile east of Cotopaxi.

5 Cabins with Kitchen	Pay Phone Available	21435 US Hwy 50 - PO Box 387
2 Cabins without Kitchens	All Units Nonsmoking	Cotopaxi CO 81223-0387
6 Camper Cabins	Recreation Room	800/562-2686
3 Motel Rooms	Elevation: 6300	719/275-9308
Central Campfire Area	Credit Cards: VMD	Fax: 719/275-2249
	Rates: $35-$65	www.coloradodirectory.com/arkansasriverkoa/
	Open: 4/15 to 10/31	

At the resort:

At resort or within 15 minutes:

Lazy J Resort & Rafting Company

Vacation in the valley solitude of the Lazy J Resort which sits on the banks of the Arkansas River. With beautiful views of the Sangre de Cristo mountains, the resort offers modern cabins, camper cabins and motel rooms in one- and two-bedroom units. Bring your own bedding and cooking utensils for the camper cabins. Some of the modern log cabins and motel rooms have kitchenettes; and one unit has a fireplace. Nearby are large, grassy lawns for children to play on and families to relax on. Enjoy cool mountain breezes, fresh air and unforgettable scenery daily.

A full-service restaurant specializing in American and Mexican foods, a playground, a volleyball court, horse shoe pits and a heated swimming pool are other amenities. The gift shop features Colorado specialty items, T-shirts, snacks, souvenirs and rafting supplies. Whitewater raft trips for every level, run by the resort, are Lazy J's specialty. They proudly boast an excellent safety record. Take a wild and wet half- or full-day trip. Overnight or custom journeys can be arranged. "Saddle and Paddle" combination trips includes both horses and rafts. If you prefer river fishing, cast your line from near your cabin, or hike to one of the many nearby fishing areas.

Indoor and outdoor group meeting areas, and shady RV sites are also available.

Location: Thirty miles west of the Royal Gorge on Highway 50, near milepost marker 242.

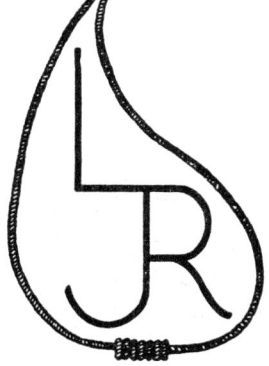

3 Cabins with Kitchen	Pay Phone Available	Cheryl Jeffries, Owner
8 Camper Cabins	Recreation Room	PO Box 109
5 Motel Rooms	Elevation: 6200	Coaldale CO 81222-0109
1 Room with Fireplace	Credit Cards: VM	719/942-4274
1 Room with Woodstove	Rates: $30-$70	www.coloradodirectory.com/lazyjresort/
Central Woodstove	Open: All Year	
Central Campfire Area		

At the resort:

At resort or within 15 minutes:

Whispering Pines Resort

The roaring Arkansas River runs for a mile right through Whispering Pines Resort in Texas Creek. On the south side of the river, the newly remodeled motel rooms and rustic camper cabins have a breathtaking view of the Rocky Mountains from the river's banks. If you stay in the camper cabins, bring your own bedding and cooking supplies. Hot showers and clean restrooms are provided. Kick back in the shade and watch the rafters paddle past.

It almost goes without saying that the trout fishing is excellent and the whitewater rafting is great — all right from Whispering Pines and continues down the Arkansas River through the Royal Gorge. Return again to Whispering Pines on their bus. Nearby, you can horseback ride, golf, visit tourist attractions, and get all your groceries, camping supplies and fishing tackle in the nearby shops.

RV and tent sites are also available. When making your lodging reservations be sure to also book a raft trip.

Location: On Highway 50, milepost marker 250, near Texas Creek.

6 Camper Cabins	Pay Phone Available	Hal Davenport, Owner & Bob Hinshaw, Mgr.
4 Motel Rooms	Recreation Room	24871 HWY 50 W
	Elevation: 7200	Texas Creek CO 81223
	Credit Cards: VM	888/275-3827
	Rates: $35-$45	719/275-3827
	Open: 5/1 to 9/15	Fax: 972/289-4984
		www.coloradodirectory.com/whisperingpinesresort

At the resort:

At resort or within 15 minutes:

San Isabel to Westcliffe

Map: M-17 & L-15

When silver was king in 1881, the Denver & Rio Grande Railroad expanded from Cañon City west and built **Westcliffe**. After silver went bust, Westcliffe managed to hang on as a ranching and farming community. Just north of town is Lake DeWeese, in the bowl of the Wet Mountain Valley, which offers fishing and water sports. Grape Creek, which flows below the reservoir, has rainbow and brown trout. **San Isabel** is home to Lake San Isabel in the San Isabel National Forest, an ideal place for picnicking, fishing and hiking. Lakes of the Clouds, at 11,200', are accessible by four-wheel drive or hiking in 5 miles. But the trip is worth it as the remote beaver ponds below the lakes have brook and cutthroat trout while the upper lake has rainbow trout. In the winter, try cross-country skiing and snowshoeing in the area. The new Frontier pathways Scenic and Historic Byway connects Colorado City, Rye, San Isabel, Westcliffe and Pueblo via Colorado highways 165 and 96. Visit nearby Rye to see the Robbers Roost Western Museum where you can see Buffalo Bill's saddle and the guns that won the 'West'. This area has one of Colorado's most intriguing attractions: Bishop's Castle built solely by Jim Bishop. The artist has created a huge stone and iron castle complete with a metal dragon whose nose is a woodstove chimney. If you're nearby, a visit to the ever expanding castle promises to be memorable.

Fun Things to Do

- City Park Golf Course, Pueblo (719) 561-4946
- Colorado State Fair & Events Center, Pueblo (800) 876-4567
- El Pueblo Museum, Pueblo (719) 583-0453
- Greenway & Nature Center, Pueblo (719) 549-2414
- Hollydot Golf Course, Colorado City (719) 676-3341
- Lake Pueblo State Recreation Area (719) 561-9320
- Pueblo West Golf Course (719) 547-2280
- Robbers Roost Western Museum, Rye (719) 489-3559
- Walking Stick Golf Course, Pueblo (719) 584-3400

Alpine Lodge, Cabins & Dinner Restaurant

Bordering the San Isabel National Forest, Alpine Lodge is nestled among pine and aspen trees in the Sangre de Cristo Mountains. The quaint mountain cabins sleep up to four people in two bedrooms. All have kitchens equipped with stoves, refrigerators, cooking utensils and dishes. The cabins also feature private baths with all towels and linens provided. The cabins are electrically heated and insulated for year round comfort.

For your evening meal try Alpine Lodge's restaurant, specializing in charbroiled steaks, seafood, sandwiches and delicious homemade soup and pies. The only television at the lodge is in the lounge. Over 100 miles of trails in the San Isabel National Forest and Sangre de Cristo Wilderness area await you for hiking and horseback riding during the summer and snow-shoeing and cross-country skiing in the winter. Start hiking on the trails from your cabin door to dozens of mountain streams and lakes. Or drive to Lake DeWeese for fishing or boating. Climb many of the nearby 13,000' to 14,000' peaks in a day without technical equipment and don't be surprised to see eagles soaring high above you. Photograph the wild-

flowers splashing color through the meadows and mountainsides. In the fall, hunt elk, antelope, deer, bighorn sheep and wild turkey.

Cabins are available for daily or weekly stays. Alvarado Campground is adjacent to lodge for camping.

Location: Ten miles southwest of Westcliffe on County Road 140, off Highway 69, between milepost markers 55-56.

5 Cabins with Kitchen	Pay Phone Available	David & Marian Leugers, Owners
	Recreation Room	6848 CR 140
	Elevation: 9000	Westcliffe CO 81252
	Credit Cards: VM	888/783-5557
	Rates: $48	719/783-2660
	Open: All Year	E-mail: alpinelodg@aol.com
		www.coloradodirectory.com/alpinelodgewestcliffe/

At the resort:

At resort or within 15 minutes:

Lodge at San Isabel

Snug in the mountains next to the trout-stocked Lake San Isabel, these cabins are ideal for groups and family reunions. The lodge is well-established and family run. Each cabin sleeps four people and some have king beds. Bring your own dishes and cooking utensils. The lodge provides towels every day and linens every three days. Three of the cabins have kitchens for housekeeping and sleep from four to six people. Get away from it all at this scenic, quiet mountain lodge just a few steps from picturesque Lake San Isabel.

The Lodge's full service restaurant, open from 8 a.m. to 9 p.m. daily, specializes in great burgers and Mexican dishes. If you prefer, order take-out and eat in the privacy of your cabin. Also on-site is a small gift shop full of curios. Ask your hosts about summer whitewater rafting tours. Go horseback riding, hiking and mountain biking on the surrounding national forest trails. Catch a glimpse of the past when you explore the old gold mines. Enjoy jeeping, motorcycling or ATV riding on Greenhorn Mountain. In the fall, hunt elk, antelope, deer, bear, mountain lion, big horn sheep and wild turkey. Or enjoy the yearly turning of the aspen. The lodge is on Ophir Creek snowmobile trail system which consists of 90+ miles of groom trails running from Ophir Creek to Greenhorn Mountain. No visit to Rye is complete without a stop at Robber's Roost Western Museum where you can see Buffalo Bill's saddle and the guns that won the West.

Location: Ten miles north of Rye on Highway 165, near milepost marker 19. Eighteen miles from I-25.

---

3 Cabins with Kitchen	Pay Phone Available	Dave & Shirley Harmon, Owners
6 Cabins without Kitchens	Recreation Room	59 CR 371
Central Fireplace	Elevation: 8600	Rye CO 81069
	Credit Cards: VM	719/489-2280
	Rates: $45-$95	www.coloradodirectory.com/lodgesanisabel/
	Open: 4/15 to 11/1	

At the resort:

At resort or within 15 minutes:

Pine Lodge

Open year around, Pine Lodge is within walking distance of beautiful Lake Isabel in scenic San Isabel National Forest. The five cabins are comfortably furnished, and four have full kitchens. One cabin has a fireplace as well. Linens and towels are provided.

May through October a restaurant, gift shop, store and paddle boat rentals are within minutes walk from the lodge. The San Isabel area offers plenty of opportunities for relaxing as well as experience numerous mountain adventures. In the winter, ski and snowmobile on 90 miles of groomed trails, sled, ice fish and hunt. In the summer hike, mountain bike, fish for trout and boat. Visit Bishop's Castle, four wheel drive the back roads or golf in the high country.

All units are non-smoking.

Location: Twenty-two miles south of Pueblo and 20 miles north of Wlsenburg. From I-25 take exit 74, go 18 miles west on Highway 165 (up the mountain) to San Isabel, on right side of Highway 165 near milepost marker 19.

4 Cabins with Kitchen
1 Cabin without Kitchen
1 Room with Fireplace
Central Hot Tub
Central Campfire Area

Pay Phone Available
All Units Nonsmoking
Elevation: 8600
Credit Cards: VM
Rates: $65-$85
Open: All Year

John & Sharon Messec, Owners
PO Box 596
Rye CO 81069
719/489-2686
Fax: 719/489-3162
E-mail: pinelodge@aculink.net
www.coloradodirectory.com/pinelodge

At the resort:

At resort or within 15 minutes:

Scenic Highways of Legends

Including Cuchara, La Veta, Stonewall, Trinidad & Walsenburg —
Map: O-16, O-17, P-16, P-19, N-18

The Scenic Highway of Legends (Highway 12) was designated as a Colorado State Byway in 1987 and a National Byway in 1988. Like its name, the highway passes through numerous towns which played a part in forming Colorado's fascinating historical legacy. **Stonewall**, another town on the highway, is near a rock wall that rises 250 feet above town which is part of the Dakota Sandstone formation. In the 1880s, Stonewall was the site of a stand-off between settlers and the government over the Maxwell Land Grand. Today, this is a peaceful, pristine area where the spring waters are said to be enchanted. Nearby Monument Lake is nestled among the pines and high altitude lakes. A legend here tells of two Indian chiefs who, in search of water for their thirsty tribes, met and embraced in peace, crying for the lack of water. A lake formed at their feet and a volcano erupted, enclosing the two chiefs in rock in the center of the lake. Today both this lake and nearby North Lake offer fishing and other year round outdoor activities. **Cuchara** was home to settlers who found the soil ideal for growing potatoes. In 1908 George Mayes and his wife moved here and decided the valley was ideal for a summer resort and modern Cuchara was born. The Cuchara Valley Ski Area offers many winter activities, including downhill skiing. **La Veta**, settled in 1862, began when Colonel John M. Francisco and his partner Henry Daigre build a fort here for commerce and protection. Visit the Fort Francisco Museum. Threats from Native Americans managed to be resolved without bloodshed and the town survived with the coming of the railroad. **Walsenburg** sits at the gateway to Cuchara Valley and was settled in the late 1800s. Fred Walsen opened a large general store, became a community leader and incorporated the town's 320-acre site.

Fun Things to Do

- Cuchara Valley Ski Area (888) 282-4272
- Grandote Peak Golf Course (719) 742-3391
- Lathrop State Park & Golf Course (719) 738-2376
- Trinidad State Park (719) 846-6959

Chicosa Canyon Cabin and Bed & Breakfast

You'll be welcomed to this charming country inn that is as unique as southern Colorado. Chicosa Canyon Bed & Breakfast is a century-old, native stone ranch that sits on 64 peaceful, canyon acres. Choose between accommodations in the house or in a romantic cabin with wood burning stove and panoramic views of the mountains. The cabin sleeps 4 and includes a private bath, refrigerator and microwave. With its secluded front porch situated in front of a beautiful rock formation, the cabin offers privacy and a place to relax. The 3 rooms in the ranch: the Rose Room, Heartland and the Quilted Attic, have charming period antiques and quilts or down comforters. Rooms may be rented with private or shared bath.

After the hearty breakfast, set off for a hike. From here, you'll discover the secrets of the Anasazi and Apache, coal miners, pioneers and cowboys who chiseled history into the sandstone canyon walls. Birders will delight at the variety of western birds and humming birds that flock here in spring to join the canyon wren. Boarding facilities for your horse are on-site and there are many scenic trails to ride. Area activities include fishing, seasonal bird and game hunting, hiking and mountain biking. In the winter, a ski resort is less than an hour away. The nearby city of Trinidad offers testimony to its colorful history in museums, restaurants, and even a golf course. A trip down the Scenic Highway of Legends is also recommended. After your day of vacationing, relax and read in the solarium or take a soak in the hot tub. In the evening, be sure to step outdoors and contemplate the star-filled sky.

Accommodations are non-smoking & a 2 night minimum is preferred. Lodging

prices include a full breakfast. Supervised children 5 and over & pets are welcomed in the cabin. Chicosa Canyon is available for receptions, reunions, retreats & other special occasions!

Location: I-25 at exit 23 west 4.9 miles, west on County Rd 40, keep right.

1 Cabin with Kitchen	Phone in Lobby	Stan Braithwaite & Keena Unrah, Owners
3 Lodging Rooms	Bed & Breakfast Available	32391 CR 40
1 Room with Woodstove	All Units Nonsmoking	Trinidad CO 81082
Central Hot Tub	Recreation Room	719/846-6199 & Fax
Central Fireplace	Elevation: 6200	E-mail: chicosa@ria.net
	Credit Cards: VM	www.coloradodirectory.com/chicosacanyonbb/
	Rates: $75-$95	
	Open: All Year	

At the resort:

At resort or within 15 minutes:

Cuchara River Cabins & Campground

Nestled in the heart of the Sangre de Christo Mountains, Cuchara River Cabins & Campground offers both cabins and suites. The tastefully furnished one- and two-bedroom units feature private bathrooms, full or queen beds and mini-dish color television. Five cabins have a full, standard kitchen. Fourteen spacious, full service RV/campsites in a country setting with mature shade trees, campfire rings and picnic tables are also available along the peaceful Cuchara River. Because this valley has not been over-commercialized, its breathtaking natural beauty and peaceful atmosphere make this an ideal place to relax and reconnect with life.

The large outdoor area includes a campfire circle for evening gatherings and picnic tables. Walk to downtown La Veta, only one block away, for restaurants and small town shopping. Family reunions and group gatherings will find the numerous lodging options ideal for different tastes. Area activities include skiing, hiking, horseback riding, mountain biking, boating, hunting and fishing. Throughout the year, there are numerous arts, crafts and music festivals the whole family will enjoy. Try a day trip along Highway 12, the Scenic Highway of Legends, or play a round at the nearby world-class golf course. No matter how you spend your day, you can return here to let the soft melody of the Cuchara River lull you to sleep.

Some units are non-smoking. Ask about the off season rates. Pets and children are welcome.

Location: 404 South Oak is only one block from downtown La Veta.

4 Cabins with Kitchen	Pay Phone Available	David Enke & Anne Jenkins, Owners
1 Cabin without Kitchen	Some Units Nonsmoking	PO Box 397
4 Motel Rooms	Elevation: 7200	La Veta CO 81055-0450
Central Campfire Area	Credit Cards: None	800/375-2656
	Rates: $45-$75	719/742-5303
	Open: All Year	E-mail: crc@rmi.net
		www.coloradodirectory.com/cuchararivercabins

At the resort:

At resort or within 15 minutes:

Cuchara Vacation Rentals

Specializing in exceptionally nice, clean properties, Cuchara Vacation Rentals has private homes and condominiums available. Some of the units have telephones while fourteen of them have fireplaces and six have wood stoves. Eight guest houses and 11 lodging rooms are offered, all with linens provided. Units will accommodate from 2 to 14 people. The fully equipped kitchens have microwaves, dishwashers and cooking utensils.

Located in southeast Colorado, the Cuchara Vacation Rentals are only a day's drive from many Texas, Oklahoma and Kansas cities. The Cuchara Valley is on the Scenic Highway of Legends, nestled at the base of the Spanish Peaks Mountains. Area activities include hiking, skiing, golfing, fishing, mountain biking, boating, horseback riding and hunting.

Rates are for up to four people. Ask about the off-season rates. Some rentals are non-smoking.

Location: In southeast Colorado (about 80 miles south of Pueblo, off I-25).

11 Vacation Homes	Some Units Nonsmoking	Jay & Sandra Harmon, Owners
12 Lodging Rooms	Elevation: 8850	654 Road 401 - Pinehaven
17 Rooms with Fireplaces	Credit Cards: None	La Veta CO 81055
6 Rooms with Wood Stoves	Rates:	719/742-3340
	Open: All Year	Fax: 719/742-3340 call 1st.
		www.coloradodirectory.com/cucharavacation

At the resort: At resort or within 15 minutes:

La Plaza de Los Leones Inn, Cafe & Gifts

Built in 1907, La Plaza Inn was originally known as the Oxford Hotel with a reputation of being one of the Rocky's finest hotels — and not much has changed! The 16 guest rooms all have private toilet facilities. Most rooms have a tub and shower, but there is a shower "down the hall" for those rooms with only a tub. Each room is decorated with a different theme, from southwestern to Victorian. Choose between the alluring lavender and lace of the Bridal Suite or the collection of antlers and wildlife art in the Buck Room. The Family Farm room boasts a massive brass night stand and bunk beds.

La Plaza Inn offers continental breakfasts for all guests or a full, hearty breakfast served on the main floor in the inn's on-site cafe. The Plaza Cafe offers fresh donuts and a cafeteria style buffet for breakfast, lunch and dinner. Tortilla Flats Steak house & Cantina, also on the main floor, offers high quality, grain-fed beef for the best steaks west of Omaha! Watch the tortilla factory turn out tortillas, sip frozen Margaritas, and enjoy some southwestern cuisine, or try the steaks, ribs and chops for a cowboy-size meal. The town of Walsenburg offers restaurants, shops and festivals throughout the year. Golf enthusiasts will appreciate La Veta's Grandote Golf Course, a Tom Weiskopff championship course, a short drive away. Just three miles away is Lathrop State Park which has over 1,100 acres for hiking, biking, boating, fishing, wind surfing and water skiing. Walsenburg sits at the northern entrance to the Scenic Highway of Legends — a drive you should be sure to explore!

The inn also has a large meeting room ideal for wedding receptions, meetings, and family reunions. The room has a small dance floor, a large, built-in projection screen and can accommodate up to 100 people. Ask about the romantic honeymoon suite. All rooms are non-smoking.

Location: In Walsenburg on West 6th Street

16 Lodging Rooms	Phone in Lobby	Marti Henderson, Owner
	Bed & Breakfast Available	118 W 6th St
	All Units Nonsmoking	Walsenburg CO 81089
	Recreation Room	719/738-5700
	Elevation: 6000	Fax: 719/738-6220
	Credit Cards: VM	www.coloradodirectory.com/laplaza/
	Rates: $50-$70	
	Open: All Year	

At the resort:

At resort or within 15 minutes:

River's Edge Bed & Breakfast

Let time flow by while vacationing on the banks of Cuchara River at River's Edge Bed & Breakfast. All five rooms have queen beds and western decor in this deluxe lodging resort. Choose among various combinations of queen bed and shared bath, queen bed with private bath or suite with private bath. You may also rent the entire home for larger groups. Enjoy varying gourmet breakfasts every morning before starting your day.

Located on the Scenic Highway of Legends at the base of Spanish Peaks Mountains, River's Edge is near cross country skiing, downhill skiing, snowmobiling, sleigh riding, hiking, golfing, mountain biking, horseback riding, hunting and fishing. Meals in addition to the breakfast are available with advance reservations. A hot tub and laundry room are available as well.

Long term stays, large parties and special catering are available. Ask about the low season rates available for April, May, October and November. All rooms are non-smoking. Pets and guest horses are welcomed.

Location: On the banks of the Cuhcara River, the last building on the right side of the block long village of Chuchara. From Walsenburg drive 11 miles on US Highwaat 160, then 13 miles southwest on State Highway 12 to Cuhcara.

1 Vacation Home	Phone in Rooms	Mike Moore, Owner
5 Lodging Rooms	Bed & Breakfast Available	90 E Cuchara Ave
Central Hot Tub	All Units Nonsmoking	Cuchara CO 81055
Central Fireplace	Recreation Room	719/742-5169
Central Campfire Area	Elevation: 8650	Fax: 719/742-3111
	Credit Cards: VM	E-mail: rebb@rmi.net
	Rates: $100-$125	www.coloradodirectory.com/riversedgebb
	Open: All Year	

At the resort:

At resort or within 15 minutes:

Stonewall Inn & RV Park

Escape to the rustic atmosphere of Stonewall Inn where the off-highway resort offers peace and quiet of a restful getaway in the mountains near the Scenic Highway of Legends. Evergreen, which sleeps seven, is a two-story log cabin with a fireplace, living room, a bedroom with a double bed and a loft with a double bed and twin bed. Santa Fe and Sequoia are small cabins (cabinette) with a double bed. Sequoia sleeps two and Santa Fe, with an extra bedroom, sleeps four. The newly remodeled cabinettes, Cheyenne, Cuchara, Dakota, Durango, Edelweiss and Sierra have two double beds and each sleeps four. Pendleton and Susnell are cabinettes with a living room and bedroom with two double beds which sleep up to five. All units have fully equipped kitchens, satellite television and private baths.

Kids will enjoy the new playground and basketball court while everyone will appreciate the central campfire area for nightly campfires, talking, singing and roasting marshmallows. Monument and North lakes are within five to 10 minutes away and both offer plenty of fish for the eager angler. Other activities in the area include boating, hiking, horseback riding, mountain biking, golfing, big game hunting, downhill and cross country skiing, snowmobiling and ice fishing. Relaxing is part of every day.

Full hookup RV sites with satellite television are also available. No smoking or pets are allowed in the rooms.

Location: Thirty-four miles west of Trinidad on Highway 12 near milepost marker 38 in small town of Stonewall.

12 Cabins with Kitchen	Pay Phone Available	Fred & Linda Cucinelli, Owners
1 Vacation Home	All Units Nonsmoking	6673 Hwy 12
1 Room with Fireplace	Elevation: 8000	Weston CO 81091
Central Campfire Area	Credit Cards: VMD	719/868-2294 & fax ph 1st
	Rates: $55-$85	www.coloradodirectory.com/stonewallinn
	Open: 5/15 to 11/15	

At the resort:

At resort or within 15 minutes:

Yellow Pine Ranch & Livery

Since 1927, families have enjoyed Yellow Pine Ranch & Livery's western heritage and hospitality. The ranch is located high in a mountain valley and bordered on two sides by the unspoiled wilderness of the San Isabel National Forest. All the cabins at Yellow Pine Ranch offer a rural setting with majestic views of the Sangre de Christo Mountain Range. The cabins are individually decorated with hand-made curtains, quilts on comfortable beds, clean linens and plump towels. Each unit has a fully equipped kitchens and either shower or tub and shower combinations. For a true getaway, none of the units has a telephone or television. Six cabins have fire places and one has a wood stove. Among the cabins available are a couple which sleep six to eight, several which can accommodate four to six, and two for couples only. Outside the cabins are either beautiful flower beds or flower boxes. Daily maid service, daily linen service and daily towel service are not provided, and they request that you leave dishes clean upon departure.

Majestic views, rivers, streams and stocked ponds surround Yellow Pine Ranch which is a family owned/operated and family oriented resort. Fish right outside your door. From Memorial Day through Labor Day, horse drawn wagon rides with guitar playing cowboys are offered for ranch guests. Horseback riding opportunities includes trail rides. You will also enjoy the hay rides, barbecue cookouts and bonfire parties. Within minutes are a museum, golf courses, mountain bike trails. Cuchara Village is within walking distance.

Ranch guests receive 20 percent discounts on all resort activities. The outdoor, covered picnic shelter accommodates 50 and an indoor cooking area is available. With advanced arrangements, catered meals can be supplied. Yellow Pine Ranch is open during the Christmas holidays for a truly special getaway. Pets are allowed only by advance agreement with the managers.

Location: On State Highway 12

9 Cabins with Kitchen	Phone in Lobby	Jo Anne VanLue, Manager
6 Rooms with Fireplaces	Elevation: 8500	15880 State Hwy 12
1 Room with Woodstove	Credit Cards: None	Cuchara CO 81055-1310
Central Campfire Area	Rates: $70-$110	719/742-3528
	Open: 5/1 to 10/31	www.coloradodirectory.com/yellowpineranch/

At the resort:

At resort or within 15 minutes:

South Fork Area

Including Wagon Wheel Gap — Map: N-10 & N-9

South Fork is where the south fork of the Rio Grande joins the main body of the Rio Grande. It is situated at the western edge of the San Luis Valley, one of the biggest intermountain valleys in the world. Since the late 1880s, South Fork, at 8,250', has been a logging and lumbering community. The Rio Grande River between South Fork and Del Norte has been designated Gold Medal trout water which means it offers the greatest potential for trophy trout fishing success in Colorado. The town, at the foot of Wolf Creek Pass with its deep-power ski resort, is near numerous, year-round recreational possibilities. Whether you hike it or drive it, the surrounding mountains have deer, elk, grouse, ptarmigan, bighorn sheep, snowshoe rabbits, and even an occasional bear, bobcat or cougar! The nearby town of **Wagon Wheel Gap** was the scene of several early Indian battles and it's said Kit Carson's brother-in-law farmed here in 1840. The town's railroad station is listed on the National Register of Historical Places. The Silver Thread Scenic Byway begins at South Fork, continues through Wagon Wheel Gap and Creede and ends at Lake City.

Fun Things to Do

- Chinook Smokehouse (888) 890-9110
- Spruce Lodge Rafting (800) 228-5605
- Wolf Creek Ski Area (970) 264-5629

AspenRidge Cabins & RV Park

The boundless quiet is calming at Aspenridge which sits on the picturesque Silver Thread Scenic Byway. The modern cabins have kitchens, bathrooms and cable television. All linens, pots and pans are furnished. Cabins have one or two bedrooms all with double beds. The town of South Fork is surrounded on three sides by the Rio Grande National Forest and some of the largest, undisturbed wilderness areas in the country — the outdoor activities here are countless.

The game room and the indoor and outdoor group meeting areas are great for family reunions and kids. A coin laundry is on-site for your convenience. Nearby, the Rio Grande River boasts excellent, open and gold medal trout fishing. If you prefer, your hosts can supply you with a map to the many local lakes whose deep, calm waters await your expert casting. Hike into the unusual Wheeler Geologic Area, a haunting landscape of pinnacles, canyons and arches accessible only by foot. Rent a horse nearby and take an unforgettable trail ride into nature at its finest. You'll find plenty of old logging and mining roads which make for exhilarating four-wheel drive or mountain bike trips. Make Aspenridge your vacationing and fishing headquarters in southern Colorado. Their hot tub is only open in winter.

RV sties are also available.

Location: Off Highway 149, near milepost marker one, a half mile northwest of the junction at Highway 160.

6 Cabins with Kitchen	Pay Phone Available	Charles & Brenda Murray, Owners
1 Vacation Home	Some Units Nonsmoking	0710 W Hwy 149
1 Room with Woodstove	Recreation Room	South Fork CO 81154
Central Hot Tub	Elevation: 8180	719/873-5921 & fax
Central Woodstove	Credit Cards: VMD	www.coloradodirectory.com/aspenridgecabins/
Central Campfire Area	Rates: $45-$85	
	Open: All Year	

At the resort:

At resort or within 15 minutes:

Blue Creek Lodge, Cabins, RV Park & Restaurant

This is a vacationer's paradise — a haven for fishing enthusiasts, hunters, skiers, hikers and photographers. Blue Creek Lodge features modern housekeeping cabins, dormitory beds and lodge rooms with a private bath. All cabins have a stove, refrigerator, dishes, pots and pans, linens and carpeting. Three cabins have one room with double beds and private baths, one has a deck. The three bedroom cabin has a fireplace and one and half baths for large families. The efficiency has a king size bed and bath.

The lodge offers hospitality with home-cooked meals in its full-service restaurant. Treat yourself at the soda fountain, carouse in the game room and stock up on curios from the gift shop. Have your hair styled at Thressia's Beauty Salon right on the property. In the winter, try inner tubing, ice skating, snowmobiling and cross-country or alpine skiing at the Wolf Creek Ski Area. In the spring and summer months, enjoy the high rivers in a raft. If you're planning a tamer vacation, go hiking, rock hounding or fly fishing in the Rio Grande River across the road, or in the many mountain lakes nearby. Bring your own horse or rent one nearby for trips into the back country. In the fall, come hunt in some of the finest elk and deer country in the Rocky Mountains!

RV sites and trailers are also available. Children age 5 and under stay free. Ask about their weekly rates. One night deposit is required with reservation.

Location: Off of Highway 149, near milepost markers 11-12, halfway between South Fork and Creede.

11 Cabins with Kitchen	Recreation Room	Bill & Thressia Philbern, Owners
1 Vacation Home	Elevation: 8735	HC 33
6 Lodging Rooms	Credit Cards: VM	South Fork CO 81154
28 Beds in Bunkhouse	Rates: $34-$70	800/326-6408
1 Room with Fireplace	Open: All Year	719/658-2479
Central Fireplace		Fax: 719/658-2915
Central Campfire Area		www.coloradodirectory.com/bluecreeklodge/
All Units Nonsmoking		

At the resort:

At resort or within 15 minutes:

Chinook Lodge & Smokehouse

Vacation beneath tall pine trees in the heart of the Rocky Mountains at Chinook Lodge's turn-of-the-century, rustic modern log cabins with clean showers. The one and two bedroom housekeeping cabins feature kitchens and native rock fireplaces. All have antique furniture.

The small artesian shop contains snacks, hunting and fishing licenses. To whet your appetite, the Smokehouse & Deli makes tasty smoked ham, turkey and fish, and serves lunch daily. Be sure to try the old fashioned beef jerky, from regular to super-hot. The South Fork area is ideal for fishing and hunting. The Wolf Creek Ski Area is a short 25 minutes away, boasting the best downhill and cross country skiing in the South Fork area. The nearby Gold Medal waters of the Rio Grande River and numerous mountain lakes area an angler's dream come true. The roaring Rio Grande is also fun for "blue water" rafting trips during the summer.

Shaded, 32-foot wide RV sites are also available. Reservations are encouraged. Pets are allowed for free with advanced arrangements. Guest horses are welcomed.

Location: At the east edge of South Fork on Highway 160, near milepost marker 186.

6 Cabins with Kitchen	Pay Phone Available	Clayton & Kristy Trickle, Owners
1 Cabin without Kitchen	Elevation: 8300	PO Box 1214
6 Rooms with Fireplaces	Credit Cards: VM	South Fork CO 81154-0530
	Rates: $38-$58	719/873-9993
	Open: All Year	E-mail: ardee@amigo.net
		www.coloradodirectory.com/chinooklodge

At the resort:

At resort or within 15 minutes:

Cottonwood Cove Lodge, Cabins, Cafe, Jeeps, & Rafts

Nestled in thousands of acres of untouched mountains, near the clear, icy waters of the Rio Grande River, Cottonwood Cove has housekeeping cabins with one to three bedrooms, fireplaces, linens and kitchens with supplies. Several of the cabins are along the Rio Grande, or choose a lodge room. An authentic, 1940s guest ranch, Cottonwood Cove is in a picture perfect setting, ideal for a refreshing escape from everyday life. Relax in the cool shade of cottonwood, aspen and pine trees while admiring the view of the surrounding mountains across the way.

The lodge, built in 1945, has a cozy family room, a cafe specializing in home-made pies, a recreational room and gift shop. The restaurant is open for breakfast, lunch and dinner. Cottonwood Cove provides excursions on horseback to nearby scenic areas. You're sure to catch many gold medal trout in newly stocked fish ponds, in the Rio Grande as well as in the surrounding mountain lakes. Jeep and self-guided "blue-water" raft rentals available. Mountain bikers will delight in the close proximity of the Wolf Creek Ski Area, Wheeler Geological National Monument and hundreds of miles of national forests roads here.

Between November and April, cabin availability is limited. Full hookup RV sites are also available.

Location: On Highway 149, near milepost marker 13.

24 Cabins with Kitchen	Pay Phone Available	Tom & Mona Hensley, Managers
3 Vacation Homes	Elevation: 8448	HC 33 Wagon Wheel Gap
6 Lodging Rooms	Credit Cards: VMD	South Fork CO 81154
9 Rooms with Fireplaces	Rates: $39-$119	719/658-2242
Central Fireplace	Open: All Year	Fax: 719/658-0802
Central Woodstove		E-mail: cottonwoodcove@amigo.net
Central Campfire Area		www.coloradodirectory.com/cottonwoodcovelodge/

At the resort:

At resort or within 15 minutes:

Foothills Lodge

At the beginning of the Silver Thread Scenic Byway sits Foothills Lodge and your vacation destination. Choose between modern log cabins with aspen paneling, kitchens and woodburning fireplaces or uniquely decorated lodge apartments with kitchens. Your vacation home can range from one to two bedrooms and have anywhere from one queen size bed to four double beds depending on the accommodation. All but one cabin have kitchens and many can sleep up to eight people. You will enjoy hot showers, carpeting, fresh towels daily, gas heat, Colorado cable television and direct dial telephones. Weekly cleaning is available for stays two weeks or longer.

The indoor hot tub is a popular place to gather after a day of hunting, fishing, skiing, snowmobiling, sightseeing or loosing yourself in a good book. Small children will enjoy the playground, while children-at-heart will enjoy Gold Medal fishing in the Rio Grande just minutes away. South Fork, at the edge the San Luis Valley, is a convenient jumping off point to a variety of nearby recreation activities: Wolf Creek Ski Area, hiking, trout fishing and sightseeing in the beautiful countryside. Adjacent to the lodge you can enjoy a meal at the Hungry Logger Restaurant or Croaker's Saloon. Open all year round, Foothills Lodge is a great escape from it all — and is relaxing!

If traveling with a toddler cribs are available. Pets are not allowed at the lodge.

Location: On Highway 160 at milepost marker 160. At the south end of South Fork.

6 Cabins with Kitchen	Phone in Rooms	Sid & Priscilla Ham, Owners
8 Lodging Rooms	Elevation: 8200	PO Box 264
1 Motel Room	Credit Cards: VMAD	South Fork CO 81154-0264
5 Rooms with Fireplaces	Rates: $40-$85	800/510-3897
Central Hot Tub	Open: All Year	719/873-5969 wp & Fax
		E-mail: fhlodge@amigo.net
		www.coloradodirectory.com/foothillslodge/

At the resort:

At resort or within 15 minutes:

Goodnight's Lonesome Dove Cabins & Campground

Surrounded by the San Juan Range of the Rocky Mountains and 2 million acres of Rio Grande National Forest, Goodnight's offers six housekeeping cabins. The completely furnished, log cabins are delightfully cozy. All cabins are non-smoking with central heat and have double beds, equipped kitchens, private baths and satellite cable television. Five of the cabins have two rooms, and can sleep up to four people. The other cabin can sleep up to seven. RV sites are also available through the fall.

A country store on site will meet all your basic grocery needs, including fishing tackle, fishing and hunting licenses. The gift shop features handmade gifts, shirts and Colorado souvenirs. The year-round family activities will appeal to the sports enthusiast and nature lover alike. Try hiking, fishing, horseback riding, rafting, mountain biking or simply relaxing in the cool mountain air. Area attractions include exploring the old mining town of Creede, Chimney Rock, Great Sand Dunes National Monument and Mesa Verde. Visit Pagosa Springs and soak in the natural hot springs. Take a narrow-gauge train trip or a four-wheel drive tour through the back country. Hunters can come here year-round to enjoy nature's bounty. In the winter, ski Wolf Creek Ski area, noted to have the most snow in Colorado. Other winter activities include snowmobiling, cross-country skiing, ice fishing, ice skating and sleigh rides. Sled and tube rentals area also available. During the summer attend the non-denominational Alpine Resort Ministry Sunday Church service. No matter how you spend your day, be sure to save time for a relaxing break in the new hot tub at Goodnight's Cabins, or kick back with a video movie rental.

Pets are allowed.

Location: About 6 miles southwest of South Fork. On Highway 160 at milepost marker 180.

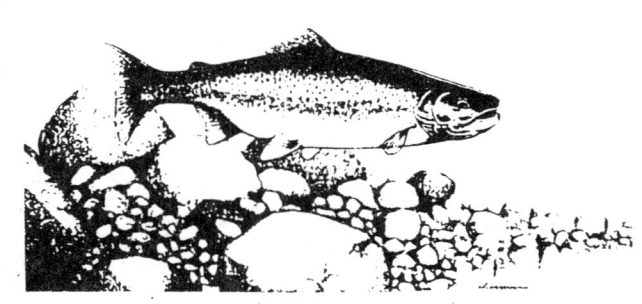

6 Cabins with Kitchen	Pay Phone Available	Robert & Connie Goodnight, Owners
Central Hot Tub	All Units Nonsmoking	PO Box 157
Central Woodstove	Recreation Room	South Fork CO 81154-0157
Central Campfire Area	Elevation: 8500	800/551-3683 (DOVE)
	Credit Cards: VM	719/873-1072
	Rates: $65	Fax: 719/873-5442
	Open: All Year	www.coloradodirectory.com/goodnightcabins/

At the resort:

At resort or within 15 minutes:

Inn Motel & Cabins of South Fork

Comfortably nestled among the San Juan Mountains, the Inn Motel is a beautiful knotty pine lodge in a cozy mountain setting. The 16 large, clean rooms in the modern lodge have scenic, river front views. Three two-bedroom cabins with full kitchens, living area, fireplace and daily maid service are also available. One cabin has a fireplace. Free local calls and cable television with free HBO and ESPN are provided. Free continental breakfast is offered to all guests.

The inn is walking distance to restaurants , gift and tackle shops and a grocery store. You'll be near fishing, whitewater rafting, boating, mountain biking, hiking, hunting, cross-country skiing, downhill skiing and snowmobiling. Within a short drive are four wheel drive tours, a museum and golf course.

Pets are welcomed at the Inn Motel for a small fee with advanced arrangements. Some of the units are non-smoking.

Location: At the junction of US Highway 160 and Colorado Highway 149.

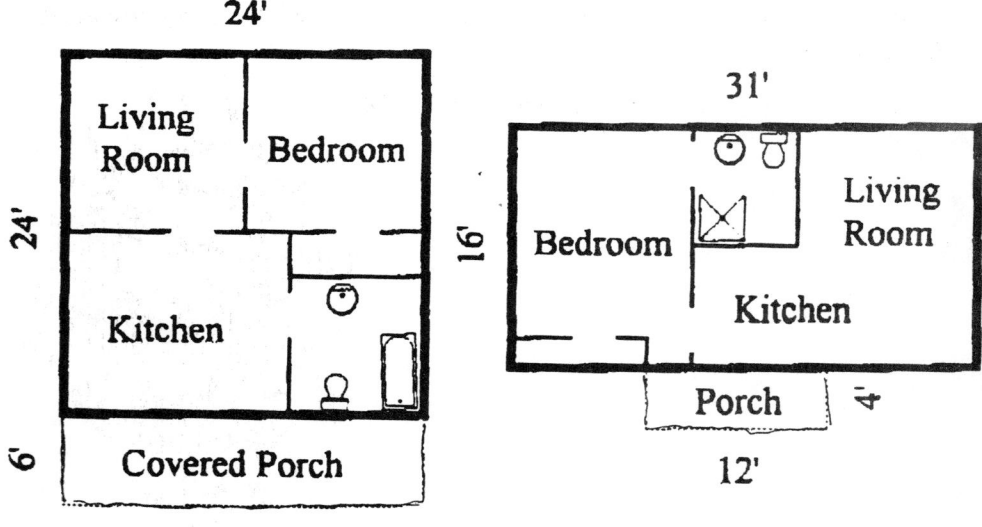

3 Cabins with Kitchen	Phone in Rooms	Brett & LaQuita Zielke, Owners
16 Motel Rooms	Some Units Nonsmoking	Box 474
1 Room with Woodstove	Elevation: 8150	South Fork CO 81154-0474
Central Hot Tub	Credit Cards: VMAD	800/233-9723
	Rates: $40-$65	719/873-5514
	Open: All Year	Fax: 719/873-1321
		www.coloradodirectory.com/innmotelcabins/

At the resort:

At resort or within 15 minutes:

Rainbow Lodge, Cabins & RV Park

At Rainbow Lodge, choose among 16 modern housekeeping cabins or 13 lodge rooms. 'Rough it' in the spacious, one or two-bedroom log cabins with fireplaces, cable television, and fully equipped kitchens. The one or two-bedroom lodge rooms have queen beds, cable television and telephones.

The lodge is within walking distance of both the South Fork of the Rio Grande and the Rio Grande rivers, which are great for beginning river rafters and anglers. In fact, the entire area is a fishing haven with numerous mountain lakes nearby, all easily accessible in a two-wheel-drive car (four-wheel-drive vehicles are not needed). The mountains surrounding South Fork are home to a variety of wildlife, for hikers, sightseers and hunters alike to appreciate. Take any of the numerous hiking trails to explore nature's wonders here. In the winter, visit nearby Wolf Creek Ski Area, known as much for its pristine snow as its lack of crowds. Ask about the sleigh rides and snowmobile tours as well. Restaurants and evening entertainment are a short drive away. There is a grocery and large sporting goods store next door, and under the same ownership as this lodge.

RV sites are also available from May through October. Pets are welcomed at Rainbow Lodge.

Location: On Highway 160, at milepost marker 186.

16 Cabins with Kitchen	Rates: $36-$66	Teri & Robert Byrd, Managers
13 Motel Rooms	Open: All Year	PO Box 224
14 Rooms with Fireplaces		South Fork CO 81154-0224
Central Woodstove		888/873-5174
Central Campfire Area		719/873-5571
Recreation Room		Fax: 719/873-5125
Elevation: 8250		E-mail: cobyrd@amigo.net
Credit Cards: VMAD		www.coloradodirectory.com/rainbowlodge/

At the resort:

At resort or within 15 minutes:

Riverbend Resort Cabins & RV Park

In a mountain setting on the South Fork of the Rio Grande River, Riverbend Resort has one-mile river frontage, modern, well-heated cabins with fully equipped kitchens and fireplaces. Three cabins — Aspen, Ponderosa and the Columbine — feature an upstairs loft that sleeps 4 to 8 people. The larger cabins can accommodate up to 15 people each. All cabins have bed and bath linens, color television, microwaves, charcoal grills, decks and breath-taking views of the river. Ponderosa, spruce and aspen trees dot the resort. In 1983, Riverbend was transformed into Kamp Komfort for the movie National Lampoon's Vacation. Visit part of the movie set that still remains.

Riverbend sports horseshoes, a playground and planned group activities. Fish on the trout-stocked river or in many of the nearby mountain lakes. Riverbend is bordered on two sides by national forest and is in the heart of the San Juan Mountains, which offer fantastic hiking, mountain biking, horseback riding, and hunting for trophy elk, deer and bear. While the kids play in the game room, you can relax in the hot tub after a day of view-filled hiking. Darlene is a fiber artist and has added a weaving studio and gallery. In winter, enjoy Wolf Creek ski area only a 20 minute drive away. Cross country ski or snowmobile the many groomed trails in the area.

Grassy RV sites overlooking the river are available. Children under 4 stay free. Ask about their off season rates. The resort has room for your horse. Well behaved pets are allowed in the cabins for a small fee.

Location: Three miles southwest of South Fork on Highway 160, near milepost marker 183.

11 Cabins with Kitchen	Pay Phone Available	Martin & Darlene Danko, Owners
30 Beds in Bunkhouse	Some Units Nonsmoking	Box 1270
11 Rooms with Fireplaces	Recreation Room	South Fork CO 81154-1270
Central Hot Tub	Elevation: 8350	800/621-6512
Central Fireplace	Credit Cards: VMAD	719/873-5344
Central Campfire Area	Rates: $47-$150	Fax: 719/873-5770
	Open: All Year	E-mail: riverbend.resort@juno.com
		www.coloradodirectory.com/riverbendresort/

At the resort:

At resort or within 15 minutes:

Spruce Lodge, Cabins, B&B, Rafting and RV Park

If you're an outdoor sports enthusiast, Spruce Lodge is the place to stay. The resort is at the foot of the San Juan Mountains near the Rio Grande River and only 17 miles from Wolf Creek Ski Area. Built in the 1920s, the Lodge is a quaint, historic log building that blends modern conveniences with turn-of-the-century charm. Choose between comfortable, rustic guest rooms in the main lodge or modern motel rooms, including television and telephone with or without a fully equipped kitchenette, in the adjacent chalet. There are also two new 2 bedroom cabins with kitchens, plus two vacation homes. Smoking or non-smoking units are available and all room rates include a delicious breakfast.

Play miniature golf on-site. Ask your hosts about unguided rafting on the Rio Grande — there are mild, fun family trips for beginners. After a day of rafting, soothe your tired muscles in the spacious, indoor hot tub or relax in front of the large river rock fireplace in the main lobby. Other area activities include trout fishing, horseback riding, hiking, hunting and four-wheel driving. Rent a mountain bike and ride the back country trails. Winter sports abound as well, from cross-country and downhill skiing to snowmobiling. Several fine restaurants and a variety of shops are located close by.

Ask about the large meeting area in the lodge for your family reunion. Full hookup RV sites are also available.

Location: North side of Highway 160, at the east end of South Fork, near milepost marker 187.

2 Cabins with Kitchen	Some Units Nonsmoking	Josef & Daniela Schroeck, Owners
2 Vacation Homes	Recreation Room	PO Box 156
4 Lodging Rooms	Elevation: 8180	South Fork CO 81154-0156
10 Motel Rooms	Credit Cards: VMAD	800/228-5605
Central Hot Tub	Rates: $45-$55	719/873-5605 & fax
Central Fireplace	Open: All Year	www.coloradodirectory.com/sprucelodge/
Central Campfire Area		
Bed & Breakfast Available		

At the resort:

At resort or within 15 minutes:

Steamboat Springs & North Park Areas

Including Columbine, Cowdrey, Hahns Peak, Hayden, Rand & Walden — Map: C-9, A-9, B-9, A-11, C-12, B-12 & C-8

A famous ski center, **Steamboat Springs** in the Yampa Valley offers much more than just winter sports. Fish Creek Falls is a breathtaking 283' waterfall and historic bridge. From the falls you have access to hiking and mountain biking trails that lead to the Continental Divide. From town, drive northeast to the Mount Zirkel Wilderness Area where the elevation ranges from 7,000' to 13,000' in a 141,000-acre undeveloped area, ideal for hiking, fishing and hunting. The Yampa River Trail System runs adjacent to downtown. Steamboat Springs was supposedly named in 1865 when French trappers riding through thought they heard the chugging of a steamboat. But it was a hot springs that chugged until 1908 when the railroad blasted out the rock chamber over the springs. Northern Utes (the Yampsatika) summered in the area as early as the 1300s. Whites first settled here in 1875 and although they used skis to get around in the winter, it wasn't until 1913 that they started skiing for fun and the rest is history. Be forewarned, however, according to local legend, the "Yampa Valley Curse" means visitors are cast under a spell that compels them to return again and again. The Elk River flows from north of Steamboat Springs passing through clark and Routt National Forest. North Park's grassland are rimmed on three sides with a limitless view around the basin to contrasting peaks — Medicine Bow, Rabbit Ears, Never Summer and Park mountain ranges. Fishing, hunting and hiking are the primary sports. **Walden** with a popular of 1000 is the business hub of North Park. Northwest of Walden is Lake John where fishing is very good. Very few folks know that northeast of Walden are sand dunes.

*[Even though Rand and Walden are east of Steamboat and rightly in the **North Park** area, we have taken the liberty of including them in this chapter. These are diverse areas from Steamboat. But then also are **Clark**, **Columbine**, **Hahns Peak** and **Hayden**. Such is the independent character of the towns in this rugged and independent northwest part of Colorado. Yet for you, dear reader, we have contained them into this chapter.]*

Fun Things to Do

- Hahn's Peak Area Historical Society (970) 879-3825, Winter 824-5176
- Mount Zirkel Wilderness Area (970) 879-1870
- North Park Ranger District(970) 723-8204
- Pearl Lake State Park (970) 879-3922
- Stagecoach State Park (970) 736-2436
- Steamboat Lake State Park (970) 879-3922
- Steamboat Springs Golf Course (970) 879-4295
- Steamboat Springs Ski Area (800) 922-2722
- Tread of Pioneers Museum (970) 879-2214

Elk River Guest Ranch

On the banks of the upper Elk River, surrounded by Routt National Forest and near the pristine Mount Zirkel Wilderness area, Elk River Guest Ranch is an excellent place to get away from it all. Enjoy a private cabin encircled by the outstanding scenery of the Elk River Valley. These cabins offer wood stoves, private baths and full kitchens with comfortable furnishings. The cabins, with daily maid service, have one or two bedrooms and can sleep six to eight people. Bring along your camera to capture wildlife, wild flowers, rushing rivers, billowing high country meadows and, in the fall, aspen in all their colorful, golden glory.

For those who truly want a luxury, no-hassles vacation, ask about the three meals a day delivered to your own cabin! The ranch will prepare you for hunting season or fishing all summer long on Steamboat and Pearl Lakes or on the more than 100 mountain lakes and 900 miles of nearby streams. Elk River Guest Ranch also offers horseback rides of varying lengths, including a lunch trip to Pearl Lake. In the winter, try cross-country skiing or snowmobiling on the 25 miles of groomed trails or downhill ski in Steamboat Springs. Unwind in the large hot tub and join your hosts around the nightly, summer campfires after a day of high country adventures.

RV Sites are available. Reservations must be made in advance with 50% deposit.

Location: Twenty miles north of Steamboat Springs. Off County Road 129, on County Road 64 (Seed House Road)

4 Cabins with Kitchen	Phone in Lobby	Bill & Kathy Hinder, Owners
1 Room with Fireplace	Recreation Room	29840 Rd 64
1 Room with Woodstove	Elevation: 7300	Clark CO 80428
Central Hot Tub	Credit Cards: VM	800/750-6220
Central Campfire Area	Rates: $125-$175	970/879-6220
	Open: All Year	Fax: 970/879-6220
		E-mail: ergr@cmn.net
		www.coloradodirectory.com/elkriverranch/

At the resort:

At resort or within 15 minutes:

Elkhead Ranch

Nestled in the Elkhead Valley, enjoy exploring on Elkhead Ranch's 10,000 acre historically designated 1883 cattle ranch. The valley offers the chance for complete seclusion and privacy from the hurried pace of life. Accommodations range from a fully equipped, ranch style lodge, to a secluded tipi on the banks of the creek, and a high country cow camp for the more adventurous. The lodge is a five bedroom ranch house, perfect for a family reunion or special gathering. For the horse enthusiast you can bring your own horse, there are indoor box stalls, outdoor paddocks, a round pen, and a full size roping arena set in the shade of Cottonwood trees.

The choice is yours, take a trail ride either Western or English gear or practice arena roping. For the fishing buff there is a private reservoir stocked with bass and 10 miles of private Creek frontage that is stocked with trout — fishing licenses are not required. The Ranch is surrounded by an abundance of cottonwood trees, lush hay meadows, rolling sagebrush covered hills, aspen spotted ridges, and numerous kinds of wildlife abound. Other summer activities on the ranch include hiking, canoeing, photography, and mountain biking. In summer the PRCA Rodeo in Steamboat Springs runs every Friday and Saturday night. Fall and winter activities include big game hunting, cross-country skiing and snowshoeing.

Rates include three meals, use of a horse and unlimited fishing.

Location: Forty miles northwest of Steamboat Springs and 16 miles north of Hayden, drive north on Walnut Street, then west on County Road 76, follow signs. 12 miles northeast of Elkhead Reservoir.

1 Vacation Home	Phone in Rooms	Heather Stirling, Owner
1 Room with Fireplace	All Units Nonsmoking	8102 RCR 56
1 Room with Woodstove	Recreation Room	Hayden CO 81639
	Elevation: 7500	970/276-3920
	Credit Cards: None	Fax: 970/276-3377
	Rates: $150-$300	E-mail: elkhead@ranchweb.com
	Open: All Year	www.coloradodirectory.com/elkheadranch

At the resort:

At resort or within 15 minutes:

Glen Eden Resort

In the heart of ranch and recreation country, Glen Eden has "contempo-rustic" townhomes (duplexes) along the Elk River, combining natural, rustic materials with contemporary interior design. This is an upscale resort. All accommodations are completely furnished, from firewood to forks. There are TVs in all of the cabins and VCRs in some of the cabins for your viewing pleasure. The townhomes have moss rock fireplaces, two bathrooms, two bedrooms, a fully-equipped kitchen, covered sun porch and views of spectacular Mount Zirkel and Sand Mountain.

The log-styled pine lodge has a dining room, tavern, saloon and a conference room. For those nippier days, swim in the heated pool or soak in one of two hot tubs. Many activities available at the resort — playing tennis, mountain biking and private trout fishing on the Elk River and in high-country lakes. Fly fishing instruction is also available. Additional activities include rafting and extensive trails for snowmobiling. Your hosts can arrange horseback hunting trips to Colorado's largest elk populations minutes away. You can also go horseback riding minutes away and go boating on nearby Steamboat Lake. The Mount Zirkel Wilderness area, 12 miles away, and Routt National Forest, three miles away, are perfect for summer hiking and winter cross-country skiing. Take a picnic in historical Hahn's Peak or ask your hosts about the many sightseeing opportunities.

The resort is closed for one week each April. Call ahead for more information. Kids under 17 stay free.

Location: In Clark on County Road 129, near milepost marker 17, 18 miles north of Steamboat Springs.

26 Cabins with Kitchen	Pay Phone Available	Rich Landon, GM
6 Vacation Homes	Some Units Nonsmoking	PO Box 908
26 Rooms with Fireplaces	Elevation: 7200	Clark CO 80428-0908
4 Rooms with Wood Stoves	Credit Cards: VMAD	800/882-0854
Central Hot Tub	Rates: $95-$165	970/879-3907
Central Fireplace	Open: 4/18 to 4/11	Fax: 970/870-0858
Central Campfire Area		E-mail: eden@amigo.net
		www.coloradodirectory.com/glenedenresort/

At the resort:

At resort or within 15 minutes:

Lake John Resort

The four cabins at Lake John Resort have spectacular views overlooking Lake John. All are modern, clean and spacious. Each cabin is furnished with a kitchenette with refrigerator, electric range, cooking utensils, dishes and silverware, as well as electric heat, linens, towels and light blankets.

Lake John is an angler's paradise offering some of the best trout fishing in the state. The rainbows and cutthroats at Lake John are plump and sassy — lots of fun to catch and even better to eat! Boat rentals are available on-site. In addition, the lake is near national forest and public lands which offer great areas for big and small game hunting as well as waterfowl hunting. Come here to hike, mountain bike, horseback ride, cross country ski, snow mobile or just soak up Mother Nature at her finest. Other resort amenities include a new, full service restaurant and a store with bait, tackle, fishing and hunting licenses, drinks, snacks ice and free coffee every morning.

Full hookup RV sites and tent sites are also available.

Location: In north central Colorado, 17 miles northwest of Walden.

4 Cabins with Kitchen	Pay Phone Available	Bill & Tish Willcox, Owners
Central Campfire Area	Recreation Room	PO Box 902
	Elevation: 8200	Walden CO 80480-0902
	Credit Cards: VM	970/723-3226
	Rates: $50	Fax: 970/723-3236
	Open: All Year	E-mail: ljr@frii.com
		www.coloradodirectory.com/lakejohnresort/

At the resort:

At resort or within 15 minutes:

Mended Wing Guest House

Hidden away from the business of life, among a grove of pine and aspen trees, is Mended Wing Guest House. Experience a mending of the spirit, mind and soul as you drink in the panoramic views of Mt. Zirkel, Steamboat Lake and Hahn's Peak. Accommodations include king and queen sized beds with down comforters, wool blankets and thick terry robes that stand ready for a trip to the hot tub. The unit also includes a fully equipped kitchen. The loft, accessible by ladder, has a full bathroom all its own and a queen bed with all the same luxury of the master suite. The master suite features a raised sleeping area. A full bath serves both the living room and bedroom. The living room has a queen sofa bed, wood stove and dining area all with views of Mt. Zirkel wilderness. The main level of the master bedroom includes a sitting area, an extra sink, vanity and a cozy library to wile away the hours reading, sketching or relaxing.

The winter season here is a wonderland of activities from snowmobiling to cross-country skiing. Want to try something different? How about a dog sled tour where you'll glide along charted trails with a master guiding his team of dogs. Try ice fishing in the winter and warm weather casting in the summer at Steamboat Lake.

Location: Twenty-four miles north of Steamboat Springs. On County Road 129, at milepost marker 24.

1 Vacation Home	Phone in Rooms	Andy & Paula Maneotis, Owners
1 Room with Hot Tub	All Units Nonsmoking	PO Box 773267
1 Room with Woodstove	Elevation: 8150	Steamboat Springs CO 80477
	Credit Cards: VM	970/870-1522
	Rates: $150	www.coloradodirectory.com/mendedwinghouse
	Open: All Year	

At the resort:

At resort or within 15 minutes:

Midnight Ranch

The pavement ends at Midnight Ranch and the adventure begins. Located 33 miles north of Steamboat Springs the guest cabin is on 240 acres high in the mountains, surrounded by open, wild flower meadows, tall pine trees and thick groves of aspen. The secluded log-post and beam cabin has three bedroom, two baths, fireplace, full kitchen and a washer and dryer. The cabin is decorated in country antiques and provides a unique vacation experience. The cabin comfortably sleeps nine.

In the summer, enjoy trophy fly fishing on the private 10 acre lake (catch and release only), or use the corral and pasture if you want to bring your own horses. Steamboat Lake has boat rentals, while Hahn's Peak Lake and Pearl Lake are great

for fishing. ATV, horseback and mountain bike rentals are close by, or just take a hike and explore one of the many forest service trails. In the winter, bring your four wheel drive vehicle to the guest cabin. Take advantage of the groomed cross country ski trials on the Ranch. Bring your own snowmobiles or rent them nearby. Back country skiers will enjoy exploring the 10,300-foot Hahn's Peak while others might like the downhill slopes at Steamboat's resort. The pavement ends at Midnight Ranch and the adventure begins!

Midnight Ranch Guest Cabin is ideal for a family vacation, business retreat, small conference or wedding.

Location: From Steamboat Springs drive north on County Road 129 for 33 miles.

---

1 Vacation Home	Phone in Lobby	Steve Coolidge & Tonja Coates
1 Room with Woodstove	Elevation: 7600	PO Box 744
Central Campfire Area	Credit Cards: None	Clark CO 80428-0744
	Rates: $150	970/870-3456
	Open: All Year	E-mail: midnight@cmn.net
		www.coloradodirectory.com/midnightranch

At the resort:

At resort or within 15 minutes:

Sky Valley Lodge

Vacation in the warm and inviting elegance of an English country manor at Sky Valley Lodge. Adjacent to Lake Catamount on the edge of Rabbit Ears Pass and tucked into the side of a mountain, you'll appreciate the stunning, sweeping view of the valley below. The twenty-four rooms are divided twelve each between an upper and lower lodge. The lodges have been recently updated with a new kitchenette and new furnishings in almost all rooms. During the winter, snuggle down on feather beds for a cozy treat.

Contemporary gourmet continental breakfast is served daily in the dining room where full breakfast and lighter fare luncheon/dinner menus are available. Family-style dinners with selected entrees may be reserved each morning. Kids can play in the special nook near the dining room while you relax in the bar/lounge. Just seven minutes from Steamboat, the lodge has daily shuttles to take guests downtown for dining and shopping, and to a ski-in, ski-out slopeside hotel where you can store your equipment in the lockers while taking a break from the runs. Warm weather activities includes hiking, biking, hot air ballooning and rodeo watching. In the winter, after enjoying downhill or cross-country skiing, be sure to relax in the sauna or take a dip in the outdoor hot tub. Soak in the soothing water and view the Milky Way in all its splendor.

Sky Valley Lodge is great for family reunions, weddings and private parties.

Location: On Highway 40 one and a half miles up from base of Rabbit Ears Pass, at milepost marker 141, looking over Steamboat Springs.

24 Lodging Rooms	Phone in Lobby	Steve Myler, Manager
Central Hot Tub	Bed & Breakfast Available	PO Box 773132
Central Fireplace	All Units Nonsmoking	Steamboat Springs CO 80477-3132
Central Woodstove	Recreation Room	800/538-7519
	Elevation: 7600	970/879-7749
	Credit Cards: VMAD	Fax: 970/879-7752
	Rates: $79-$173	E-mail: info@steamboat-lodging.com
	Open: All Year	www.coloradodirectory.com/skyvalleylodge

At the resort:

At resort or within 15 minutes:

Steamboat Lake Outfitters

At the foot of Hahn's Peak, Steamboat Lake Outfitters is high in Colorado's Rocky Mountain across from beautiful Steamboat Lake State Park. Stay in one of the four rustic log housekeeping cabins. The units sleep four to eight people. Each cabin is completely furnished with a kitchen and full bathroom. Take in the tranquillity of the Valley on your cabins deck with a barbecue grill. All linens and towels are furnished.

Experience the back country of Colorado by horse back, all-terrain vehicle, or snowmobile on one of the guided tours through the wild and scenic areas of Routt National Forest, the Continental Divide, and Zirkel Wilderness Area. Hourly, daily and extended tours in Northern Colorado and Southern Wyoming are available. The general store is well-stocked with groceries, hunting and fishing licenses, tackle, gifts and a liquor store. Be sure to try the home cooked specials and sub-sandwiches in the deli or stop in for breakfast. Gasoline and propane are also available. Fish on three lakes or miles of mountain brooks and alpine streams. Ride your mountain bike or hike on the nearby trails during the milder months, while in the winter, take Routt County's best snowmobile tours. The downhill skiing at Steamboat Springs is some of the best in the country.

Pets are allowed for a fee.

Location: Twenty-five miles north of Steamboat Springs and 7 miles from Clark; on County Road 129, near mile-post marker 24, across from Steamboat Lake.

Location: Twenty-five miles north of Steamboat Springs and 7 miles from Clark; on County Road 129, near mile-post marker 24, across from Steamboat Lake.

---

4 Cabins with Kitchen

Pay Phone Available
Elevation: 8200
Credit Cards: VMAD
Rates: $85
Open: All Year

Chad Bedell & Don Markley, Owners
PO Box 749
Clark CO 80428-0839
800/342-1889
970/879-5878
Fax: 970/879-5147
E-mail: slomail@cmn.net
www.coloradodirectory.com/hahnspeakranch

At the resort:

At resort or within 15 minutes:

Steamboat Log Cabins at Perry-Mansfield

Perry-Mansfield is truly a unique vacation spot: it is both the oldest performing arts camp in the country and a cabin resort. The modern log cabins are on 73 wooded acres of beautiful, secluded and wooded, Strawberry Park, one of the more beautiful areas in the region. The snug cabins, which sleep up to 10 people, contain electric baseboard heat, wood-burning fireplaces, full kitchens with microwave, color TV, coffee maker and bathrooms. All linens and firewood are included. Facilities make a snug mountain home during your visit.

Perry-Mansfield was a focal point for American modern dance in the 1930s. Dance pioneer Agnes de Mille was inspired to choreograph her famous ballet "Rodeo" after attending a local square dance at a county schoolhouse not far from Perry-Mansfield. The performing arts tradition continues — in the summer, be sure to attend their lovely theater and dance productions put on by the camp's students. The area is ripe for hiking, fishing or swimming in the nearby natural hot springs pool. In the winter, enjoy snowshoeing, cross-country skiing, sledding and downhill skiing at Steamboat Springs.

The rustic conference facility is ideal for business meetings and family reunions.

Location: In Steamboat Springs, go north on 7th from Lincoln, turn right on Missouri and continue to North Park. Follow North Park for one and a half miles. Perry-Mansfield is on the left.

7 Cabins with Kitchen	Pay Phone Available	Rhonda Graham
1 Room with Woodstove	Elevation: 7000	40755 RCR 36
	Credit Cards: VMAD	Steamboat Springs CO 80487-9298
	Rates: $105-$350	970/879-1060800/538-7519
	Open: All Year	970/879-1730 Mike Lomus
		Fax: 970/870-9436 resort & fax
		E-mail: info@steamboat-lodging.com
		www.coloradodirectory.com/steamboatlogcabins

At the resort:

At resort or within 15 minutes:

Whistling Elk Ranch

Get a chance to be "city slickers" for a day on this working cattle ranch in North Park where you can help with cattle drives and branding when they occur. Whistling Elk's deluxe, modern cabins feature full kitchens and bathrooms, wood-burning fireplaces, electric heat and two bedrooms. Towels, linens, firewood, cooking utensils and coffee makers are provided. All cabins are non-smoking. Located at the base of Owl Mountain, days here are sunny and warm while the nights are cool and comfortable.

Daily activities at the ranch can include working up an appetite being a real ranch hand helping with the chores or relaxing and taking in the wonderful scenery. The ranch also sponsors a "back country camp," where you ride in by horseback or mountain bike and spend the night under a blanket of dazzling stars. Morning greets you with a breathtaking view of Parkview Mountain and the smell of a delicious western breakfast. Fish on the trail or back at the ranch in the 3 miles of private stream or the stocked pond on the ranch's 1,600 acres of private land open to guests. Explore the ranch's many trails, either on a gentle horse, on foot, your mountain bike, or by cross-country skis. Photograph wildlife, including elk, mule deer, black bear, moose, coyotes and eagles. Ask about guided big-game hunts in season. In the evening, gaze at stars from the secluded outdoor hot tub after "working" all day. Whistling Elk offers a vacation far from crowds in the beauty and solitude of the Rocky Mountains.

Location: Ninety miles west of Fort Collins on Jackson County Road 27, 9.5 miles southwest of Highway 14; or 4.3 miles northeast of Highway 125.

3 Cabins with Kitchen	Phone in Lobby	John Ziegman & Mical Hutson, Owners
3 Rooms with Wood Stoves	All Units Nonsmoking	PO Box 2
Central Hot Tub	Elevation: 8700	Rand CO 80473-002
Central Campfire Area	Credit Cards: None	970/723-8311 Z's hp & Fax
	Rates: $95	E-mail: micalhut@aol.com
	Open: All Year	www.coloradodirectory.com/whistlingelkranch/

At the resort:

At resort or within 15 minutes:

Strasburg

Map: H-22, F-19, G-26

The last railroad spike of the Kansas Pacific's line to Denver was driven near **Strasburg** in 1870. On I-70, there's a myriad of things to see and do. Located on Colorado's high plains, Strasburg is a convenient stopping point while traveling. Watch for the abundant wildlife on the surrounding plains. In Strasburg, visit the Comanche Crossing Museum. Denver International Airport is only 30 minutes west of Strasburg via I-70. As you travel I-70 west, you can watch the beautiful Rocky Mountains rise majestically up out of the plains. Nearby, in the town of Genoa, is the Genoa Tower Museum where you can see six states from the tower on a clear day. The museum also has a large collection of fossil skulls, guns, bottles, Indian artifacts and oddities like two-headed calves and jackalopes! Northeast from Flagler is the Flagler Reservoir and State Wildlife Area where you can fish and picnic while protected wildlife wander in the reserve. The Kit Carson County Carousel in Burlington, is a fully restored and operating, hand-carved 1905 wooden merry-go-round. One of fewer than 170 such carousels left in the country, this gaily painted, charming antique was a toy of the American Victorian middle class and is a National Landmark.

Fun Things to Do

- Burlington Old Town Museum (800) 288-1334, (719) 346-7382
- Comanche Crossing Museum (303) 622-4668
- Flagler Reservoir & State Wildlife Area (719) 765-4422
- Pioneer Schoolhouse Museum, Limon (719) 775-2350
- Uhrich's locomotive Train Machine Shop (719) 622-4431
- Welcome Center at Burlington (719) 346-5554

Strasburg Inn B&B, Gifts & Antiques

The Strasburg Inn in eastern Colorado offers late 19th-century charm in its relaxing parlor complete with a library to browse. The Inn was established in 1915 to serve the growing community which the railroads accessed in 1870. The eight bed and breakfast rooms have queen or double beds, color televisions, shared baths and air conditioning for hot summer evenings. Each room is decorated with antiques and local crafts. The Sundance Suite, a large, one-bedroom suite with a sitting room and a private bath, microwave and refrigerator, is tucked under the eaves of the large inn which provides an at-home atmosphere. The suite also has a VCR for add convenience. The included continental breakfast for all guests features fresh, home-baked pastries, fresh juice and steaming hot coffee.

In days gone by, travelers staying at the inn also found a grocery store, barber shop and dining room on the first floor. Today, the Strasburg Inn has a full-service antique and gift shop with unique items sure to please. There is also a laundry on-site and playground across the street. The Inn is located in historic Strasburg where, on Aug. 15, 1870, the tracks were laid to connect the Atlantic Coast to the Pacific Coast. Learn all about this event and other historical moments at the nearby Comanche Crossing Museum. Other places to visit while in town are Urich's Locomotive and the Llama Ranch where you can tour and see the llamas for free. Other area attractions include fishing, golfing, boating and hunting in season. Pets are welcomed to accompany you to the Strasburg Inn.

Location: Thirty-five miles east of Denver in Strasburg on Main St. Thirty minutes to Denver International Airport.

8 Lodging Rooms	Pay Phone Available	James Beasley & Sandy McIlheney
	Bed & Breakfast Available	PO Box 296
	Some Units Nonsmoking	Strasburg CO 80136-0296
	Recreation Room	303/622-4314
	Elevation: 5380	www.coloradodirectory.com/strasburgbb
	Credit Cards: None	
	Rates: $35-$50	
	Open: All to Year	

At the resort:

At resort or within 15 minutes:

Summit County

Including Breckenridge, Dillon, Frisco, Green Mountain Reservoir, Heeney, Keystone, & Silverthorne — Map: G-13, F-12, E-11 & F-13

It almost goes without saying that Summit County offers the best in downhill and cross-country skiing as well as snowboarding at its many ski resorts. There's more than just countless opportunities for winter adventures here, though. Charmingly restored, gingerbread Victorian houses lining its streets earned **Breckenridge** a National Historic District designation. Set amidst mountain splendor and the Continental Divide for a backdrop, this former mining town was established in an 1859 gold rush — the first permanent settlement on Colorado's Western Slope. Named in honor of Vice President John C. Breckenridge (in order to get a post office more easily), the town, when the Civil War broke out and the vice president supported the Confederacy, was re-named Breckenridge. In addition to the diverse terrain on the ski resort's three mountains, Breckenridge, at an elevation of 9,603', has the only Jack Nicklaus-designed municipal golf course, renown musical organizations, and miles of hiking trails. Be sure and check out the human maze at Peak 8 — a fun place to get lost! Surrounded by Arapaho National Forest, the city has fishing on the Upper Blue River or the nearby Mohawk Lakes. Go sailing on Lake **Dillon** or shop in more than fifty **Silverthorne** Factory Outlet Stores. Rent a mountain bike in **Frisco** and enjoy extensive **Summit County** bike path system of 47 trails! Four 14ers (mountain peaks 14,000' and higher in elevation) can be climbed nearby. Boating and fishing are popular at **Green Mountain Reservoir** by Heeney, 20 miles north of I-70.

Fun Things To Do

- Alpine Slide, Breckenridge (970) 453-5000
- Breckenridge Activity Center (970) 453-5579
- Breckenridge Golf Club (970) 453-9104
- Breckenridge Ski Area (970) 453-5000
- Country Boy Gold Mine Tour, Breckenridge (970) 453-4405
- Dillon Ranger District Office, Silverthorne (970) 468-5400
- Frisco Historical Society, Frisco (970) 668-3428
- Summit Historical Society Tours (970) 453-9022

Alpen Hütte Lodge

This beautiful lodge on the Blue River, at the foot of the Continental Divide, is styled after European mountain lodges. Alpen Hütte offers clean, comfortable rooms that sleep up to eight people. Lockers are available in each room for secure storage. Most rooms have bunks; however, if you prefer, ask for a queen sized bed.

Ideal for groups, retreats and reunions, the lodge offers guests the use of the commercial kitchen facilities available all year. Don't worry about noise; the lodge enforces a midnight curfew to ensure a good night's sleep. Alpen Hütte is right on the Summit County Bike Path System, with over 50 miles of paved roads. Those who want more adventurous rides can rent a Trek mountain bike to traverse the mountain highland's unsurpassed mountain views. Hiking trails wind through towering evergreens, along majestic mountains, rivers and mountain lakes. Fish in Gold Medal waters a few steps from your back door, or venture into the Eagle's Nest Wilderness. In the winter, ski on the many downhill ski areas nearby, including Arapahoe Basin, Keystone, Copper Mountain, Breckenridge, Vail and Loveland. Or you can cross-country ski on groomed trails at Nordic centers and in the wilderness areas. The free county-wide shuttle bus stops here as does the East-West Greyhound bus. The lodge is directly across from a new recreation center with four swimming pools, a hot tub and a sauna.

The lodge has facilities for the handicapped.

Location: Off I-70 at exit 205 (Dillon/ Silverthorne Exit) Go north one block and turn right at stop light (there is a Wendy's). Immediately turn Left on Rainbow Drive, drive 4 blocks on left side of street.

15 Lodging Rooms	Pay Phone Available	Eric Hagmayer & Maribeth McLee
60 Beds in Bunkhouse	All Units Nonsmoking	PO Box 919
Central Fireplace	Recreation Room	Silverthorne CO 80498-0919
	Elevation: 8700	970/468-6336
	Credit Cards: VM	Fax: 970/262-1109
	Rates:	E-mail: ahutte@colorado.net
	Open: All Year	www.coloradodirectory.com/alpenhuttelodge

At the resort:

At resort or within 15 minutes:

MarDei's Mountain Retreat Bed & Breakfast

MarDei's chalet architecture is influenced by and features a European design interior. Guest rooms have king, queen, full or twin beds with down comforters. Choose between a dorm room with four single beds and shared bath, rooms with a double bed and shared bath, a room with a queen sized bed and private bath or a large room with a king and single beds, private bath, balcony and fireplace. Breakfast is served daily and is included in the price.

Cross-country or downhill ski the Summit by purchasing a pass to all four close by resorts. Other winter activities include going on a sleigh ride, snowmobiling, ice skating and heli-skiing. During the summer try fishing, sailing, biking, golfing, rafting, four-wheel driving, horseback riding, hiking, playing tennis, hot air ballooning and even llama trekking! Fishermen, sailors, hikers and backpackers will like nearby Lake Dillon's miles of shoreline and hiking trails. After it all, relax in the outdoor hot tub or unwind by the fireside and take in a movie.

Location: From I-70 take Frisco (exit 203), south to Main Street (4th stop light), right on Main Street to first stop sign (4th Avenue), turn left, go two blocks, on the right side of road of corner of 4th and Teller.

20 Lodging Rooms	Phone in Lobby	Amy & Michael Wolach, Owners
2 Beds in Bunkhouse	Bed & Breakfast Available	PO Box 1767
3 Rooms with Hot Tubs	All Units Nonsmoking	Frisco CO 80443-1767
14 Rooms with Fireplaces	Recreation Room	888/658-5337
Central Hot Tub	Elevation: 9000	970/668-5337
Central Fireplace	Credit Cards: VM	E-mail: mardies@colorado.net
	Rates: $35-$225	www.coloradodirectory.com/mardeismtnretreat
	Open: All Year	

At the resort:

At resort or within 15 minutes:

Melody Lodge

Built around 1940, Melody Lodge was originally a dance hall and bar with several "fishing cabins" during the construction of the Green Mountain Reservoir. On the way to Heeney, look for the cabins with the red roofs, where the Blue River meets Green Mountain Reservoir. The two-room cabin, with a shower- bath, is fully furnished. The front room has a full bed plus a sofa bed. The second room is a fully equipped kitchen/dining area with all the necessary utensils. The two bedroom suite, in the upstairs of the lodge features a full bath, kitchenette, and private entrance. The one bedroom cabin has a woodburning fireplace with rustic charm. Linens, pillows, towels, dishes, pots and pans are provided in both cabins and the suite. Television is available in the suite and one bedroom cabin.

Being located in the valley between the magnificent Gore Range and the Williams Fork Mountains, Melody Lodge has a wealth of activities available for the outdoor enthusiast. View wildlife and country flora while walking to nearby Green Mountain Reservoir or rent our fishing and pontoon boats! Try fly fishing the Gold Medal trout waters of the Blue River or enjoy a peaceful canoe or paddleboat ride, only 100 yards from the lodge. The nearby Eagle's Nest Wilderness area is great for hiking; or for the more adventuresome, raft the nearby Colorado and Blue Rivers. Hunt in Arapahoe National Forest in season. Or just relax and enjoy peace and quiet and the beautiful views.

Location: From I-70 take Highway 9 north for 17 miles out of Silverthorne. At Green Mountain Reservoir/ Heeney sign, turn left on Heeney Road and go one and a half miles, on the right.

3 Cabins with Kitchen	Phone in Lobby	Debra Gregory-Mitchener & Dale Mitchener,
1 Lodging Room	Elevation: 8100	Ownrs
1 Room with Fireplace	Credit Cards: VM	1534 Heeney Rd 30
1 Room with Woodstove	Rates: $60-$100	Silverthorne CO 80498
Central Hot Tub	Open: May 25 to 11/31	888/8MELODY (863-5639)
Central Campfire Area		800/468-8495
		E-mail: melodylg@colorado.net
		www.coloradodirectory.com/melodylodge

At the resort:

At resort or within 15 minutes:

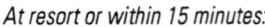

Telluride Area

Including Norwood — Map: M-5 & L-3

Snug in a box canyon along the San Miguel River, **Telluride** offers both superb downhill skiing and many outdoor adventures in a pristine wilderness. The first thing you'll notice when arriving in town are the lofty, jagged peaks, some reaching to nearly 14,000' in elevation, towering over the quaint Victorian town. Like many other small mountain towns, Telluride came into existence because of gold and silver strikes in 1875. In the 1880s, Telluride got its name when a rare sulfurous element, tellurium, appeared in local gold deposits. From the early days, this tiny town had a reputation for "hell-raising" with its gambling and a red light district, prompting the nickname "to-hell-u-ride." Though those wild days are in the past, adventures still abound here. Nowadays, you can downhill and cross-country ski, snowmobile and trek into the back country in the winter. In the summer, explore nature on foot, horseback or mountain bike. You'll find great fishing on the Dolores and San Miguel Rivers as well as at Trout and Woods Lakes. Those who love to four-wheel drive will find plenty of scenic, high mountain passes to traverse, including the stunning trip over Ophir Pass into Silverton. Telluride is the town of festivals, including the Bluegrass Festival in late June, the Jazz Celebration in early August, the Film Festival in early September and the Hang Gliding Festival in late September. The small town of **Norwood** is only 30 miles northwest of Telluride on Colorado Highway 145 and a whole lot less expensive! South of Norwood the fishing and boating are good at Miramonte Reservoir State Wildlife Area.

Fun Things To Do

- Telluride Golf Club (970) 728-6366
- Telluride Historical Museum (970) 728-3344

Annie's Country Bed & Breakfast

The house specialties at Annie's are peace, quiet and sourdough bread and pastries! Built during the lean years following the First World War, this working ranch has seen only a few changes for the sake of convenience such as electricity, indoor plumbing and central heat, thus retaining it's historic and true country feel. The outhouse and fireplace are still in place and working, but the outhouse is used only for reading per county rules. Choose a room with either a private or shared bath. Beds in the guest rooms feature linens dried in the high country sun and pure mountain air; flannel and down for the cool nights, cotton during the warmer season. King, queen, double or single beds are available. Experience true Colorado hospitality on this "Currier & Ives" style working ranch.

Wake to the mouth-watering aroma of a full cowboy breakfast with sourdough specialties. Lunch and dinner are served on request. The common room has games and reading material available. You won't find a TV here! Fish at the property or drink in the beauty of nature from the gentle hiking trails nearby. Other activities include big game hunting, arrowhead hunting and four-wheeling. Enjoy the thousands of acres of Federal Lands from 14,000' peaks to desert terrain, either within a fifteen minute drive. The B&B is a pleasant alternative to the pricey condos of Telluride any time of the year. Take some time to visit nearby Telluride, Silverton and Ouray — each is a unique mountain town with something different to offer, from downhill and cross-country skiing to shopping to natural hot springs.

Location: Take Highway 145 to 44ZN Road, between milepost 99-100, then take 44ZN a half a mile north. Make a right turn onto ranch lane, then .25 miles.

1 Vacation Home	Phone in Lobby	Anne Shaffer, Owner
4 Lodging Rooms	Bed & Breakfast Available	PO Box 495
Central Fireplace	All Units Nonsmoking	Norwood CO 81423-0495
	Recreation Room	970/327-4331
	Elevation: 7014	E-mail: annes@independence.net
	Credit Cards: None	www.coloradodirectory.com/anniecountrybb
	Rates: $35-$45	
	Open: All Year	

At the resort:

At resort or within 15 minutes:

Lone Cone Elk Ranch Bed & Breakfast

A bed and breakfast guest ranch, Lone Cone Elk Ranch is open year round. The ranch is located in the small agricultural town of Norwood where cattle ranches and farms dot the landscape. The complete downstairs of the two-story home is yours during your stay. It includes two bedrooms, a bathroom with a shower, a spacious living area with a fireplace and a private entrance. There is a television in the common area family room for your convenience. In addition there are two rooms upstairs.

Choose between two options: the bed and breakfast plan which includes accommodations and breakfast, but no ranch activities; or the guest ranch plan which includes home-cooked meals, accommodations and ranch activities. Listen to our bull elk bugle in the fall and watch the baby calves in the spring. Other ranch activities center on fishing, hiking, wildlife watching, taking photos and relaxing in some of the most beautiful areas the San Juan Mountains have to offer. In the fall, Lone Cone Elk Ranch specializes in trophy deer and elk hunting on national forest hunting grounds. This is a wonderful chance to experience first-hand what life is like on a working ranch.

Location: One mile west of Norwood, take Grand Avenue in town which turns into Z42 Road at the west edge of Norwood.

4 Lodging Rooms	Phone in Lobby	Sharon & Bob Hardman, Owners
Central Fireplace	Bed & Breakfast Available	PO Box 220
	All Units Nonsmoking	Norwood CO 81423-0220
	Recreation Room	888/ELK-RACH
	Elevation: 7000	970/327-4300
	Credit Cards: None	Fax: 970/327-4343
	Rates: $45	www.coloradodirectory.com/loneconeelkranch
	Open: All Year	

At the resort:

At resort or within 15 minutes:

Winter Park

Located in the beautiful Fraser Valley and enclosed by the Arapaho National Forest, **Winter Park** is home to numerous activities. Don't be fooled by the name because Winter Park is also a summer playground. You'll discover an exhilarating alpine slide, excellent fishing, breath-taking hiking, fun white-water rafting and dazzling scenery. There is also an extensive mountain bike trail system covering some 500 miles of mapped trails and 200 miles of marked trails using old logging and ranching roads sure to delight two-wheeler beginners or experts. Drive over the spectacular Berthoud Pass which crosses the Continental Divide at 11,301'. Or take the Rollins Pass Road in a four-wheel drive, following the original railway over the Divide which was used for 24 years until the Moffat Tunnel was completed in 1927. Anglers will be drawn to both the beautiful settings and the rainbow, brook, mackinaw and cutthroat trout and kokanee salmon in the lakes and rivers of the Arapaho National Forest.

Fun Things to Do

- Alpine Slide (970) 726-5514
- Berthoud Pass Ski Area (800) SKI-BERT
- Cozens Ranch House Museum (970) 726-5488
- Grand County Historical Museum (970) 725-3939
- Pole Creek Golf Course (970) 726-8847

Berthoud Pass Recreation Area

On top of the Continental Divide overlooking the picturesque Fraser River Valley, Berthoud Pass Recreation Area is a summer and winter paradise. During the summer ride the scenic chair lift to the top of the peaks for a panoramic view of several mountain ranges. Great mountain biking and hiking abound. Bring your camera to capture the beautiful summer bounty of wild flowers. As one of Colorado's first ski areas, Berthoud Pass is carrying on the skiing and snow boarding tradition of affordable, uncrowded, family winter fun. The terrain offers something for everyone with the addition of a quad chairlift to the new west side, tripling the skiable terrain.

Enjoy a hearty lunch at Pauly's Pub, featuring reasonable menu prices (including a 99-cent bowl of chili), daily lunch specials and a bird's eye view of the Continental Divide. Berthoud Discount Sports Outlet offers savings of 30%-70% off fleece, ski wear, skis, snowboards, goggles, sunglasses and t-shirts.

Call to find out about the special events that take place during the summer and winter seasons. Ski lessons are available for beginners through advanced for both boarding and skiing.

Location: Less than an hours drive from Denver, only 15 minutes from Winter Park, on US Highway 40.

Steve Bromberg, General Manager
PO Box 3314
Winter Park   CO   80482
800/754-2378
303/569-0100
Fax: 303/569-3472
E-mail: berthoudpass@rkymtnhi.com
www.coloradodirectory.com/berthoudpass/

Arapahoe Ski Lodge

Get away from it all at the family owned and operated Arapahoe Ski Lodge, conveniently located in downtown Winter Park, just three miles from the ski area. The 11 cheerful rooms each have one or two queen beds and a private tub/shower bath.

The bar-lounge and recreation/television rooms have fireplaces for warm, relaxing comfort. Other amenities include a dining room, indoor pool, spa and sauna — a perfect way to end a day of skiing. In summer, early and late ski season Arapahoe Ski Lodge is a bed and breakfast resort. During prime ski season, room rates include dinner and breakfast. Summer activities in the Fraser Valley include the Alpine Slide, golf, white water raft tours, rodeo, hiking and mountain biking trails. The lodge offers indoor bike storage.

A $400 deposit per room, per week is required within 10 days after the reservation is made. Ask about the special lift ticket prices for regular, early and late ski seasons.

Location: In down town Winter Park.

"A warm welcome in ski country"

Celebrating Our 25th Ski Season • 1974-1999

11 Lodging Rooms	Bed & Breakfast Available	Rich & Mil Holzwarth & Jan Roman
Central Hot Tub	All Units Nonsmoking	PO Box 44
Central Fireplace	Recreation Room	Winter Park CO 80482-0044
	Elevation: 8700	800/338-2698
	Credit Cards: VMAD	970/726-8222
	Rates: $74-$162	Fax: 970/726-8222
	Open: 11/14 to 4/13	E-mail: askil@rkymtnhi.com
		www.coloradodirectory.com/arapahoeskilodge

At the resort:

At resort or within 15 minutes:

Hideaway Lodge, Bistro & Pub

The Hideaway is a European style lodge with nine nicely decorated rooms upstairs. The rooms are bed and breakfast accommodations. The lodge was originally a corporate retreat for Burlington Northern executives in the 1960s and went through several transformations until it was recently renovated from top to bottom.

The full service restaurant downstairs has a huge sun deck and serves lunch and dinner daily, with such features as wild game, vegetarian dishes, seafood buffets and Sunday brunch. The Pub offers evening entertainment and happy hour specials. Catering on or off the property is available, cooked by the chef-owners! The pub also has video and pinball games as well as a pool table. Hideaway is right on U.S. 40 in Winter Park and is just minutes away from many activities. Cross country ski and mountain bike on trails beginning at the lodge. Fish on site. No matter how you spend your day, be sure to end it with a relaxing soak in the hot tub.

Hideaway specializes in weddings, family reunions and off-property catering.

Location: Downtown Winter Park.

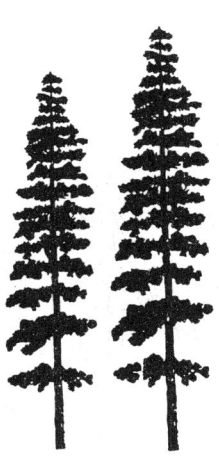

9 Lodging Rooms
Central Hot Tub

Bed & Breakfast Available
Recreation Room
Elevation: 9100
Credit Cards: VMAD
Rates:
Open: All Year

Geoffrey Schober & Ed Raegner
PO Box 1450
Winter Park   CO   80482-1450
970/726-1081
Fax: 970/726-0366
www.coloradodirectory.com/hideawaylodge/

At the resort:

At resort or within 15 minutes:

Hurd Creek Ranch Lodge, Cabin Rental & Fishing Club

This high country lodge has newly remodeled cabins on one of the oldest working ranches in Grand County. Boasting a spectacular view, the lodge offers two cabins and lodge rooms. The charming studio log cabin has a fireplace while the deluxe-view cabin has one bedroom. Both can accommodate up to four with modern kitchens and full baths. The lodge sleeps 17 people in five bedrooms with three full and two half baths. The lodge's kitchen is fully equipped for your cooking pleasure.

The lodge features a great room centered around a large fireplace, a sun room on the first floor for a perfect place to relax, a six-person hot tub and a wet bar. Located in Ranch Creek Valley near Tabernash, the lodge is only fifteen minutes from Winter Park Resort and all its winter and summer activities. Views of the ski area, the Continental Divide and Byers Peak over the open meadow is a sight not to be missed.

Sorry, no pets are allowed.

Location: About 3 miles from US 40, take a left at the "T", go .8 miles to the "Y", take right fork for 1.1 miles.

2 Cabins with Kitchen	Pay Phone Available	Steven & Andrea Paulk, Owners
1 Vacation Home	Elevation: 8620	PO Box 516
1 Room with Hot Tub	Credit Cards: VM	Tabernash CO 80478-0516
1 Room with Fireplace	Rates: $125-$250	800/471-5122
Central Fireplace	Open: All Year	Fax: 970/726-8934
Central Campfire Area		E-mail: flaws@rkymtnhi.com
		www.coloradodirectory.com/hurdcreekranch/

At the resort:

At resort or within 15 minutes:

Sitzmark Lodge Chalets/Cabins & RV Park

Open year round, and operating since 1968, Sitzmark offers plenty of outdoor fun. The secluded, housekeeping chalet-cabins sleep six and have fully equipped kitchenettes, fireplaces and cable television. Cabins have two double beds, refrigerator, microwave, and cable television. All accommodations have phones. Linens are provided for both the chalets and cabins. Maid service is available upon request.

Fish on the private, stocked trout lake and along the Frasier River during the summer. Rent a horse from the nearby stables or bring your own to ride in Arapahoe National Forest's natural wonders. Hike on the many trails as well. Nearby, enjoy cookouts under the pines, the heated swimming pool, the playground and the full service restaurant. Try the Alpine Slide in Winter Park for downhill summer fun, whitewater rafting, mountain biking, four-wheel driving, playing miniature golf and exploring local museums are all part of the Winter Park experience. Chair-lift rides to the top of the mountain for hiking and mountain biking are also offered in the summer. Of course, in the winter, the downhill skiing at Winter Park, Mary Jane ski, Silver Creek and Berthoud Pass areas is a major attraction. Other activities include snow-cat tours, inner tubing, cross-country skiing, dog sled rides, snowmobiling and horse-drawn sleigh rides.

Pets are allowed. A rustic RV and camping park is planned.

Location: On Highway 40, at milepost marker 228.

3 Cabins with Kitchen	Phone in Rooms	Harold L Baker, Owner
4 Lodging Rooms	All Units Nonsmoking	PO Box 65
4 Beds in Bunkhouse	Elevation: 8700	Winter Park CO 80482-0065
Central Campfire Area	Credit Cards: VMAD	970/726-5453
	Rates: $50-$100	www.coloradodirectory.com/sitzmarklodgechalets
	Open: All Year	

At the resort:

At resort or within 15 minutes:

Snow Mountain Ranch®/YMCA of the Rockies

On a vast 5,100 forested acres near the western entrance to Rocky Mountain National Park, Snow Mountain Ranch has 215 lodge rooms and 50 cabins and vacation homes. Limited cabin availability to non-members of YMCA of the Rockies (mainly available September through May). The cabins have two to five bedrooms with fireplaces and kitchens equipped with cooking utensils and dishes. Ask about the newly renovated Aspenbrook and Silver Sage Lodges, and the new Independence Reunion Cabin.

Snow Mountain Ranch is designed for group and family fun. Recreation, family programs, team-building, and youth day-camp offer year-round fun. Swim in the large indoor pool, relax in the sauna, practice on the climbing wall, play tennis and miniature golf or roller skate in the skating rink. Enjoy outdoor seasonal adventure with hiking, horseback riding mountain biking, fishing, snowshoeing and cross-country skiing. The Nordic Center offers over 100km groomed trails with lessons and equipment rental. On-site ski or snowboard rental is available for trips to nearby Berthoud Pass, Silver Creek and Winter Park ski areas. Snow Mountain Ranch also has a gift shop, restaurant/snack bar and library.

Snow Mountain Ranch can accommodate groups of 1,500 people at its conference facilities. Camp sites and full hookup RV sites are also available.

Location: Between Winter Park and Granby on Highway 40, near milepost marker 219.

38 Cabins with Kitchen	All Units Nonsmoking	Kent Meyer, Managing Dir.
7 Vacation Homes	Recreation Room	PO Box 169
215 Lodging Rooms	Elevation: 8800	Winter Park CO 80482-0169
45 Rooms with Fireplaces	Credit Cards: None	303/443-4743 Denver
Central Fireplace	Rates: $62-$270	Fax: 303/449-6781
Central Campfire Area	Open: All Year	E-mail: info@ymcarockies.org
		www.coloradodirectory.com/ymcasnowmountain

At the resort:

At resort or within 15 minutes:

Woodspur Lodge

In a convenient location to numerous mountain activities, Woodspur Lodge offers 32 rooms in Winter Park. Single, double and family accommodations all include private bathrooms and daily maid service. The lodge is nestled in Arapaho Forest and has views of the Continental Divide.

The main lodge boasts a large fireplace, library, recreation room, two outdoor Jacuzzi's, sauna and private bar amid a rustic feeling and a spectacular mountain view. In addition to skiing the slopes at Winter Park and other downhill resorts nearby, you can take a sleigh ride, go snow tubing, ice skate, snow mobile, snowshoe and cross country ski. In the summer, come to golf, horseback ride, hike, four wheel drive, white water raft, fish, play tennis or racquet ball, mountain bike, rent a moped or take a thrilling ride on the alpine slide. No matter when you vacation here, you'll find plenty to do at Woodspur Lodge.

The basic rates include home cooked, all you can eat, breakfasts and dinners. Free van service to and from the slopes is provided.

Location: West of US 40 at Vasquez, over railroad right on Van Anderson to Lodge.

32 Lodging Rooms
Central Hot Tub
Central Fireplace
Central Campfire Area

Phone in Lobby
Bed & Breakfast Available
All Units Nonsmoking
Recreation Room
Elevation: 9100
Credit Cards: VMD
Rates: $146-$156
Open: All Year

Carol & Rob Gordon, Owners
PO Box 249
Winter Park   CO   80482-0249
800/626-6562
970/726-8417
Fax: 970/726-8553
E-mail: woodspur@coweblink.net
www.coloradodirectory.com/woodspurlodge/

At the resort:

At resort or within 15 minutes:

Resort	Town/Area	Page	CENTRAL	PRIVATE																		
7-11 Ranch	Gunnison Area	158				•	i	$	•	•		•	•			•	•	15		•	•	•
A Bed & Breakfast on Maple Street	Mesa Verde Area	187	•		•		i					5	10	5								
Adventure Bound River Expeditions	Glenwood Springs Area	128																				
Allenspark Lodge	Peak-to-Peak Scenic Highway	206	•		•		i					3	1				•			•	10	5
Almont Resort	Gunnison Area	159		1	•	•	i	$				•	10	10	•		•	15		•		•
Alpen Hütte Lodge	Summit County	282					i					•	5	5	5	5	•		15	15		
Alpine Lodge, Cabins & Dinner Restaurant	San Isabel to Westcliffe	246			•		i						15	15			•			•		•
Alps Boulder Canyon Inn	Peak-to-Peak Scenic Highway	207		7	•		io					•		15		15	•			10		
Anderson's Wonder View Cottages	Estes Park Area	91	•			$					•	3	10	15	15	15				10		
Annie's Country Bed & Breakfast	Telluride Area	286			•	$		•				•	5							15		
Antler's Pointe Log Cabin Suites "On the River"	Estes Park Area	92		8								•	2	7	5	6				10		
Antlers Rio Grande Lodge	Creede	57					io	$	•	•		•	2		10		•	15		5	5	•
Appenzell Inn — A Suites Resort, The	Estes Park Area	93		29							•	1	1	1		1	1	2		5	10	
Arapaho Ranch Cabins	Peak-to-Peak Scenic Highway	208				$	i					•	5				•					
Arapahoe Ski Lodge	Winter Park Area	290	•		•		i				•	5	5	15	5		1	5	5	5	5	15
Arkansas River KOA & Loma Linda Motel	Royal Gorge Area	242				•	io	•	•	•	•	•	5		5		10					•
Arkansas Valley Adventures Rafting & Cabins	Collegiate Peaks Area	29				•	io			•		1	7		•	2	•	7				15
Ashley House Bed & Breakfast	Denver Mountain Area	66	•		•		i					5	5	10	15	10	5	10				
Aspen Winds	Estes Park Area	94	•	16								•	5	8	5	7				10		
AspenRidge Cabins & RV Park	South Fork Area	258	•				i		•			10	10		5	10	10	15		15	10	15
Avalanche Ranch Cabins	Aspen & Crystal River Valley	8				$	io	$				•	5	15			•			1		
Baldpate Inn, The	Estes Park Area	95		1	•		i					1	5	10	15	15	•					15
Barb's Bed & Breakfast	Estes Park Area	96		2	•		i					•	5	7	5	6	15			10		
Bauer's Spruce Island Chalets	Denver Mountain Area	67				$	o					•	10	8		8	•					
Be Our Guest Bed & Breakfast	Pagosa Springs	199		1	•	$	io	$				•	10	15	10		2			15	15	5
Bear Paw Lodge	Durango & Vallecito Lake Areas	71				$						1	1			1	5			10	15	5
Beaver Meadows Resort Ranch	Poudre River Canyon	231		1	•	$	io	$	•	•		•	•	15		•	•			•		15
Berthoud Pass Recreation Area	Winter Park Area	289																				
Big Thompson Timberlane Lodge	Estes Park Area	97	•	8			i				•	•	5	15	15	15				10		
Black Canyon Inn	Estes Park Area	98		12	•		i				•	5	5	5	5	5	10					
Blue Creek Lodge, Cabins, RV Park & Restaurant	South Fork Area	259			•		io		•	•		•	2		10		•	2		•	•	15
Boulder Brook on Fall River	Estes Park Area	99	•	8								•	3	6	5	6	15			5		10
Braham's Inn Bed & Breakfast	Grand Mesa Area	149			•	$	i	$						5								15
BRB Crystal River Resort	Aspen & Crystal River Valley	9				$	o		•	•	•	•	10	5	•		5			10	10	5
Bridges' Stagecoach Country Inn	Hot Sulphur Springs	172	•		•		i					1	15		1	10	•		15	•	•	1
Bruce Spruce Ranch & Faris House Lodge	Pagosa Springs	200				$	o	$	•	•		•	•				•			•		5

For definitions of glyphs, see page 2. Numbers in table indicate driving time in minutes to activities near the resort.

Resort	Town/Area	Page
Brynwood on the River	Estes Park Area	100
Buford Hunting & Fishing Lodge and Store	Meeker	184
Bunny Lane Cabins	Collegiate Peaks Area	30
Cabin at Quiet Waters	Collegiate Peaks Area	31
Call of the Canyon	Central City to Georgetown	23
Carolyn's B&B Cabins At Windmill Meadow Ranch	Pikes Peak Area	214
Casa Milagro Bed & Breakfast	Hot Sulphur Springs	173
Cascade Hills Motel & Cabins	Pikes Peak Area	215
Chair Mountain Ranch	Aspen & Crystal River Valley	10
Chicosa Canyon Cabin and Bed & Breakfast	Scenic Highways of Legends	250
Chinook Lodge & Smokehouse	South Fork Area	260
Circle H Lodge Bed & Breakfast	Grand Lake & Granby Area	135
Circle S Lodge	Durango & Vallecito Lake Areas	72
Club Hotel, The	Central City to Georgetown	24
Collegiate Peaks Vacation Home Rentals	Collegiate Peaks Area	32
Colorado Cottages	Estes Park Area	101
Colorado Vacation Homes	Collegiate Peaks Area	33
Conejos Cabins	Conejos River Canyon	48
Conejos River Guest Ranch	Conejos River Canyon	49
Conestoga Wagon Cabins & RV Campground	Central City to Georgetown	25
Cool Water Ranch Cabins	Durango & Vallecito Lake Areas	73
Cottonwood Cove Lodge, Cabins, Cafe, Jeeps, & Rafts	South Fork Area	261
Cottonwood Meadows Cabins & Fishing Guides	Conejos River Canyon	50
Crazy Horse Camping Resort & Jeep Rentals	Collegiate Peaks Area	34
Crested Butte International Hostel	Crested Butte	62
Cristiana Guesthaus Bed & Breakfast	Crested Butte	63
Cross Creek Ranch	Eagle River Valley	85
Crystal Lake Resort Bed & Breakfast & Trout River Grill	Denver Mountain Area	68
Crystal Meadows Ranch, Cabins & Campground	Grand Mesa Area	150
Crystal Springs Cabins	Peak-to-Peak Scenic Highway	209
Cuchara River Cabins & Campground	Scenic Highways of Legends	251
Cuchara Vacation Rentals	Scenic Highways of Legends	252
D'Mara Resort	Durango to Vallecito Lake	74
Daven Haven Lodge	Grand Lake & Granby Area	136
Dolores River Cabins & RV Park	Mesa Verde Area	188
Dripping Springs Bed & Breakfast Inn and Cabins	Estes Park Area	102

For definitions of glyphs, see page 2. Numbers in table indicate driving time in minutes to activities near the resort.

Resort	Town/Area	Page
Durango East KOA, Kamping Kabins™ & Kamping Kottage™	Durango to Vallecito Lake	75
Eagle Cliff House Bed & Breakfast	Estes Park Area	103
Eagle Manor, The — A Bed & Breakfast Place	Estes Park Area	104
Echo Basin Dude Ranch Resort & RV Park	Mesa Verde Area	189
Edgewater Heights Cottages	Estes Park Area	105
El Colorado Lodge	Pikes Peak Area	216
Eleven Mile Motel Cabins	Pikes Peak Area	217
Elk Point Lodge	Durango & Vallecito Lake Areas	76
Elk River Guest Ranch	Steamboat Springs Area	269
Elkhead Ranch	Steamboat Springs Area	270
Elkhorn Lodge & Guest Ranch	Estes Park Area	106
Estes Park Bed & Breakfast	Estes Park Area	107
Estes Park Center®/YMCA of the Rockies	Estes Park Area	108
Ferro's Blue Mesa Trading Post & Outfitters	Gunnison Area	160
Fireside Cabins & RV Park	Estes Park Area	109
Fireside Inn	Pagosa Springs	201
Foothills Lodge	South Fork Area	262
Forest Creek Cabins	Collegiate Peaks Area	35
G R Bar Ranch Cabins	Grand Mesa Area	151
Glen Echo Resort	Poudre River Canyon Area	232
Glen Eden Resort	Steamboat Springs Area	271
Glen Isle Resort Lodge & Cabins	Denver Mountain Area	69
Gold Camp Recreational Resort	Collegiate Peaks Area	36
Golden Eagle Ranch	Eagle River Valley	86
Goldminer Hotel, Rocky Ledge Cabin & The Nederhaus	Peak-to-Peak Scenic Highway	210
Goodnight's Lonesome Dove Cabins & Campground	South Fork Area	263
Grand Mesa Lodge	Grand Mesa Area	152
Granite Peaks Ranch	Durango & Vallecito Lake Areas	77
Green Mountain Falls Resorts	Pikes Peak Area	218
Green Snow Oasis Cabins & Shop	Mesa Verde Area	190
Green Willow Motel Cottages	Pikes Peak Area	219
Hideaway Lodge, Bistro & Pub	Winter Park Area	291
Hideout Cabins & Campground	Glenwood Springs Area	130
High Plains Drift Inn Bed & Breakfast	Conejos River Canyon	51
Historic Wit's End Guest Ranch	Durango & Vallecito Lake Areas	78
Hot Sulphur Springs Resort and Spa	Hot Sulphur Springs	174

For definitions of glyphs, see page 2. Numbers in table indicate driving time in minutes to activities near the resort.

For definitions of glyphs, see page 2. Numbers in table indicate driving time in minutes to activities near the resort.

Resort	Town/Area	Page
Mesa Lakes Resort	Grand Mesa Area	153
Midnight Ranch	Steamboat Springs Area	274
Minnesota Creek Bed & Breakfast	Grand Mesa Area	154
Minturn Inn, The	Eagle River Valley	87
Mount Elbert Lodge & Cabins	Collegiate Peaks Area	40
Mountain Chalet Aspen	Aspen & Crystal River Valley	11
Mountain Greenery Resort	Poudre River Canyon Area	234
Mountain Haven Inn & Cottages	Estes Park Area	114
Mountain Home Bed & Breakfast	Estes Park Area	115
Mountain Home Lodge	Conejos River Canyon	53
Mountain Lakes Lodge & Log Furnishings	Grand Lake & Granby Area	139
Mountain Shadows Bed & Breakfast	Estes Park Area	116
Mountaindale Cabins & Campground	Pikes Peak Area	222
Mule Creek Outfitters/M Lazy C Ranch	Pikes Peak Area	223
National Park Resort Cabins & Campground	Estes Park Area	117
Nonehshe Cabins	Grand Lake & Granby Area	140
O-Bar-O Cabins	Durango & Vallecito Lake Areas	80
Oso Grande Ranch	Pagosa Springs	203
Outpost Cabins, Motel & RV Park	Mesa Verde Area	193
Ox-Yoke Riverside Resort-The River Runs Through It	Lake City	179
Pando Cabins	Eagle River Valley	88
Phoenix Gold Mine Tour	Central City to Georgetown	22
Piedra River Resort	Pagosa Springs	204
Pine Grove Cabins	Peak-to-Peak Scenic Highway	211
Pine Lodge	San Isabel to Westcliffe	248
Pine River Lodge	Durango & Vallecito Lake Areas	81
Piñon Valley Ranch	Collegiate Peaks Area	41
Pleasant View Resort & Rocky Mountain Jeep Rental	Lake City	180
Pollard's Ute Lodge Cabins	Meeker	185
Pomotawh Naantam Ranch	Grand Mesa Area	155
Ponderosa Cabins	Mesa Verde Area	194
Ponderosa Campground & Cabins	Conejos River Canyon	54
Poudre River Resort	Poudre River Canyon Area	235
Prock Elk Ranch	Black Canyon Area	17
Prospect Mountain Ranch	Aspen & Crystal River Valley	12
R Running Bar C Guest Ranch & Circle Divide Outfitters	Creede	58

For definitions of glyphs, see page 2. Numbers in table indicate driving time in minutes to activities near the resort.

For definitions of glyphs, see page 2. Numbers in table indicate driving time in minutes to activities near the resort.

For definitions of glyphs, see page 2. Numbers in table indicate driving time in minutes to activities near the resort.

Resort	Town/Area	Page																				
Woodland Brook Cabins	Collegiate Peaks Area	46	•				•	2	5	5	5	15	2	5	5	10	5		15	15
Woodspur Lodge	Winter Park Area	295	•		•	i	•	5	5	15	15	5	5	•	5	5	5	•	•	
Yellow Pine Ranch & Livery	Scenic Highways of Legends	256				0	•			15	•	•	2				•	•		15
Yolande Placer Cabins	Aspen & Crystal River Valley	15			•		•	5		5	5		5				5			15

For definitions of glyphs, see page 2. Numbers in table indicate driving time in minutes to activities near the resort.

About The Authors

Hilton and Jenny Fitt-Peaster are Colorado residents who spend their entire summer personally visiting almost every cabin, cottage, lodge and country bed & breakfast resort in Colorado. They have been doing this since 1981 and are now widely acknowledged as the **foremost experts on this subject**.

In 1988, the authors founded the Colorado Cabin Resort and Lodge Associations, which merged with the Colorado Campground Association in 1991 to become the Colorado Campground and Lodging Owner's Association of today. The Fitt-Peaster's served as the association's first full-time executive directors for almost 20 years.

Each year since 1980, Jenny and Hilton with their daughter Rebekah publish *The COLORADO DIRECTORY — more Cabins, Lodges, Country B&Bs, Campgrounds & Fun Things To Do than any other guide.* As brokers, they also own and operate Colorado Cabin Resort & Campground Realty, Inc. — the only Colorado real estate agency specializing exclusively in these properties statewide since 1983.

Hilton served on the Colorado Tourism Board Advisory Council for ten years, 1983–93.

By an official industry-wide vote in 1995, Jenny was elected as an inaugural Director-at-Large of the new Colorado Travel & Tourism Authority. She received more votes than any other elected director. She was re-elected in 1996 and in 1997 and served on the Board until March 1999.

In 1992 the authors established Rocky Mountain Vacation Publishing, Inc. to publish the first edition of this unique book to share their secrets with you.

NOTES

NOTES

NOTES